THE HUMAN TRADITION IN
MODERN JAPAN

Kobayashi Kiyochika, *Blowing the Fire; The Painter's Gesture; Eye of the Needle; Haircut* (from the series: 100 Faces: Supplement to Thirty-two Faces). *Courtesy of the Santa Barbara Museum of Art, Gift of Mr. and Mrs. Roland A. Way.*

THE HUMAN TRADITION IN
MODERN JAPAN

EDITED BY
ANNE WALTHALL

NUMBER 3

SR Books

Lanham • Boulder • New York • Toronto • Oxford

Published by SR Books
An imprint of Rowman & Littlefield Publishers, Inc.
A wholly owned subsidary of The Rowman & Littlefield Publishing Group, Inc.
4501 Forbes Boulevard, Suite 200
Lanham, MD 20706

PO Box 317
Oxford
OX2 9RU, UK

This SR Books edition of *The Human Tradition in Modern Japan* is an unabridged
republication of the edition first published by Scholarly Resources, Inc. in 2002.

Copyright © 2002 by Scholarly Resources, Inc.
First SR Books edition 2004

British Library Cataloguing in Publication Information Available

The original edition of this book was catalogued by the Library of Congress as follows:

The human tradition in modern Japan / edited by Anne Walthall.
    p. cm. — (The human tradition around the world : no. 3)
    Includes bibliographical references and index.
    ISBN 0-8420-2911-7 (alk. paper) — ISBN 0-8420-2912-5 (pbk. : alk. paper)
    1. Japan—Biography. I. Walthall, Anne, 1946– II. Series.

    CT1836 .H86 2001
    920.52—dc21   2001034411

Printed in the United States of America

⊖™ The paper used in this publication meets the minimum requirements of American
National Standard for Information Sciences—Permanence of Paper for Printed Library
Materials, ANSI/NISO Z39.48-1992.

About the Editor

ANNE WALTHALL, whose Ph.D. is from the University of Chicago, teaches Japanese history at the University of California, Irvine. After many years spent studying peasant uprisings and village life in eighteenth- and early-nineteenth-century Japan, she shifted her interests to the field of women's history. Her current research involves a comparative study of court women and palace life in Asia. In addition to numerous articles, Walthall is the author of *Social Protest and Popular Culture in Eighteenth Century Japan* (1986), *Peasant Uprisings in Japan: A Critical Anthology of Peasant Histories* (1991), and *The Weak Body of a Useless Woman: Matsuo Taseko and the Meiji Restoration* (1998). With Hitomi Tonomura and Wakita Haruko, she is editor of *Women and Class in Japanese History* (1999).

I believe in aristocracy, though—if that is the right word, and if a democrat may use it. Not an aristocracy of power, based upon rank and influence, but an aristocracy of the sensitive, the considerate and the plucky. Its members are to be found in all nations and classes, and all through the ages, and there is a secret understanding between them when they meet. They represent the true human tradition, the one permanent victory of our queer race over cruelty and chaos. Thousands of them perish in obscurity, a few are great names. They are sensitive for others as well as for themselves, they are considerate without being fussy, their pluck is not swankiness but the power to endure, and they can take a joke.

—E. M. Forster, *Two Cheers for Democracy* (1951)

Contents

Introduction: Tracking People in the Past   xi
  Anne Walthall

I   The World of Shogun, Samurai, and Court, 1600–1868, 1

1   Shinanomiya Tsuneko: Portrait of a Court Lady   3
  Cecilia Segawa Seigle

2   Mori Yoshiki: Samurai Government Officer   25
  Luke Roberts

II   The Meiji Restoration and the Transformation of State and Society, 43

3   Nishimiya Hide: Turning Palace Arts into Marketable Skills   45
  Anne Walthall

4   The Ishizaka of Notsuda: A Family in Transition   61
  M. William Steele

III   Building the Modern State, 77

5   Hatoyama Haruko: Ambitious Woman   81
  Sally A. Hastings

6   Jahana Noboru: Okinawan Activist and Scholar   99
  Gregory Smits

7   Kinoshita Yoshio: Revolutionizing Service on Japan's National Railroads   115
  Steven J. Ericson

IV   Twentieth-Century Vicissitudes, 135

8   Matsuura Isami: A Modern Patriarch in Rural Japan   137
  Gail Lee Bernstein

9   Yoshiya Nobuko: Out and Outspoken in Practice and Prose   155
  Jennifer Robertson

10 Takahashi Masao: Flexible Marxist   **175**
    Laura Hein

V   World War II and the Postwar World, 193

11 Yokoi Shōichi: When a Soldier Finally Returns Home   **197**
    Yoshikuni Igarashi

12 Misora Hibari: The Postwar Myth of Mournful
    Tears and Sake   **213**
    Alan Tansman

Index   **231**

Introduction: Tracking People in the Past

ANNE WALTHALL*

> The historian is like the ogre of fairy tales: where he smells human
> flesh, there he finds his quarry.
>
> —Marc Bloch[1]

In explaining the Japanese to an English-speaking audience, best-selling novels such as *The Rising Sun* and *Memoirs of a Geisha* demonstrate that the all too perduring myths of the exotic Oriental still circulate in popular culture. Drawing on stereotypes of fanatical loyalty, sexual perversion, and conformity, they depict the Japanese as treacherous, ruthless, and hypocritical when they are not self-sacrificing, obsequious, and weak. All too few English-speakers have had a chance to read about the lives of ordinary Japanese people or to meet them in everyday situations. These essays offer a prophylactic against myth. They follow up the scent of vanished humanity in the records that real people have left of their experiences and aspirations to bring out the variety of Japanese life, and variety is necessary to challenge stereotypes.

Scholars themselves have tended to overlook the lives of ordinary individuals. Japan's modern history is often viewed either as a triumph of state formation, economic development, and social cohesion or, conversely, as the product of authoritarian leadership, economic exploitation, and social coercion. Although it is important to generalize about the historical processes of centralization, industrialization, urbanization, and modernization, a focus on large concepts can easily obscure the impact these had on the people who lived through them. Furthermore, historians have been known to keep one ear so perpetually cocked to the distant rumble of future upheavals that they are deaf to the voices of the moment. A woman kicking up her heels in 1926, for example, could have had no idea that fifteen years later her country would be at war with the United States. Her actions may have contributed to the right-wing revulsion against "urban decadence" and thus to the spread of militant nationalism, but is it really fair to assess her life solely in those terms?

*I wish to thank Kathryn Ragsdale for her valuable comments.

Dissatisfied with research projects that focus on large-scale models of human behavior and social life, the authors of the essays in this volume seek a human-scale perspective. They deal with individuals, reconstitute the meaning of their experiences, and put a human face on history.

Historians of Japan have by no means neglected biography as a genre. Some have written books about a single individual; others have collected stories about a number of people in a single volume. (See the Suggested Readings for some of these collective biographies.) Their focus, however, has been primarily on people whose achievements brought them nationwide and sometimes international fame. Most have dealt with extremely brief periods. Yet the lives of ordinary people yield at least as much drama as the deeds of the great, even if not on the same scale. The essays that follow unearth the stories of men and women, most of them unknown outside their family and locality, who lived in Japan between the seventeenth and twentieth centuries. The purpose is to weave together studies of individuals while preserving a sense of generational differences. Their experiences bridge the divides between the sexes, between the local and the national, between rural and urban, and illustrate what it was like to live through crucial moments in the history of modern Japan.

Although the individuals whose biographies are related here often sat on the sidelines of national history, telling their stories contributes to a changed understanding of that history. Biographies of ordinary men and women introduce readers not only to the many varieties of human experience, the anguish, and the hardships but also to the achievements and the pleasures of being alive. They incorporate the material details of everyday life into the master narrative of a nation's becoming, challenge assumptions regarding what is historically important, and offer a supplement made up of the seemingly trivial and unimportant. After all, it is in the details that we find the strongest whiff of humanity, that we rescue individuals from the abstractions they become in history. The goal is to integrate these details and these lives into the historical narrative, based on the premise that their presence might encourage readers to recognize the insufficiency of texts that in focusing solely on great figures or large-scale processes tell only part of the story. To paraphrase Joan Scott, adding ordinary people to history occasions its rewriting: "They provide something extra and they are necessary for completion, they are superfluous and indispensable."[2] They witness reverberating national events that happened elsewhere but from the perspective of private joys and tragedies. The writing of their biographies thus enlarges history itself.

Another goal of this volume is to challenge the all too common assumption that lives are led in a continuous and unilinear manner, that what a person does with his or her life is necessarily prefigured by what went before. Even within the limitations imposed by family and society, people still have to make choices and confront circumstances very different from their expectations. Constructing a narrative tends to smooth out discontinuities. One that follows a chronological framework implies a linearity where none in fact existed, subordinates explanation to what happens next, and makes it appear that an individual's actions at any one stage of his or her life were preordained. It is important to disrupt this even tenor, to emphasize disjunctures between different moments in a life. People inhabit a number of communities throughout their lives. These communities are the products of work and struggle, they are inherently unstable, and they are not always retrievable. What passes for identity at one moment may not be sufficient decades down the road. Furthermore, there is no one way to tell a life; each biographer brings to the project a different perspective and a different set of questions.

Historians know that "the past is a foreign country." How much more foreign can it be when the people in a nation's past speak a language and inhabit a space different from our own? In writing history the problem is always to make the past comprehensible to the present while retaining the strangeness of the past (or alterity, to use postmodern language) and the distinctive features of a culture. Yet a sensitivity to distinctiveness presents its own problems.

In today's world, every national unit and a good many subnational ones take considerable pride in defining their attributes differently from everyone else's. Why do the Russians act the way they do? How do the French define flair? Pundits and a goodly number of people in the bars and coffee shops throughout Japan expound at length on the issue of their national identity, made all the more pressing now because most people in industrialized societies dress, work, and even eat in ways that are similar the world over. Who are the Japanese? In some sense, this question underlies every book written on Japan. At the same time, however, it all too easily slides into issues of what make the Japanese unique. Nothing wrong with that, so long as it is clearly understood that every nation is unique in one way or another. When the question becomes, what makes the Japanese uniquely unique? then the answer might well presume a conformity of behavior and attitudes where little in fact exists. The biography of any individual must necessarily challenge too easy assumptions about what "the Japanese" will do or how they will feel in any particular circumstances. By presenting the inherent diversity of individual lives within Japan's changing historical context over the last few centuries, the biographies in this volume both retain and refine various meanings of what it is to be Japanese.

A collection such as this cannot pretend to be comprehensive or even representative. Some readers may wonder, why this person and not that one? Why begin with a seventeenth-century princess and end with a popular singer treated like royalty by her fans? Neither is ordinary, in fact, to the extent that ordinary denotes common; that designation would have been angrily rejected by Shinanomiya, proud heiress to an imperial line that stretched back over a thousand years (Chapter 1). Yet like the vast majority of women in her day she remains absent from the public record. Were it not for her magnificent though never published diary, nothing more would be known about her than her name on genealogical charts. By searching through this diary we can uncover patterns of human relationships quite different from those usually assumed to have defined family life in early modern Japan. Shinanomiya and Mori Yoshiki (Chapter 2) prove that people do not have to be modern to lead lives full of incident and interest. Conversely, no one in postwar Japan is ignorant of Misora Hibari, a singer whose enduring popularity, at least with one segment of the population, owes much to her identification with the ordinary people who suffered during World War II and its aftermath (Chapter 12). She sang as though for them, and through her songs she recast the misery they had all experienced.

Close examination shows that no life is entirely ordinary. Every individual makes some contribution to the human tradition, whether it be in striving for success or merely in surviving. Some periods, however, are more compelling than others. For this reason, one major emphasis in this volume is on the last half of the nineteenth century, when Japan tried to build a modern state and promote industrialization within the context of a predatory foreign environment. A second focus is on the meaning of modernity in the twentieth century. In addition, the authors in this volume have sought to balance stories about men and women without aiming at a strict numerical parity. Within the limited space available, they have also tried to go beyond the mainstream of Japan's historical experience to seek out stories about the lives of people on the margins. Yoshiya Nobuko refused to conform to the norms of conventional womanhood (Chapter 9). While Jahana Noboru's life should not be read as representative of the problems faced by Japan's minorities, he yet serves to remind us that their stories too offer an essential supplement to the history of modern Japan (Chapter 6).

The first people we meet in these pages lived in a world radically different from contemporary Japan. The imposing castle walls in the center of Tokyo, which now enclose the imperial palace, were built by the first Tokugawa shoguns early in the seventeenth century as a symbol and celebration of their rule over Japan. Except for fire breaks, they preferred narrow twisting streets unsuitable for wheeled vehicles or armies. Since none except officials were allowed to ride horses, everyone else walked or rode in palanquins. Only the shogun and a small circle of advisers had any say in national politics. They paid little attention to domanial affairs deemed the prerogatives of the daimyo or even to village governance so long as taxes were paid and peace maintained. Hereditary status, social inequality, and to a certain extent sex segregation were the order of the day. Men and women at the imperial court, in villages and among the urban poor interacted considerably more freely than did samurai or merchant men and women whose dwellings typically assigned specific spaces to each sex. The economy was agrarian based. Cottage industries supplied manufactured goods, and commerce flourished. Whether in the countryside or the city, people enjoyed drinking and singing, and when the opportunity presented itself, traveling, seeing spectacles, and going to the theater.

This was not an idyllic world. Hereditary status restrictions could be stifling to people born on the lower rungs of society and social inequality infuriating. Genteel poverty was the lot for most members of the ruling class. Heated only by a charcoal brazier or an open fire, houses were frigid—not a problem when there was no plumbing to freeze. Candles and oil lamps provided a feeble glow when the sun went down. Life expectancies were short; medical treatment, chancy. Even among the aristocracy at least half of all children died before the age of five. Some years the crops failed, and people starved.

During the nineteenth-century age of imperialism, the outside world that the shoguns had previously managed to keep at bay became an ever increasing threat to Japan. Once it became clear that the divisions of rule between shogun and daimyo compromised Japan's security, the ruling class united behind the young Emperor Meiji. Commoners had no choice but to follow. The centralization of government threw many erstwhile samurai bureaucrats out of work, but it also enabled the creation of a modern army and a system of compulsory education for every boy and girl. The state took the lead in everything from industrialization to the inculcation of patriotic values and a strong sense of national identity. The following chapters show, however, that the citizens of the new Japan were not simply passive recipients of government directives. Each in his or her own way demonstrated initiative in dealing with the unpredictable and the unexpected.

The transformations of the late-nineteenth century brought Japan into the modern age. Both men and women found that they had to make choices of where to live, with whom to live, what occupation to pursue. Movement from place to place became faster and safer. The introduction of electricity for commercial purposes in 1883 made buildings brighter, leading eventually to the neon signs of the 1920s that lit up the night and lured people to new forms of entertainment, such as revues and movies. Regardless of what the government wanted its citizens to know and believe, it could not stop the importation of new ideas:

arguments for greater political participation for the masses, for economic justice, for a redefinition of human relations circulated throughout the country.

Modernity has its dark side as well. In Japan's case, the early twentieth century brought a growing gap in the practice of everyday life between urban and rural areas, yet the increased contact between the two made it easy for people in the countryside to blame their troubles on a moral critique of all that was specifically modern about the city—the hedonistic pursuit of leisure, the concern with superficial appearances in architecture and dress, and a generalized degeneracy that found its characteristic expression in the self-evident promiscuity of any woman who did not devote herself to husband and children. Modern institutions and technologies proved to be two-edged swords. Standardized compulsory education can be used to indoctrinate students into a vision of the world in which Japan has few friends but many enemies and Japan is superior to all others. A centralized government with new means of control and communication at its disposal can go from being authoritarian to totalitarian, demanding a complete commitment, body and mind, from its citizens to combat evils within and without. Modern warfare dehumanizes the enemy. Machine guns, torpedoes, and bombers make it easy to commit mass murder without ever catching sight of the victims until a single cataclysmic bomb can kill 140,000.

The people who inhabit the pages of this book experienced both the benefits and the costs of changing circumstances. They had to make choices without the advantage that hindsight confers on the biographer. None of them was a saint; they all had human needs and complications. While each life had its own central drama, each also shares certain themes with other lives.

A theme that dominates the first sections of this book is the change from status to class and what that meant for individuals. Shinanomiya and Mori Yoshiki led their entire lives as members of the aristocracy and ruling class because that was what their ancestors had done. Even after most status distinctions were abolished in 1869, for better or worse many people continued to identify or be identified with their old familial status. Jahana Noboru, for example, never escaped the taint of his peasant background in his dealings with the Okinawan aristocracy. In other circumstances a continuing consciousness of status distinctions gave rise to some interesting contradictions, for example, when Nishimiya Hide, a former samurai woman, found herself beholden to a servant turned shopkeeper (Chapter 3). Once the old sureties of a guaranteed position and livelihood disappeared, one's standing in society became determined less by birth (though that never completely disappeared as a criterion) and more by income. Entertainers who had once been viewed as only slightly better than nonhumans (*hinin*) became the new aristocracy of talent.

Another theme concerns the new occupations for men and women created in the course of Japan's modernization. From the social work performed by Ishizaka Mina (Chapter 4) to the building of railroads that involved Kinoshita Yoshio (Chapter 7), from factory work to clerking, the differentiation and specialization that made Japan's industrial revolution possible created many different kinds of jobs, some more lucrative than others. Nishimiya Hide's son made shoes (Chapter 3); Yokoi Shōichi's training as a tailor provided him with the skills to survive in the jungle (Chapter 11). The state took a hand in this as it did in other areas of human endeavor, forcing even traditional fields such as education to become more regularized and its practitioners, Hatoyama Haruko (Chapter 5) and Takahashi Masao (Chapter 10), for example, to become more professionalized. Career bureaucrats appeared on the scene, along with career politicians. For some people new avenues of employment became a way to better themselves; Ishizaka Shōkō worked for the sake of his community, Kinoshita Yoshio for his company; a few made the nation their reason for striving to succeed.

A third theme involves the standardization and homogenization imposed by the modern state that made movement much easier than before. Not only did transportation improve, but also the social and legal barriers disappeared that had previously prevented people from changing occupations or even residences. In some cases, movement was involuntary, as when Yokoi Shōichi ended up on Guam. Few of the people depicted in this volume were born in Tokyo; most, however, migrated there either as children or young adults. The capital became such a magnet that by the 1970s, 25 percent of the population lived in or near it. The people who inhabit these pages, Misora Hibari, for example, show how this happened and what was the attraction. In addition, some had family members who emigrated to the United States, to Manchuria, or to Southeast Asia.

A fourth theme that runs through these lives is the changing structure of the family and relationships among family members. Volumes have been written about the traditional Japanese house (*ie*), a male-centered corporate entity passed down from one generation to the next in the male line (Ishizaka Shōkō is proof positive that sometimes it was necessary to adopt an heir to keep it going). The promulgation of the civil code in 1898 enshrined this system in law and codified a system of household registration designed to identify and place every inhabitant in the Japanese islands. Yet the individuals who populate these pages lived in household situations that varied according to status, class, period, and personal inclination. As we see in the cases of Ishizaka Shōkō and Matsuura Isami, even the vaunted patriarchal authority suffered setbacks when children became estranged from their fathers or when fathers hesitated to enforce their will. Despite the challenge to its structure in the form of a new kind of domestic space created in the early twentieth century, Jennifer Robertson's account of Yoshiya Nobuko shows how the *ie* proved flexible enough to provide a secure living arrangement for a lesbian couple after World War II.

In the pages of this book we see how the roles of men and women within the family varied according to time, class, and region. Generally speaking it can be said that Ishizaka Shōkō and Hatoyama Haruko's fathers, who lived in earlier periods and rural areas, had more opportunity to invest time and effort in their children, though here, too, individual inclination has to be taken into account. Even in the twentieth century, Matsuura Isami, who worked at home, could pay attention to what was going on within his family (Chapter 8). After a child has grown up and left home to get married, it is easier to stay involved in her life if she lives close by. When men have to commute to work, Matsuura's daughters learned that child-rearing becomes a mother's responsibility, although when help is cheap and socially acceptable, servants may also be involved. One of the hallmarks of modern life, the differentiation of work space from living space, has meant that parental involvement in child-rearing has become strictly maternal.

Some readers may wonder at the importance given to education in these pages. Surely only a bunch of professors would pick so many subjects who put such effort into getting to college. Given the extremely limited opportunities for education beyond the six years mandated in 1907, many young people who might have wanted to go to middle school or even high school could not. In this regard, the men and women who appear in this volume are truly exceptional. Certainly, not all Japanese strove so hard for scholastic achievement. Yoshiya Nobuko's father is just one example of a father who felt that too much education would harm his daughter's chances in the marriage market, whereas Matsuura Isami was certain it would not. Even in the early postwar period, many fathers refused to allow their daughters to take advantage of the new opportunities for women in previously all-male institutions because they viewed educating women as a waste of time and money. Nonetheless, in coming to an understanding of the diverse meanings of modernity, it is worth comparing the content of what Shinanomiya, Nishimiya Hide, and Ishizaka Shōkō learned before the Meiji Restoration of 1868 with what Hatoyama Haruko and Takahashi Masao learned afterward, both in terms of the transformation from Chinese-centered learning to

Western-centered and the differences between what was considered appropriate for men compared to women.

The people who march through these pages did not make history. They tried to make a living for themselves and their loved ones, but the range of their actions was extremely circumscribed. They had no power to affect the public events of their day, from the relatively bloodless restoration of the emperor to direct rule in 1868 to the bloodbath of World War II. Nonetheless, they found their lives irrevocably changed. In living through revolution, war, depression, and prosperity, they adapted in ways that thirty, sometimes ten, years earlier would have been deemed highly unconventional if not unthinkable. That they managed to thrive speaks to the resiliency of the human spirit and its amazing adaptability.

NOTES

1. This quotation from the famous French historian may be found in Robert Darnton, "Looking the Devil in the Face," *New York Review of Books*, February 10, 2000, 14.

2. Joan W. Scott, "Women's History," in *New Perspectives on Historical Writing*, ed. Peter Burke (Cambridge and Oxford: Polity Press, 1991), 49.

SUGGESTED READINGS

Ivan Morris, in *The Nobility of Failure: Tragic Heroes in the History of Japan* (1975), sets the standard for collective biography, telling the story of nine men plus the kamikaze pilots (no women) who lived between the fourth century C.E. and 1945. A similar type of book is *Heroic with Grace: Legendary Women of Japan*, edited by Chieko Irie Mulhern (1991). *Five Political Leaders of Modern Japan* by Oka Yoshitake (1986) highlights the public achievements and some private foibles of the men largely responsible for creating the modern state.

Other texts focus on war heroes or victims, as in Rodney Barker's *The Hiroshima Maidens: A Story of Courage, Compassion, and Survival* (1985). Phyllis Birnbaum has recently published a collective biography about five notable women in prewar Japan, *Modern Girls, Shining Stars, the Skies of Tokyo* (1999), and Robert J. Lifton created a powerful book about men's lives in *Six Lives, Six Deaths: Portraits from Modern Japan* (1979). In *Personality in Japanese History* edited by Albert M. Craig and Donald H. Shively (1970; 1995), fourteen eminent historians examine the interplay between famous men and significant events in the early modern and modern eras. *Great Historical Figures of Japan*, edited by Murakami Hyoe and Thomas J. Harper (1978), takes the widest field of vision, providing short fact-filled biographies of historically important men and women from ancient to modern times. *Britain and Japan: Biographical Portraits*, edited by Ian Nish (1997), examines the men who contributed to building the modern Japanese state.

PART I

THE WORLD OF SHOGUN, SAMURAI, AND COURT, 1600–1868

For over two hundred and fifty years Japan enjoyed what many people at the time termed "the Great Peace." Under the benevolent if arbitrary rule of the Tokugawa shoguns, no major wars either domestic or foreign disrupted state and society. The most obvious blemish on public security arose in the form of peasant uprisings. In that Japan's rulers tried to restrict social mobility and contact with most foreigners, some Westerners then and since have been prone to assume that the country must have stagnated.

Desiring order above all, the Tokugawa shoguns devised a system in which status would be hereditary; no man or woman was to change jobs or even residences. The shoguns placed the military as the ruling class at the top of a ranked ordering of occupations. Comprising 6.4 percent of the population, the military included both daimyo, the rulers of domains, and their vassals, the samurai who guarded them and staffed administrative offices. They lived chiefly in castle towns. The story of Mori Yoshiki (Chapter 2) tells of one such soldier–bureaucrat. Directly below the military in importance were the peasants, some 85 percent of the population, officially valued because they produced food, but also exploited because they were immobile and unarmed. They lived in villages. Then came the artisans, also useful because they made tools for peasants and swords for samurai. At the bottom were the merchants, officially despised because they produced nothing. Both artisans and merchants lived in towns. Outside the status system was the emperor and his court in Kyoto on the one hand, and the outcasts, nonhumans, on the other. While the outcasts disposed of dead animals and guarded prisoners, the emperor was expected to devote himself to ritual. The chief duty of his courtiers was to preserve the cultural practices of their ancestors. As we see in Chapter 1, this responsibility included appreciating nature as well as managing estates.

The shoguns' hortatory directives to rulers and commoners to remain in place did not prevent change. With little to entice them from their villages and distract them from their work, peasants devoted themselves to improving their lot. Agricultural productivity soared, and cottage industries flourished. Some peasants ended up as landless laborers; others became very wealthy indeed, as we see in later chapters. Merchants made themselves indispensable to daimyo, acting as financiers

1

and marketing agents for domain products. The result was a commercial revolution that threatened to erode the status system underpinning the political order. Low-ranking samurai whose stipends had never been adequate turned to by-employments to supplement their income, making cricket cages, paper hair ties, and other products. For them, the calling to serve their lord, the daimyo, became increasingly irrelevant. The political history of the Tokugawa period includes repeated attempts to reform the system for the benefit of the rulers; the self-interest of commoners and samurai alike doomed these efforts to failure.

Shinanomiya, the subject of Chapter 1, and Mori Yoshiki, the subject of Chapter 2, led very different lives, one as the daughter of an emperor, and the other as a samurai. Yet they did share the security of a guaranteed income, and neither performed manual labor. This social and financial stability does not mean that their lives were without incident, suffering, and disappointment. Recovering their stories illuminates the circumstances within which they maneuvered, the roles then appropriate to men and women and the relations between them, and the politics of the time. The world they inhabited is gone forever outside television dramas. Nonetheless, it had a tremendous impact on the way Japan became modern.

CHAPTER I

Shinanomiya Tsuneko

Portrait of a Court Lady

CECILIA SEGAWA SEIGLE

Politically, economically, and socially the emperor remained hidden during the period from 1600 to 1868. Most emperors found the burden of office so onerous that they retired as quickly as they could. Some historians have argued that most Japanese people did not know they existed at all. Dutch emissaries in the seventeenth and eighteenth centuries emphasized the emperor's ecclesiastical role. Westerners who tried to establish diplomatic relations with Japan in the nineteenth century addressed the shogun as "king." They were baffled to learn that he was not Japan's sole legitimate ruler. The first Tokugawa shogun had ordered the imperial court to devote itself to literary and cultural pursuits. Guaranteed a modest if secure income by the military overlords, successive emperors took advantage of this directive to revive ancient court ceremonies and rituals. When the shogun's government started to totter in the face of domestic turmoil and foreign threat in the 1850s, ideologues seeking an alternative principle of rule turned to the imperial court. At this point the cultural and symbolic capital it had amassed earlier, through activities such as those performed and witnessed by Shinanomiya, made it possible for the emperor to step out from the shadows and become politically charged.

Shinanomiya's diary offers an intimate glimpse of life in the rarified world of this politically ineffectual but culturally crucial aristocratic society during the last half of the seventeenth century. Through its lens we view tempests in teapots, political wrangling over largely honorary appointments, considered all the more precious for that very reason. Although court life remained in thrall to its antecedents in the ninth century, within the confines of this tradition, Shinanomiya had considerable freedom to do as she pleased. At first glance her concerns may appear entirely frivolous or so universally human as to transcend time and place. Nonetheless, only the daughter of an emperor could have exhibited her particular blend of leisure and managerial practices, relations with father and husband, or combination of pragmatic and aesthetic responses to the world around her.

Professor emerita of the University of Pennsylvania, Cecilia Segawa Seigle has published a number of translations of modern Japanese literature as well as Yoshiwara: The Glittering World of the Japanese

3

Courtesan *(1993). This essay is drawn from her book*, Kōjo Shinanomiya no nichijō seikatsu: Mujōhōin-dono gonikki wo yomu *(The everyday life of Imperial Princess Shinanomiya: Reading the Mujōhōin-dono diary) (2001).*

𝒯he story of Princess Shinanomiya Tsuneko (1642–1702), the sixteenth daughter born to Retired Emperor Gomizunoo (1596–1680), begins with her first diary entry on 1666/1/1 and ends on 1700/3/24, two years before her death.[1] A limited amount of supplementary information is obtainable from the diaries of her husband, Konoe Motohiro, and her brother, Ordained Prince Myōhōin.[2] The latter's records attest to her active life in court society prior to her marriage, and to the marriage itself on 1664/11/12. Information concerning her childhood, however, is totally lacking.

Although Shinanomiya had many important relatives, she herself is scarcely known today. As the genealogical chart (Figure 1) indicates, she had four siblings who were emperors: Emperor Meishō (r. 1629–1643) was her half sister, and Emperors Gokōmyō (r. 1643–1654) and Gosai (r. 1654–1663) her half brothers. Emperor Reigen (r. 1663–1687) was her full brother. Other brothers and a good many of her sisters became abbots and abbesses to reduce competition for the throne and claims on the royal income. In addition, her only daughter Hiroko was married to the sixth shogun, Tokugawa Ienobu (1662–1712). In later years, Shinanomiya's son Iehiro and a grandson Iehisa followed in her husband's footsteps to become Regent to an adult emperor (Kanpaku), Regent to a child emperor (Sesshō), and Chancellor (Dajōdaijin). Both eventually achieved the exalted position of Jugō (or Jusangō, an honorary rank next to Emperor, Empress Dowager, and Empress, conferred on both men and women), although Iehiro declined the honor.

Shinanomiya's mother was Shin-Chūnagon, of the Sono (Fujiwara) family, who became Gomizunoo's last favorite consort and gave birth to six children: four boys and two girls. Twenty-eight years Gomizunoo's junior, she was an elegant, gentle woman whom the emperor loved until she died, a fifty-four-year-old grandmother. Her children and her son-in-law Motohiro were devoted to her. All of them except Emperor Reigen formed a tight-knit, satellite group around the sun of Gomizunoo and saw one another constantly for social and cultural activities at his court.

Three salient characteristics stand out in Shinanomiya's personality and life. First, within the conventional moral dictates of her rarified environment, Shinanomiya enjoyed complete freedom in her activities. In the days when women's lives are often perceived as having been restricted and repressed throughout society, she gave full play to her limitless energy and curiosity, celebrating life and the beauty around her.

Figure 1
The 27 Children of 108th Emperor Gomizunoo, 1596–1680; r. 1611–1629
Who Survived Infancy and Their Mothers

MOTHERS (in order of rank):

a. Tōfukumon'in, daughter of Shogun Tokugawa Hidetada, 1607–1678

b. Shin-Chūnagon (Shin-Kōgimon'in), given name Sono Kuniko,1624–1677

c. Hōshunmon'in, given name Kushige Takako, 1604–1685

d. Mibu'in, given name Sono Mitsuko, 1602–1656

e. Gon-no-Chūnagon, daughter of Yotsutsuji Hidetsugu

f. Sochi, daughter of Minase Shiroshibe

g. Oyotsu, daughter of Yotsutsuji Kimitoo

PRINCES	PRINCESSES
g. Kamonomiya, 1618–1622	g. Monchi, abbess at Enshōji, 1619–1697
d. 110th Emperor Gokōmyō, 1633–1654	a. 109th Emperor Meishō, 1623–1696
d. Morizumi, abbot at Rinnōji, 1634–1654	a. Teruko, m. Konoe Hisatsugu, 1625–1651
f. Seishō, abbot at Ninnaji, 1637–1678	a. Akiko, Third Princess, 1629–1675
c. 111th Emperor Gosai, 1637–1685	c. Rishō, abbess at Hōkyōji, 1631–1656
c. Seishin, abbot at Daikakuji, 1639–1696	d. Gashi, m. Nijō Mitsuhira, 1632–1696
b. Gyōjo, abbot at Myōhōin, 1640–1695	c. Mitsuko, abbess at Rinkyūji, 1634–1727
c. Onjin, Prince Hachijō, 1643–1665	d. Genshō, abbess at Daishōji, 1637–1662
e. Sonkō, abbot at Chion'in, 1645–1680	d. Sōchō, abbess at Reiganji, 1639–1678
c. Dōkan, abbot at Shōgoin, 1647–1676	c. Richū, abbess at Hōkyōji, 1641–1689
b. Shinkei, abbot at Ichijōin, 1649–1707	b. Shinanomiya, m. Konoe Motohiro, 1642–1702
b. Sonshō, abbot at Shōren'in, 1651–1694	e. Songa, abbess at Kōshōin, 1654–1683
e. Seiran, abbot at Kajii, 1651–1680	b. Eikyō, abbess at Daishōji, 1657–1686
b. 112th Emperor Reigen, 1654–1732	

Second, her devotion to her father Gomizunoo continued well into her adulthood, supplanting the sense of responsibility normally attendant upon the status of wife or mother. Only gradually did her loyalty transfer itself over several decades from her birth family to her husband's family, as she became transformed from a pampered princess into a mature wife and mother.

Third, her personality: She had a penchant for viewing life selectively and recognizing only what she wished to. She was capable of dealing with a critical situation if she thought she could cope with it; otherwise, she lived in total denial, repeating a mantra of congratulatory incantations: "*Medetashi, medetashi!*" (How auspicious! How felicitous!) and "May this good fortune last for thousands of generations and ten thousand years!"

FATHER AND FAMILY DURING
THE EARLY YEARS OF MARRIAGE

Shinanomiya was twenty-two when she married sixteen-year-old Konoe Motohiro (1648–1722), who eventually became Kanpaku and Chancellor.[3] The Konoe were the most distinguished of the five noblest families (*go-sekke*): Konoe, Kujō, Ichijō, Nijō, and Takatsukasa, all descendants of the Fujiwara clan that rose to prominence in the seventh century. Most of Motohiro's forefathers had held the highest political positions at the imperial court.

Gomizunoo arranged the marriage between his favorite daughter Shinanomiya and his protégé Motohiro, who had lost his father and adoptive mother as a child. Motohiro's grandfather was Gomizunoo's younger brother, who had been divested of his princely status and succeeded to the headship of the Konoe family. In Shinanomiya's day, imperial and aristocratic children either entered into arranged marriages when extremely young, or were sent to prestigious Buddhist temples and nunneries to become celibate abbots and abbesses. Judging from Shinanomiya's mature age, one may infer that Gomizunoo remained indecisive for some years concerning her fate.

From the beginning of her married life, Shinanomiya enjoyed freedom of movement in the palaces of various family members. She attended banquets, lectures, and games, enjoyed gardens and villas, and joined picnics and boating parties, often without her husband. She clearly valued her birth household over her marital family.

In the 1660s and 1670s, Shinanomiya was generally very happy. She loved Motohiro and constantly referred to his activities in her diary. In the early days of her marriage, the only unsatisfactory arrangement was

Motohiro's habit of returning in the morning to the Konoe's ancestral home, in the manner of Heian-period aristocrats in the eighth to the twelfth centuries. According to her brother's diary, Shinanomiya dwelt in a mansion of her own. Unwilling to move into his wife's house, Motohiro was building a home for himself and Shinanomiya. He was a mere teenager who enjoyed the company of Shinanomiya's brothers and other friends his own age. He might have been somewhat intimidated by his wife, who was older, socially superior, and more sophisticated. Although of an imperial lineage, Motohiro himself was not royalty, and his rank was not so high as those that his ancestors had already achieved at his age. In this hierarchical society, it must have been difficult for the young husband to forget his lower standing.

The new house was finally completed, and the couple moved in on 1666/12/12. As the head of the Fujiwara-Konoe clan, however, Motohiro had to administer Shinto rites for the family protector, the Kasuga Shrine. His duties called for frequent abstentions from meat and sex as well as residence in the "omote" (official part of the household, as against "oku" or inner chambers). In fact, once he participated in a religious retreat, staying away longer than Shinanomiya found acceptable. Her only diary entry day after day was "[Motohiro is] still away!" Eight days later he finally returned with some flowers to make up for his absence. While Motohiro was at court and she was home, she often visited the nearby nunnery of her aunt Yōtokuin (younger sister of Gomizunoo) in search of companionship. Once, to mitigate her loneliness, she asked her aunt's maid to accompany her to her home and remain until she fell asleep. When she was already expecting her second baby, she was vexed enough to stay at her father's palace for two nights. She did not leave her bed until noon, when a maid came to summon her to her father.

The world of the palace was the only environment Shinanomiya had known as a child and felt comfortable with. On many occasions she remained all day at Gomizunoo's palace, partook of lunch and snacks, then visited either Tōfukumon'in (Gomizunoo's empress, daughter of the second Shogun Tokugawa Hidetada) or Reigen's consort. Later she might return to her father's for dinner and evening snacks. At times Gomizunoo summoned Motohiro to have dinner with his entourage. However, after Motohiro had had dinner and taken his leave, Shinanomiya frequently remained with her father until midnight. Motohiro's absences might have encouraged such self-indulgence, or possibly her long daily visits to Gomizunoo might have led Motohiro to spend even more time away from home.

Shinanomiya received almost daily presents from Gomizunoo, Tōfukumon'in, Gosai, Meishō, and others at court. She had obviously been spoiled by such numerous gifts since her childhood. Not that all of the gifts were valuable. Gomizunoo tended to be extraordinarily informal and down-to-earth in his daily behavior. He would give a surprisingly casual mishmash of valuable and common, sophisticated and rustic, elegant and mundane, even undignified or homely items. For example, a grass broom, salt pot, noodles, rice cakes and dumplings that were offerings at shrines and temples, or food from his dinner tray would be mixed with money, valuable clothing, and objects of art. Rarely did Shinanomiya return from a visit without presents.

According to the records that lady secretaries kept on visitors, gifts, and events at the imperial palace (*Oyudono no ue no nikki*), on occasion Shinanomiya presented fish or fruit to the emperor along with ample, proper gifts whenever protocol called for them. However, it seems she usually dispensed with meaningless gift-giving. Ever the pragmatist, she probably realized that the daily gifts exchanged at the palace were mostly perishable and excessive in quantity. She knew that, of necessity, such gifts were often redistributed among noble and royal households.

Gomizunoo loved being surrounded by people, enjoyed giving gifts to his entourage, and was generous to a fault with Shinanomiya and Motohiro. Between 1666 and 1680 (the year of his death), Gomizunoo visited the Konoe mansion at least 105 times, 16 times in 1671 alone. Every visit meant gifts of varying quality and quantity, for example, silk fabrics, furniture, toys, and daily necessities for the entire family. Some of his visits could also be very casual. Once when Shinanomiya went to present him with a branch of beautiful cherry blossoms from her garden, Gomizunoo suddenly announced that he would come see them for himself, thus forcing her to rush home to prepare for his visit. In summers, when her children and servants customarily held festival dances night after night, he wanted to come watch them. From time to time, he requested structural additions at the Konoe house at his expense. He even suggested the construction of a latticed bay window in a room facing the street because he liked to observe the outside world and the pedestrians. Once, he came to witness the construction in progress of the new rooms in the official part of the house (*omote*). Upon completion, he visited for an inspection and beamed with complacency as he checked and approved of every room (1671/12/5).

Shinanomiya owned a plot in the Hataeda hills northeast of Kyoto, where Gomizunoo and Tōfukumon'in owned hills and a villa. Shinanomiya and Motohiro had long admired the vistas that spread before the hills and the rich natural resources they contained. In 1672, Gomizunoo overwhelmed Motohiro by presenting one of the hills to him. Since it adjoined Shinanomiya's hill, this gift provided the couple with a larger property from which to enjoy the view with the whole family and on which to gather flowers, mushrooms, and other edibles.

On numerous occasions Gomizunoo gave Shinanomiya gifts of money. The villa called "Shichiku" was a property in the northern suburb of Kyoto, which the couple admired so much they had wished to purchase it. The area afforded a panoramic view of the Takagamine hills, close to the upper stretches of the Kamo River, where Shinanomiya loved to watch the water. Finally they bought the property (1673/9/28) with 500 ryō that Shinanomiya "borrowed" from Gomizunoo.[4] One can be certain, however, that her loan turned into a "gift." As discussed later, on one occasion he gave her as much as 3,000 ryō.

Even today, Shūgakuin Villa, which was designed by Gomizunoo, is considered the ultimate in rustic simplicity, combined with grand-scale landscapes. Shinanomiya had the privilege of visiting the villa with her family and bringing outside guests. At such times Gomizunoo generously sent his staff and chef to the villa to provide a complete meal. After his death, Shinanomiya received notice from the *shoshidai* (the shogun's representative in Kyoto) that her father had requested the government to grant her and Mitsuko (the other favorite daughter, an ordained nun) fiefs of 300 koku each from the land around Shūgakuin.[5] In recording the bequest, she shed tears of gratitude and longing for her father.

Motohiro and Shinanomiya had three children, Hiroko (b. 1666/3/26), Iehiro (b. 1667/6/4), and Nobuna (b. 1669/4/27). The birth of Hiroko was a new, exciting experience, and within a few weeks the proud mother began to take the baby to the palaces to show her off. When Iehiro was born, he also occasionally accompanied his mother and sister to various palaces. She always wrote, "Everyone complimented the children, saying they are adorable and growing fast." Although it was obvious that she loved her children and was proud of them, she only recorded the compliments of others and never directly expressed her own feelings. Yet she could not refrain from gazing at Reigen's or Gosai's children, suggesting that she found children delightful. At some point in her youth she had probably been taught that unreserved expressions of affection for one's own family were tasteless and vulgar.

As a young mother Shinanomiya enthusiastically kept records of the children's rites of passage, such as changing infants' clothes to colored printed kimonos, snipping hair to indicate the growth of a child, or the boy's coming-of-age ceremony at age seven. Her detailed descriptions of rituals, such as wearing a special obi in preparation for her pregnancy, provide valuable insights into court life. These accounts reflect her interest in old customs as well as her own way of following in the wake of Gomizunoo in his lifelong effort to preserve courtly cultural traditions. However, after the description of an event for the first child, she had a tendency to write "Same as before."

In the early 1670s, after the birth of her children, Shinanomiya's days were filled with social and cultural events, and Gomizunoo's empress Tōfukumon'in played an important role in this life. Always a gracious and generous hostess, Tōfukumon'in entertained Gomizunoo and his guests in a uniquely elegant and feminine way. She would amuse them by releasing a mass of fireflies over the pond in her garden, hanging beautiful lanterns all around, or floating lanterns on the pond, then offer a program of dances by the little girls in her employ and music by hired blind women. Later her style was emulated by her daughter, Emperor Meishō. In addition to the conventional gifts, several times a year Tōfukumon'in would give beautiful clothing, fabric, and other luxurious accessories to her adoptive daughters, sons, and grandchildren. Having a taste for high fashion, she dazzled Shinanomiya with gifts of magnificent apparel. "I can't stop gazing at and admiring these beautiful kimonos," she stated many a time in her diary. Intimate details about the lives of Tōfukumon'in and Meishō are found in no other document but this diary.

THE MIDDLE YEARS: MISFORTUNES AND REVERSES

The material and psychological damage caused by fire was an unavoidable reality of daily life for all classes in the period. At least four major fires in Shinanomiya's day caused large-scale damage to Kyoto royalty and aristocracy. The Konoe were spared in the major fire on 1673/5/8, only to have their house commandeered by Emperor Reigen, whose palace had burned down. This was a great honor, but it was inconvenient to have to move to a smaller house until the imperial palace had been reconstructed.

The next major fire (1675/11/25) caused extensive damage, and the citywide losses totaled 2,602 residences with more than 100 deaths. Including the Konoe mansion, sixty-seven royal and aristocratic houses, twenty-one temples, and sixty-nine of their auxiliary chapels were destroyed. The loss of treasures owned by many ancient families was immeasurable. Shinanomiya escaped with her children and mother to the temple of her younger brother Prince Sonshō, while Motohiro rushed to the imperial palace. Past midnight, when Motohiro joined the family, they finally sat down to a meal, but they could only stare at one another in a daze. At 3 A.M., a servant reported that the house was razed and the library had also caught fire. Hearing that five household managers braved the burning building to save most of the archival documents and books, Motohiro wept tears of relief and gratitude. The diary he had maintained since the age of thirteen as well as priceless family treasures and heirlooms had been lost. However, it is due to the care of the generations of the Konoe and their employees that the 200,000 Konoe family documents survive to this day.

Despite the destruction of the house and the trauma of losing their ancestors' records, the Konoe and others in the highest class of society were privileged in comparison with the ordinary citizens of Kyoto. The reconstruction was begun immediately, and the house was magically completed within thirteen months, helped by shogunal subsidies of 2,000 ryō. Gomizunoo came to inspect the grand house and was very pleased, praising it as attractive and extremely convenient. Shinanomiya repeated, "*Medetashi, medetashi!* (How auspicious! How felicitous!)." She was dissatisfied, however, that her family had received no more aid than that delivered to all *sekke* and princely houses that were fire victims. Moreover, three royally related ladies, including Princess Fushimi (Motohiro's half sister), had received an additional 2,000 ryō.[6] It must be admitted that her pique was more a matter of pride than economics.

After the 1673 fire the Konoe house had been occupied without remuneration by Emperor Reigen, so on this occasion everyone expected to see special courtesy extended to the couple, or at least so Shinanomiya claimed. Now that they were treated no differently, "Everyone is laughing and it is disreputable on the part of the emperor" (1676/2/9). It is highly doubtful that anyone was laughing at Reigen. The lack of special favor apparently displeased her, especially in light of that enjoyed by the other three ladies. Whatever the reason, the shogun's government granted the subsidies upon recommendation by the emperor's court. Here was a source of her resentment toward her brother Reigen and his administration. This incident particularly revealed the difference between the way she had been treated by Gomizunoo and by the young, inconsiderate Reigen. Even thirteen months after the reconstruction of the house, the Konoe still had some debts. "His Majesty Gomizunoo sent Kashin as a messenger hearing about the unpaid bills from the recent reconstruction. He graciously sent 3,000 ryō, saying that this was for the expenses of his visits. Motohiro's gratitude for His Majesty's kindness was extraordinary" (1678/1/8). Gomizunoo's delicacy in avoiding a direct reference to Motohiro's financial difficulty must have been touching indeed.

The summer of 1677 was a season of sorrow for Shinanomiya and Motohiro when they both experienced death in the immediate family. Motohiro's eighty-four-year-old paternal grandmother and Shinanomiya's mother Shin-Chūnagon both had been ill for some time. Motohiro had to divide his time between his grandmother and his mother-in-law while still fulfilling his official duties at the palace. Shinanomiya forfeited all her social activities to attend steadfastly to her mother. Although she probably knew that her mother was dying, she would not admit it, yet stayed stoically at her bedside.

In the early hours of 1677/7/3, Motohiro's grandmother expired. He could only look up at the sky and cry. After her funeral on the fifth, Motohiro was too exhausted to attend the interment. Just then a messenger arrived with the news of Shin-Chūnagon's death. Grief-stricken, Motohiro wrote that she had been as kind and affectionate to him as his own mother ever since he was sixteen years old.

Shin-Chūnagon had declined gradually despite the physicians' efforts, and she passed away about midnight. Gomizunoo had visited her twice on the last day, although he did not stay until she expired in order to avoid the ritual pollution caused by death. While the family grieved, the news arrived that Shin-Chūnagon had been promoted to Jugō, a rank just below that of empress. It was an honor for the entire family, and Shinanomiya and her brothers felt greatly consoled. About the Hour of the Dog (8–10 P.M.), there was a horrendous onslaught of rain and thunderclaps. Lightning had struck the granary on the palace grounds, and comments were heard that this was nature's expression of sympathy for the family in its grief.

Tōfukumon'in's death followed the year after. "Tōfukumon'in was the granddaughter of Shogun Ieyasu and it had been fifty-nine years since her entrance to the imperial court. Old people still shed tears reminiscing about the magnificent wedding procession, which was no less grand than an imperial visit. She had been extremely kind to me since my childhood, so my sorrow is boundless and I miss her very much" (1678/6/15).

On 1679/6/26 the shogun's government proposed the marriage of the seventeen-year-old Tsunatoyo, head of the Kofu branch of the Tokugawa, to the thirteen-year-old Konoe Hiroko. At first, neither Shinanomiya nor Motohiro was happy with the prospect because of their pride and disdain for the military class and because of an ancestral injunction against marital union with a military family. Once they accepted the proposal (which was difficult to refuse given the political and economic climate), however, the couple felt very pleased. Prior to Hiroko's departure for Edo, the parents and their daughter made a trip to the ancient city of Nara, their first and last long trip together. Then, following the aristocratic custom, Hiroko departed alone for Edo, accompanied only by her nurse, several female servants and companions, and hundreds of samurai guards sent by the shogun.

Taking advantage of official postmen, Hiroko wrote diligently to her parents, frequently sending luxurious gifts to everyone, including the servants. Her mother recorded the arrival of Hiroko's letters and packages but not the content of the letters. Her invariable comment was, "Everything is fine and both of them are extremely well. This is a matter of congratulations for a thousand years and ten thousand generations!"

With the death of Emperor Gomizunoo (1680/8/19), which had been anticipated for some time, Shinanomiya was forced to end her old ways and become more mature. Her half-brother Gosai rapidly became her close ally as well as Motohiro's. However, Gosai probably needed Shinanomiya and Motohiro more than they needed him. He was an elegant, cultured emperor, a man with a gentle personality. To enhance the heritage of Gomizunoo's scholarship and cultural dissemination, Gosai continued his father's periodic literary seminars and poetry meetings. He was extremely solicitous of the couple's company, constantly keeping them until late at night, while showering them with gifts. Shinanomiya developed a deep affection and respect for Gosai, but he was no substitute for Gomizunoo.

In 1681, in Edo, Hiroko gave birth to a baby girl. The news threw the Konoe family and servants alike into a frenzied excitement. With each entry in her diary, Shinanomiya repeated, *"Medetashi, medetashi!"* like a mantra, as though to ensure the family's good fortune. Two months later, however, a letter arrived, reporting the baby's death. Shinanomiya recorded only the facts without revealing her own feelings. Seventeen years later, when Hiroko's baby boy died within a few hours of his birth, she did the same. She received the letters reporting the birth and death two days apart, and she again exhibited her proclivity for disproportionate display of joyous celebration and little sorrow. Although Motohiro occasionally exploded with anger against injustice or openly slandered his political enemies, Shinanomiya refrained from disclosing her deeper, inner feelings. On this occasion, she wrote, "They are both extremely well, and everything is fine. *Medetashi, medetashi!*"

In choosing the topics of her chronicle, Shinanomiya was strictly selective. Even incidents of great historical and social significance did not appear in her diary if they were outside her immediate concerns. Her husband often sympathized with the people of Kyoto or the provinces who died from starvation in famine years. He wrote harsh words against Shogun Tsunayoshi for repeatedly issuing "Edicts against Cruelties to All Living Things" (1687–1709), which resulted in harming numerous human lives while claiming to protect animals. Shinanomiya was either unobservant or deliberately oblivious. When her monthly memorial service of *hōshō* (releasing birds or fish for mercy) was prohibited by the edict, she simply chronicled the fact without comment. She remained very much a protected princess, and she saw only what she wanted to see, ignoring illness, death, ugliness, and disagreeable behavior.

It is only fair to state, however, that she was basically a kind person with a sense of noblesse oblige toward her many servants, especially the aged help who had worked for the Konoe family or Gomizunoo for many years. Her eulogies on the deaths of old servants are more revealing of her feelings than usual (1691/1/12; 1696/7/6). Increasingly her compassion began to reach people outside her acquaintance. To give an example, once when the music of a street singer caught her attention, she sent a servant to find more about the singer. Hearing the sad history of the displaced wandering samurai and his young loyal servant who would not desert him, she was moved to tears and gave them generous amounts of money and food (1687/9/6).

After so many years, signs of Shinanomiya's shift in allegiance to the Konoe family from the imperial family manifested themselves in her criticism of Emperor Reigen. Not only his position as a reigning sovereign, but also his stern, temperamental personality had led him to stand apart from Gomizunoo's close inner circle. The Konoe's special friendship with Gosai after the death of Gomizunoo also might have irritated Reigen. Since the late 1670s, Motohiro had admonished Reigen concerning his rash dismissal of courtiers, but this resulted only in strained relations. There were also basic differences in their political philosophy. Reigen wished to reform court administration as soon as possible. Motohiro wanted to follow the will of Gomizunoo, retaining traditional policy, while cooperating with the shogun's government. In history books Reigen is portrayed as an able and cultured emperor who revived some ancient court rites, but on a personal level he seems to have been dictatorial and erratic. For a long while, he had allowed his current favorite consort, her father and brother, and other sycophants to wield power, a situation that Motohiro repeatedly lamented in his diary.

The penultimate political appointment, the Kanpaku, rotated among the five *sekke* families, Ministers of the Left usually being promoted to the position. Motohiro had served as Minister of the Center and of the Right as a younger man and served as the Minister of the Left beginning in 1677; therefore, the Kanpaku position was due him next. On the evening of 1682/2/18, a letter arrived from Retired Emperor Gosai that devastated Motohiro and Shinanomiya:

> His Majesty Gosai's letter informed us that the Kanpaku [Takatsukasa Fusasuke] decided definitely to resign. A directive from Edo communicated [to the court] the appointment of Lord Ichijō [Minister of the Right Ichijō Fuyutsune] as the next Kanpaku. This news was totally unexpected. Not understanding it, Emperor Gosai asked for confirmation and was assured of its validity. He was astonished and consequently sent a detailed confidential letter to Motohiro. From it we learned that the court is to announce the appointment tomorrow. We are totally at a loss as to what we

can do and merely remain dazed. However, if we think this over carefully, whether [the emperor] decided this or the shogun enforced this—whichever it is, what will be will be; our words will be nugatory so long as [Motohiro is] not appreciated in the world. Let it be; this is a misfortune for one individual that affects only one person. Everything, from the court matters on down, all the outrageous things now piling up are entirely the result of the emperor's lack of virtue. However, when a person is not recognized by such a world, he might as well let go of it and just watch. It could be fun. If both of us keep our wits about us, remain tranquil, and leave everything as is, it will pass—nevertheless, I shed tears, thinking if only His Majesty [Gomizunoo] were alive!

This was an amazing accusation to have been made by Shinanomiya, who had been thoroughly loyal to the imperial court and its system, and who had always been extremely careful not to speak against anyone, especially the reigning sovereign. Motohiro was especially hurt and embittered. The priest Myōhōin, his sympathetic brother-in-law, extolled the able, talented, and cultured Motohiro, then sneered at the official decision: "It is truly astonishing that such a slow, thick, and obtuse man is appointed as Kanpaku instead of the incomparably erudite authority on ancient court traditions, the peerlessly loyal Motohiro!"[7]

Everyone knew that in matters of political appointments, the shogun's government usually rubber-stamped the recommendations of Kyoto. Yet the next day three emissaries arrived at the Konoe residence with a propitiatory letter from the emperor, insisting that the decision was solely the shogun's, and asking Motohiro whether he would accept the new Kanpaku. Motohiro answered formally that he had no objection, that Ichijō Fuyutsune was an eminently suitable choice for the position. The emperor in addition sent Shinanomiya's maternal uncle and Reigen's nurse to her as his emissaries. Shinanomiya submitted exactly the same reply as Motohiro.

Sympathetic friends gathered around the resentful Motohiro and bitterly decried the waning of the court world. On the day of the investiture of the new Kanpaku, Shinanomiya wrote, "I hear it was a very festive affair. The world is truly incomprehensible and loathsome" (1682/2/24). Nevertheless, she was fundamentally a person of the establishment who tended to view matters fatalistically. A few days later she continued, "It is moving toward a better end step by step. There are secrets within secrets. . . . In the end, everything will be cleared up. *Medetashi, medetashi!*" (1682/2/29).

Nonetheless, there was no sign of improvement. Although court affairs moved on ceremoniously and smoothly, and although on the surface the Konoe were civil to everyone, Motohiro's relationship with Reigen was never completely mended. Shinanomiya remained pleasant to everyone at court and impeccable in her adherence to protocol, but her distrust of her brother remained intact the rest of her life.

A month later the future crown prince was named. To Shinanomiya's astonishment, the crown prince-designate was not the First or Second Prince, but the Fifth Prince, the son of the present favorite, a woman disliked by Motohiro. Shinanomiya clearly saw a parallel between this wrong and that done to Motohiro. Here was another case of injustice that exposed "the decline of the world and court politics." She wrote, "Truly, truly, this world is ephemeral and uncertain. The thought of First Prince's sorrow brings tears to my eyes. It is equal to the kanpaku veering in an unexpected direction. We expect the world to be just, but nothing follows the right order. It is frightening!" (1682/3/25). Thus, while she sympathized with the First Prince, she was partially consoled that even the oldest son of the emperor might suffer mistreatment.

Another incident occurred that summer when the Fifth Prince was suddenly moved into Gomizunoo's former palace. Shinanomiya was extremely upset. Amid general congratulations and celebrations, she sent gifts to the boy and his mother as dictated by protocol, but privately she wrote that Gomizunoo's mourning period of three years was not yet over. "Why? What is the hurry? I wonder and mourn over this changeable world. It is only a little more to wait [to the end of the mourning period], so everyone is rightly whispering. This world is full of incomprehensible things. What is to become of us all!!" (1682/6/27). It was not the others but Shinanomiya who was whispering these words of resentment. In her mind, for a little boy not yet officially invested as a prince of the blood imperial (*shinnō senge*), nor formally appointed crown prince, to be moving into Gomizunoo's palace was a blasphemy against the memory of her father.

Shinanomiya and Motohiro had witnessed Reigen's quick temper and severity that history books do not discuss. In the late 1670s and the early 1680s, numerous courtiers including Konoe relatives and four successive lady secretaries (*nagahashi*) were punished or dismissed for unspecified, unexplained offenses. Motohiro often blamed the wicked scheming advisers surrounding the emperor (Reigen's favorite's family), who slandered loyal subjects, including himself. No doubt his strong resentment of Reigen colored Shinanomiya's judgment of her brother.

However, Reigen was Shinanomiya's flesh and blood, and the unpredictable emperor did make conciliatory gestures from time to time. In 1679 he had permitted his First Princess to marry his nephew, Konoe Iehiro, and the wedding took place in 1683. Shortly afterwards, the family had an audience with Reigen. "[His Majesty] was in a much better mood than I had seen recently; indeed, this is truly to be congratulated and there is nothing more we wish" (1683/12/17). This statement attests to Reigen's moodiness and his unpredictable personality feared by many people. In a number of ways, Shinanomiya's shift of allegiance from her birth family to her husband's family developed out of bitter experience with the realities of the court world.

Shinanomiya herself, however, exhibited considerable human frailty in dealing with her third child, Nobuna. Her relationship with him clearly attests to her proclivity to avoid unpleasant reality. From the day of his birth, his name was scarcely mentioned in her diary, compared with numerous entries about her two older children. On the surface, it would appear that she never formed a close attachment to him.

A year after Nobuna's birth, Shinanomiya had written that the day being auspicious, she and her husband had decided to give Nobuna away to the Yotsutsuji, another noble family, as an adopted son (as if she were giving away an unwanted puppy). In some areas of Japan there is a folk practice of deserting a sickly child and having someone care for him temporarily as a foundling to change his health and fortune.[8] This may have been what Shinanomiya and Motohiro intended, because Nobuna was actually not adopted by the Yotsutsuji family at that time. Instead, he was formally adopted twelve years later by a different nobleman, Ōimikado, former Minister of the Center. In the interim, we note glimpses of a sickly and lonely boy. "Nobuna had no movement and was in a bad humor, so Ryōsetsu [physician] stayed overnight. In the evening, there was a movement and he felt much better so we were all happy" (1674/6/17). Only once, at a festive moon-viewing party at Gomizunoo's, at someone else's suggestion was Nobuna sent for. "Everyone said he was adorable; even the lady attendants made a great fuss over him. After a while I sent him home. . . . His Majesty gave him beautiful dolls" (1671/7/16). Similar compliments and adulation for Hiroko and Iehiro had been recorded with much greater frequency.

Once when the boy was five years old, Shinanomiya returned from an outing and immediately left again to visit her aunt residing in the vicinity. "Nobuna came tripping after me; I let him stay briefly and sent him home. I stayed until 8 P.M." (1674/7/6). This brief note suggests that Nobuna missed his mother so much that he was reduced to following her about.

The year 1682 saw Nobuna's coming-of-age ceremony and official investiture at court. He then met with his adoptive family and moved to the Ōimikado mansion. He was now listed by his new rank, and his name appeared more frequently in his mother's diary. Motohiro had always shown more concern for Nobuna than his wife had. On this occasion his diary disclosed that the adoption had not been his own wish but the command of Reigen, who had acceded to the entreaties of the childless Ōimikado. Motohiro repeatedly expressed his regret for having consented to losing his son. For a year, Nobuna often visited his birth family for dinner, and he was invited to the parties given by his brother Iehiro's wife, the First Princess. One summer evening, Shinanomiya and Motohiro were entertained with music and dancing at the First Princess's moon-viewing party until 3 A.M. As dawn approached, Shinanomiya wrote, "Nobuna also had a moon-viewing tonight at the other home and we were happy for him. . . . The moon continued to be clear and beautiful, and it was particularly promising for a happy future" (1684/ 6/16).

This happiness did not continue. Only two weeks later, Nobuna was so ill that he returned to the Konoe house. We learn only from Motohiro's retrospective comments that he had been ailing intermittently for several years. Yet inexplicably Shinanomiya ignored Nobuna's health problems and never mentioned him after he returned home. Then there occurred a most uncharacteristic outpouring of recollection and emotion on 1684/10/27, at the death of the fifteen-year-old Nobuna:

> During the seventh month, Nobuna's chronic illness reappeared but by the early eighth month, he seemed to have recovered. The illness recurred shortly thereafter. Subsequently, his condition fluctuated and relapsed as he gradually lost his appetite. Usually he ate very little when he was ill, so this was not particularly surprising. Every day we hoped the next day he would be better. However, early in the tenth month, his appetite decreased alarmingly and . . . he grew very weak.
>
> By the morning of the fourteenth of the tenth month, he was exhausted. This so disconcerted us that we called in four or five doctors for examination. They all said he was beyond hope. The Former Minister of the Center Ōimikado also visited, doing everything he could, yet the boy continued to decline. About the Hour of the Dog (10 P.M.) he expired. Both Motohiro and I lost consciousness with grief. All we could do was pray that he be put to rest in the best possible condition. The Former Minister said he wanted to take the boy to his house that night, and I had no choice but to let him do as he wished. Ever since that night, my heart has been strangled and I have remained in bed. His Majesty Gosai sent words frequently asking after me. My brother Prince Myōhōin also visited me frequently and offered words of admonition and consolation. Nichigon [archbishop, Shinanomiya's maternal uncle] comes often, and Sogan [priest, family friend] stays with me, offering me words of solace morning and evening. Gradually, I have managed somehow to regain strength and appetite. Still, it is impossible to forget him. Every little thing brings back his memory, what he used to do and how he used to be. Indeed, indeed, he had not yet reached the age when he could be called a young man, and he has already gone to become a person in an ancient story. What sorrow, what pity. As I think about it, the evanescence of this life engulfs me, and the whole memory feels like a bad dream. Enough, let it be, there is nothing I can do. I say to myself, if this is predestination, my grief will never bring him back. The only thing I can do now is to devote myself to memorial services and never neglect prayers for him three times a day. Until today, I have neglected my diary but I have made up my mind to begin again to write tonight. It is the twenty-

seventh today [the day of his birth], so I ordered the memorial service of *hōshō*.

Shinanomiya had experienced a number of deaths in the family, but this was the first such expression of naked grief and remorse in her diary. It was never to be repeated. Without admitting it, she must have felt deep guilt and regret for her negligence. In 1675, when Iehiro had small-pox, Shinanomiya immediately sent for three doctors and anguished over him for fifteen days. Yet when Nobuna returned home sick, she continued to ignore the need for physicians until it was too late. Evidently she knew that he was going to die and could not accept it. In atonement she never neglected to commemorate the day of his death by releasing living fish or fowl.

It would appear that Shinanomiya lived entirely in a state of denial during times of illness or bad luck. Instead, she always concentrated on good news: "May this good fortune last forever and ever, for thousands of generations and ten thousands of years! *Medetashi, medetashi!*" Whether the incantation was efficacious or not, it was the only way she knew to deal with such situations.

SHINANOMIYA'S LATER YEARS

Times were changing, and more and more transitions were noted among the generations. During the New Year's celebrations of 1685, a sensational murder occurred in the household of the former Kanpaku. As a result, Emperor Reigen appointed the young Iehiro to substitute for the intended Master of Ceremony at one of the New Year's rites. On the day of the event, Shinanomiya wrote that "Iehiro completed his duty perfectly and the emperor was particularly impressed by his splendid performance. All the leading nobles were surprised by his accomplishment and complimented him; no greater happiness for us! . . . [long incantations here]. . . . *Truly this foretells the revival of the family name*" (emphasis added).

She had by now completely assumed the role of wife of the Konoe family head and mother of his heir, regarding the success of Iehiro as key to the revitalization of the family. In the previous eras, the Konoe were incontestably the leading family of the court world. Now, Motohiro was languishing in the position of Minister of the Left while locked in hostility with Reigen. The emperor's unpredictable behavior might suddenly deny him his rightful Kanpaku appointment. In this situation, with his faultless pedigree and outstanding talent, Iehiro was destined to become a future Regent and Kanpaku as Reigen's favorite son-in-law and leading courtier.

In addition to her roles as wife and mother, Shinanomiya was truly a woman with unexpected talents in the arts and practical matters. Her diary provides glimpses of her tending to household needs such as preparing clothes, sewing sacerdotal vestments for her brothers, dyeing and sewing mourning clothes for the family. We remember the fictional character Murasaki in *The Tale of Genji* (early eleventh century) preparing clothes for Genji and capably overseeing all household chores during his exile.

Shinanomiya was extremely knowledgeable about music, Nō dance, and Kyōgen theater. She kept detailed records of numerous court performances. She was also a good appraiser of artifacts and, true to the family tradition, a fine calligrapher. In springtime Motohiro and Shinanomiya concocted perfume made from pulverized wood mixed according to special family formulas. The perfume served as gifts for their acquaintances in Kyoto and Edo. When Emperor Gosai handed down his secret recipe for perfume (permitted to one person only), he chose Shinanomiya as his successor rather than one of his full siblings or his children.

Shinanomiya also interviewed and hired servants not only for herself but also for various emperors as well as for Hiroko and Tsunatoyo. Evidently she was a dependable judge of character. Numerous minor aristocrats and her employees, whose daughters and younger sisters gained positions through her intercession, expressed their gratitude to her in many ways. She also had a sound business sense. Every year when the villagers of her estate brought in crops, she personally supervised the transport of rice sacks from behind a screen (exalted ladies did not show their faces to commoners), then oversaw the serving of refreshments. The fact that Gomizunoo chose her, not a son or son-in-law, to take charge of her brothers' estates is also proof of her talent for management.

Inheriting her father's indefatigable curiosity and energy, Shinanomiya loved the spectacles of processions of shogunal emissaries visiting the imperial palace or the Korean embassy on their way to Edo. She would rent a house close to the boulevard where the parade was expected, stay overnight, and wait along the street for several hours (for example, see 1680/9/20; 1682/8/7; 1687/4/23). Once she was captivated by the sight of a foppish young man in the street, the likes of whom she had seen only in woodblock prints but not in person. In amazement, she described his entire outlandish outfit (1691/3/22).

Shinanomiya also inherited Gomizunoo's love of nature. In spring, she went out every day to see the cherry blossoms in all the famous areas of Kyoto and in the gardens of her acquaintances. She would write, "Today, suddenly I felt like going to view the cherry blossoms" or "to view autumn foliage." In spring and in autumn, she would follow her customary route, admiring the clouds of flowers in the eastern hills or the bro-cade of colored leaves spread across the western Kyoto temples. Although she traveled in a palanquin carried by her servants, her energy and mo-bility were astounding. She was always considerate and did not forget to allow the servants frequent rest stops and to provide them with abun-dant food and tea.

Once, while walking in the rain with her younger sister on a country road, she so admired the red maple leaves that had fallen on her wet umbrella that she had the open umbrella taken home as it was, to share the beauty of the leaves with her husband (1683/10/19). In winter she wrote, "It had snowed overnight. Wondering how the hills around the Shichiku villa might look, I left on the spur of the moment. From the tea arbor, the near and far mountains were spectacular, covered in magnifi-cent white. I completely forgot the cold" (1686/11/14). In that she never lost her sense of wonder at nature and the changing seasons, she was a true descendant of ancient court nobles.

After Motohiro finally achieved his long-awaited promotion to Kanpaku (1690), the Konoe assumed a more extravagant style of living. They attended fewer and fewer court events, sponsoring professional performances themselves instead. Their taste was catholic and mixed the popular with the sublime: court music and dances, Nō and Kyōgen, Heike chanting, popular music, and puppets. Commoner performers usually stayed overnight at the Konoe mansion. The Konoe had always permit-ted their household staff to enjoy entertainments, but the audiences, too, began to widen to include commoners and old employees of the retired and deceased emperors. The couple also performed music together. Motohiro was an excellent *koto* player and also good at flute and Pan's pipe.[9] In 1695, Shinanomiya resumed practicing *koto* after many years. A group of musically talented aristocrats gathered frequently at the Konoe house. Shinanomiya joined the performances when the musicians were family members (including her son and her brother Prince Shinkei) and close friends. Once she asked her sister Emperor Meishō if she could have Her Majesty's unused *koto*. The aging Meishō, who had become increasingly lonely and dependent on Shinanomiya's company, gladly sent it (1695/2/22). When it arrived, Shinanomiya related its long and distinguished history to her husband and son Iehiro, then sent it to be restrung (1695/3/3).

When Iehiro lost his wife, the First Princess, prematurely due to the miscarriage of their third child (1688/4/15), Shinanomiya undertook the rearing of their daughter and son. Transformed into a typical grand-mother, she was openly affectionate and doted on her grandchildren. Iehiro was a devoted son and visited his mother every day. In addition, Shinanomiya wisely sent the children frequently to their father's house, where they could spend time together. Her rearing of the grandchildren was successful: Happily married to Tokudaiji Kintomo, Tokugimi was extremely kind to her widowed grandfather Motohiro. She died at the age of thirty-five (1721/9/23), about a year before him. Iehisa became a distinguished Kanpaku.

Shinanomiya and Motohiro appear to have been unusually compatible, although toward the end, they may not have been very close. Motohiro showed no sign of philandering, and his two later children were born to two women long after his wife's death. Two months prior to her final entry in the diary, she remarked, "My Lord Kanpaku grows more powerful, younger, and more energetic; it is truly to be congratulated" (1700/1/1). In her final years she was sporadically ill; probably she felt infinitely older than Motohiro and may have been envious of her still youthful and vigorous husband. Growing more introspective, she often escaped to the Shichiku villa for a solitary appreciation of nature.

After the spring of 1700, she could write no longer. Two years later, Motohiro wrote, "At dawn, Sakurai [butler] came to my bedroom and conveyed the doctor's words, 'Her Ladyship's condition is critical.' I was astonished and rushed to see her. Her end which came about 8 A.M. was nothing to be ashamed of" (1702/8/26).

The main objective of Shinanomiya's life was the preservation of the traditional system of court society and the perpetuation of the Konoe prosperity. Under the aegis of learned emperors such as Goyōzei, Gomizunoo, Gosai, and Reigen, the seventeenth century saw special efforts made to return to the cultural traditions of the ancient court. Both Shinanomiya and Motohiro were noted exponents and collaborators in these endeavors. It was, however, also an era when peace permitted educated commoners to act as cultural arbiters and to regenerate legacies from the past to create new art. Their energy began to infiltrate into the upper class through the samurai, clergy, and aristocrats they associated with. By the end of the century, that impetus had revitalized the entire society. This energy and vitality was what Shinanomiya absorbed from the era, and it saved her from becoming a desiccated traditionalist.

Shinanomiya never mentioned any of the classical women writers, yet she might have had them in mind when she decided to write a diary of her own. In so doing, she celebrated the life she knew and lived. She made a valuable contribution to the human heritage: a rare chronicle of the generally unknown lives of aristocratic women in seventeenth-century Japan, specifically the growth of an intelligent, unconventional, and energetic woman who enjoyed and appreciated her life to the fullest extent.

NOTES

1. All of the dated citations from Shinanomiya's diary refer to "Mujōhōin-dono gonikki," a copy of the manuscript in the archives of the Historiographical Institute of the University of Tokyo. The original is at the Konoe archives (Yōmei bunkō) in Kyoto.

2. Citations from Motohiro's diary refer to "Motohirokō ki," a copy of the manuscript in the archives of the Historiographical Institute of the University of Tokyo; the original is also at the Yōmei bunkō. Her brother's diary has been published: "Gyōjo hōshinnō nikki," in *Myōhōin shiryō*, vols. 1–3 (Tokyo: Yoshikawa Kōbunkan, 1976–1978).

3. All ages in this essay follow the Western count. In Japanese records, these ages will appear as a year, or sometimes two years, older. Before World War II, the Japanese assigned babies one year at birth, then added one year with each new year. Thus, a baby born on the last day of December was two years old on New Year's day.

4. This was a princely sum; one ryō was sufficient for one person to subsist on for a year at that time.

5. One koku of rice, or 5.1 bushels, was enough to feed one man for one year.

6. Kuroita Katsumi, ed., *Tokugawa jikki*, 15 vols. (Tokyo: Yoshikawa Kōbunkan, 1929–1936; reprint ed., 1990–1991) 5,231 (1676/2/21).

7. "Gyōjo hōshinnō nikki," 2,289 (1682/2/19).

8. Iijima Yoshiharu, "Kodomo no hakken to jidōyūgi no sekai," in *Ie to josei* (Tokyo: Shōgakkan, 1985), 243, 247.

9. Heike chanting told the story of the Taira and Minamoto families locked in mortal combat in the late twelfth century that ended in the Taira defeat. The *koto* is a stringed instrument, now commonly associated with women.

SUGGESTED READINGS

Bernstein, Gail Lee, ed. *Recreating Japanese Women, 1600–1945*. Berkeley: University of California Press, 1991.

Griswold, Susan. "Sexuality, Textuality and the Definition of the 'Feminine' in Late Eighteenth-Century Japan." *U.S.-Japan Women's Journal* 9 (1995): 59–76.

Institute for Medieval Japanese Studies. *Seasons of Sacred Celebration: Flowers and Poetry from an Imperial Convent*. New York: Columbia University and Weatherhill, 1998.

Jones, Sumie, ed. *Imagining/Reading Eros*. Bloomington: Indiana University Press, 1996.

Lebra, Takie Sugiyama. *Above the Clouds: Status Culture of the Modern Japanese Nobility*. Berkeley: University of California Press, 1993.

Ruch, Barbara, ed. *Japanese Women and Buddhism*. Ann Arbor: University of Michigan, Center for Japanese Studies, forthcoming.

Seigle, Cecilia Segawa. "Shogun's Consort: Konoe Hiroko and Tokugawa Ienobu." *Harvard Journal of Asiatic Studies* 59, no. 2 (December 1999): 485–522.

Tonomura, Hiromi, Anne Walthall, and Wakita Haruko, eds. *Women and Class in Japanese History*. Ann Arbor: University of Michigan, Center for Japanese Studies, 1999.

SUGGESTED READINGS (IN JAPANESE)

Emori, Itsuo. *Reikishi no naka no Josei: Jinruigaku to hōshakaigaku karano kōsatsu*. Tokyo: Sairyūsha, 1995.

"Gyōjo hōshinnō nikki," in *Myōhōin shiryō*, vols. 1–3. Tokyo: Yoshikawa Kōbunkan, 1976–1978.

Hayashi, Reiko, ed. *Josei no kinsei*, vol. 15 of *Nihon no kinsei*. Tokyo: Chūō Kōronsha, 1993.

Imatani, Akira. *Buke to tennō*. Tokyo: Iwanami Shoten, 1993.

Iwasa, Miyoko. *Kyūtei ni ikiru: Tennō to nyōbō to*. Tokyo: Kasama Shoten, 1997.

Joseishi Sōgō Kenkyūkai, ed. *Kinsei*, vol. 3 of *Nihon joseishi*. Tokyo: Daigaku Shuppankai, 1982.

Kubo, Takako. *Kinsei no chōtei unei*. Tokyo: Iwata Shoten, 1998.

_____. "Buke shakai ni ikita kuge josei." *Josei no kinsei*, vol. 15 of *Nihon no kinsei*. Tokyo: Chūō Kōronsha, 1993. Pp. 71–96.

Kumakura Isao. *Gomizunoo tennō*. Tokyo: Iwanami Shoten, 1994.

Tsuboi, Hirofumi, et al., eds. *Ie to joseishi: Kurashi no bunkashi*, vol. 10 of *Nihon minzoku bunka taikei*. Tokyo: Shōgakkan, 1985.

CHAPTER 2

Mori Yoshiki

Samurai Government Officer

LUKE ROBERTS

Inherent status inequality structured Japanese society before most heredi-tary distinctions were officially abolished in 1873. Samurai stood at the apex, yet even this class could be broken down into countless gradations. Mori Yoshiki belonged to the upper ranks of a large, powerful domain. He filled his days doing administrative work or pursuing scholarship, his sword constantly by his side. All samurai and their daimyo lords discovered by the middle of the eighteenth century that their secure stipends and taxes on agriculture no longer sufficed to maintain an adequate standard of living. The growth of a commercial economy disproportionately benefited the en-trepreneurs, both urban and rural, who were in direct contact with the production, transportation, and distribution of goods. Like many other domains, Tosa tried to capture at least some commercial revenue through taxation, direct marketing of domanial resources, and the selling of samu-rai status to wealthy commoners. The conflicts engendered by these mea-sures sorely tried Yoshiki and his colleagues.

Yoshiki's career from redundant son to guardian of the lord's heir exposes the diverse opportunities and responsibilities accruing to a compe-tent and conscientious samurai. Along the way, we learn a great deal about a judicial system in which the government reneges on promises, reopens cases, and fudges judgments all in the name of preserving order. We catch glimpses of the relations among the classes characterized by negotiation and compromise, the tensions between the daimyo of Tosa and his Tokugawa overlord, and the rituals of rule that held the system together. At the indi-vidual level we see the importance of honor and the role of violence in the construction of samurai masculinity.

Associate professor of history at the University of California, Santa Barbara, Luke Roberts is a specialist in the history of the Tosa domain. He is the author of Mercantilism in a Japanese Domain: The Merchant Origins of Economic Nationalism in Eighteenth-Century Tosa *(1998).*

The life of the samurai named Mori Yoshiki (1768–1807) must begin by introducing his father, Mori Hirosada (1710–1773) and the place where

Yoshiki grew up. In a world of inherited status, origins were important. Mori Hirosada was a member of the mounted guard of the Yamauchi clan. The Yamauchi lords possessed the domanial country of Tosa, a mountainous province about the size of the state of Delaware, which lay on the island of Shikoku in a warm, southern clime known for palm trees and typhoons. Samurai and the many lesser retainers of the domain served their lord as government administrators, warriors, and companions. The companions, members of the *koshō* regiment, traveled with their lord once a year either to or from the city of Edo, which was four hundred miles to the east of Tosa, because the Yamauchi lord was required to live every other year in Edo in order to attend the court of his overlord, the head of the Tokugawa clan, who was feudal ruler over all of Japan. When the Yamauchi lord went to Edo, he took as many as three thousand retainers and servants along for the trip. The remainder of his samurai lived continuously in Tosa, most of them in the castle town of Kōchi, a city of around fifteen thousand people situated near the Pacific coast at the center of the realm.

Yoshiki's father, Hirosada, had served consistently in military positions, not with the companion regiment. He rose from common mounted guard to standard-bearer, to captain of a unit in the home-defense forces, thence to captain of a unit of twenty musketeers, and finally by the time of his third marriage, he became captain of a whole unit of mounted guards in the attack forces. Of course, Hirosada never saw war. There had been no warfare on the Japanese islands since the Shimabara rebellion of 1637. The rule of the Tokugawa overlords was solid and stable, and in Hirosada's day there was not even a hint of rebellion or warfare among the elite samurai. People usually referred to "the Great Peace" maintained by the Tokugawa in admiring and laudatory terms.

Hirosada, however, took great pleasure in hunting. One day in 1745 he was out hunting with friends, lying in wait on a boars' run. They had hired farmers as beaters who made a racket back in the hills to chase the animals into the ambush. A large boar came running. The samurai let loose the charges in their muskets, hitting it. The wounded and enraged boar charged; the hunters scattered to find safety in trees. Hirosada had no tree nearby, and the boar came straight at him. Having no alternative, he drew his sword and swung down at the boar, "killing it with one stroke," he wrote with great pride in his diary. This was the closest Hirosada had ever come to using the military skills he practiced regularly. They constituted part of the legacy he left to his son Yoshiki.

A more important part of that legacy may have been Hirosada's love of writing, for he was a literate and learned man. He maintained a diary rich in the happenings in the domain and his own life from the age of twenty-two until he was sixty-three, the year before his death. The diary reveals that in addition to military arts he studied the tea ceremony and incense appreciation and pursued scholarly studies under leading teachers of the domain. He also copied by hand many works on various topics, from court ceremony to war tales, and even a cookbook of favorite household recipes created by the samurai of his domain. He especially enjoyed studying old war records and the military arts of days gone by. He led a reading group of fellow samurai, in which they studied how a proper samurai was supposed to behave in various situations. In one lesson, Hirosada taught that when the need came to execute a servant, the samurai should call him out, saying, "Bring your weapons and defend yourself as you may, because I accuse you of such-and-such a crime and I will slay you." A military servant of *wakatō* status should be allowed to wield his two swords in his defense, and a military servant of the lesser *komono* status his one sword.[1] For Hirosada, the story meant that a samurai's authority lay in his superior skill in arms, in that he was naturally able to best an armed opponent. Today, most historians would note the way status issues pervade the event, giving the samurai an unfair advantage.

Hereditary status in Edo Japan was one important quality by which people defined themselves and which they often considered in determining their actions. In this time of "the Great Peace," samurai still talked about their capacity and right to use violence to exact their notions of justice, usually to enforce respect for the status system. The right to kill a commoner or servant for "rudeness" was in the law books of most domains in Japan. In reality, such personal violence was rare. When it occurred, as we shall see below, it often provoked lively debate. Few samurai in Tosa had exercised the right without being punished themselves. When Hirosada was displeased with his *komono* servants, he simply fired them. The acceptance of peace meant that the social order was maintained through habit, ritual, and suasion. When this did not suffice, bureaucratic forms of violence such as police, judges, prisons, and, occasionally, executioners constituted the means of enforcement. Samurai ran this bureaucracy that enforced the social order–status system and their own privileged position within it. The way status and government violence operated, however, was much more subtle and complex than a cursory description of the ruling ideology would have us believe.

An example of the complexities of status can be seen in the case of Yoshiki's mother, Umeno. When Hirosada married her in 1764, the lord would not recognize the marriage. The law was clear on this point: "No samurai should request to have a woman beneath his status recognized as wife. Each is free to call such a person wife without requesting formal recognition."[2] Umeno had been his household servant; she was not of samurai birth. Despite the pervasive status consciousness, however, she was recognized by samurai friends and family as, indeed, Hirosada's wife.

The marriage rites at home were formal and carried out in the presence of friends and relatives, who celebrated the occasion afterward with feasting and drinking. Umeno was twenty-five at the time and Hirosada was fifty-four. Hirosada's first two wives, both samurai, had died, and neither union had produced a male child although he did have two daughters, Otsune and Omase, each by a different mother (Omase's mother was Riso, another household servant). In lieu of a son from a wife, a child from a concubine or servant was an acceptable heir in the eyes of the domain. In lieu of even this kind of heir, domain officials also rather easily recognized the adoption of an heir from among relatives. Hirosada had been ill in 1759 and had in that year already adopted his nephew, Hirotake, as inheriting son. So, the marriage to Umeno, not acknowledged by the domain in any case, was not to make sure that any future son would be his heir. It was rather to ensure that Umeno's status was recognized by all within the household and among friends and relatives. Home life was governed by rituals. As wife, Umeno gained commanding authority over servants of the house and over Hirotake's bride Hayashi Oyoyo in her role as mother-in-law.[3]

Umeno's status may have had a hand in Yoshiki's fate. She gave birth to him in late 1768. When Hirosada died in 1773, at the age of sixty-three, Yoshiki was only five years old. As Hirosada's heir, Yoshiki's elder cousin/adoptive elder brother Hirotake became head of the household. Yoshiki seemed destined to lead the anonymous life of a samurai younger brother, a position many people of the day called a *yakkai*, a "don't-know-what-to-do-with." In 1775, however, Hirotake formally adopted Yoshiki as his son and heir. This meant that if Hirotake had later had children of his own, they would not have inherited the family headship. Given that Hirotake was still relatively young and presumably potent, this adoption has to be considered an early one. The reason may have been a desire to maintain Hirosada's bloodline, or it may reflect Umeno's authority as mother of the house, but no records survive to explain why this decision was made. From Yoshiki's perspective, one can imagine his confusion as he tried to learn the formalities of behavior with Hirotake in his changing identities as elder brother and then adoptive father. Yoshiki was seven years old at the time of his adoption and, as part of the rituals, had his first audience with the twenty-five-year-old lord of the domain, Yamauchi Toyochika. This gave him a public identity, and he was no longer a *yakkai*.[4]

Hirotake went to Edo to serve in the companion regiment where he died suddenly in 1778. This made Yoshiki the legal head of the house at age ten. In 1783 he was appointed to the lord's companion regiment and thereafter traveled to Edo and back in the biennial cycle. Edo, Japan's melting pot, was a large city with a vibrant urban culture. Its population of a million people not only dwarfed Kōchi castle town, but was more than double the population of the whole realm of Tosa itself. Being there had a great impact on Yoshiki's life. It gave him connections with influential people, and he made many of his closest lifelong friends at this time. Living in Edo also gave him ties to the samurai of other domains. Socializing with members of other domains was highly restricted (to prevent troublesome incidents) outside the private academies. Yoshiki took advantage of this loophole to exchange and copy rare manuscript books and continue his passionate study of history.

Yoshiki's first appointment came in 1788 at a time of severe hardship in Tosa and crisis in the government. For eighty years the economy of the region and the finances of the domain had been increasingly in trouble. For nearly that long, the government had been collecting surplus taxes in a futile attempt to balance the budget. Four straight years of poor harvests had led to unprecedented levels of commoner protest and rioting in the year 1787. The most significant incident occurred when two whole villages, more than seven hundred people, fled across the border into the neighboring domain, ostensibly to beg that lord to make them his subjects because their own lord was no good, but in reality to get their demands approved by the Tosa government. The Tosa officials coaxed them back only after many weeks of negotiation, in which the domain gave in to every demand of the protesters and promised not to punish anyone for the crime of disobedience. It is clear that famine had played a part in further increasing antagonism toward a government that was reputed to be corrupt and that was profligately spending money despite hardship among the people of the realm.

The lord Toyochika launched a reform of the government in 1787, attempting to cut expenses and restore a degree of popular trust in the rulers. He appointed many new and inexperienced officials with the hope that new blood would help wash out the corruption. In 1788 he ordered Yoshiki to make an official tour of the western half of the domain, stopping at each village to hear reports of conditions and demonstrate to the locals that the lord was concerned about their welfare. The headman of one of the first villages Yoshiki arrived at complained about the high expense in being forced to take care of the traveling groups of blind women entertainers (*bikuni*). He wanted their route moved to a larger village. "The Nanokawa villagers were able to be relieved of the duty to take care of the entertainers because of last year's protest when they fled to Iyo province," he pointed out. "Despite the fact that they broke serious laws [by doing so], they were brought back with a promise of forgiveness. . . . To order things just as they please for peasants who band together and flee and to order great problems for people who keep the law! People will think that if a request is made and turned down, then they should just band together and flee and then it will be approved."[5]

After the journey, Yoshiki wrote his report. In time the domain broke its promise to the Nanokawa villagers of no reprisals. Two leaders were executed and the villagers were fined.[6]

Yoshiki was on track to move up in the ranks of the companion regiment when misfortune struck. Toyochika fell ill and died in 1789 at the age of forty. His heir Toyokazu became lord, and Toyokazu's own circle of retainers became the core of the new companion regiment. After the funeral and four months of official mourning, Yoshiki and his friends were sent back to their homes.

Yoshiki's next appointment was within the domain administration, when he was made magistrate in charge of the ports of Tosa in 1793. If his office diary is any indication, there was very little work to do. Phrases such as "nothing to do today" or "the usual" appear frequently.[7] He probably spent most workdays signing documents his subordinates had created, certifying appointments of port officials and records of fish catches and export taxes. Major policy decisions were left to officials higher up, and routine events were controlled by those beneath him. As with most higher positions, his work schedule required only five or six days per month. On these occasions, Yoshiki showed up at the large government office complex in the middle of town. The rest of the time he was on call and always had to report his whereabouts in case emergencies arose.

One day in 1797 the government office complex suddenly erupted in talk that Inoue Sabanoshin, a samurai, had killed a rural samurai named Takamura Taigo.[8] Rural samurai, or *gōshi*, had the status just beneath the right of audience with the lord and thus, in samurai regard, were commoners. Four other samurai present at the murder included Mori Kumenoshin, Yoshiki's cousin, who was head of a collateral house of the Mori clan. At the end of the workday, Yoshiki immediately went to Kumenoshin to find out exactly what had happened. Kumenoshin had been drinking and eating with two other samurai friends and the rural samurai Takamura Taigo, who said that he had gotten his hands on some beef, a rare treat in those days. He invited them to partake of it with him at his home village of Amaeda, about a three-hour walk to the east. They all decided they wanted to ask their friend Inoue Sabanoshin to come along, and so they went, somewhat inebriated, to his house.

Sabanoshin already had two visitors, a rural samurai and another retainer of sub-samurai status, who had come to help resolve a dispute between Sabanoshin and his brother-in-law Yoshida Kuraji. Both Sabanoshin and Kuraji desired the same woman, the commoner daughter of a widow. Sabanoshin had asked her to become a household servant, promising that in time he would make her his wife. Then Sabanoshin got jealous of Kuraji's attentions to her and started an argument. In return, Kuraji summarily divorced his wife, who was Sabanoshin's sister. The two visitors were talking with Sabanoshin about this problem when Kumenoshin and his friends arrived. They sat waiting in a separate room while the discussions were going on. Taigo, however, walked into the other room to hear the tale. The other rural samurai knew that "there was never such a quick-tempered man as Sabanoshin." It was best to appease him. They assured him that he would get his woman soon, because he was such a fearsome man. Sabanoshin's masculinity, formed in part through his ability to control women, had been doubly threatened. He had not yet gotten the woman he wanted, and he could not "place" a woman in his control. His sister had been returned as "unsatisfactory," even though, as Sabanoshin knew, the truly unsatisfactory behavior had been his own.

Here the inebriated Taigo made a fatal mistake. Perhaps in jest, he said, "What? What could Sabanoshin cut with his stinking arm and rusty sword?" Sabanoshin then said, "Let's see if I can cut!" and thrust his sword through Taigo's sidelocks, slicing him badly. He then grabbed Taigo by the topknot and dragged him into the room where the other samurai were sitting. Everyone tried to stop the fight and let Sabanoshin have his say. He explained his anger over the insult and then said, "I leave it up to you. You tell me how I can resolve this and be a man." They all knew that a samurai would be punished severely for drawing his sword in anger, unless he had sufficient reason to assert his right to execute a person of lower status for being rude. They looked at Taigo lying on the floor, moaning and holding his head. They inspected the wound to see if it could be passed off as a razor cut. It was too big, so they decided to make a case of execution for extreme rudeness.

Sabanoshin faced Taigo, saying, "You have been criminally rude to a samurai. I cannot let this go and I am going to execute you. Do you have anything to say?" Terrified, Taigo answered that he had been wrong. Sabanoshin then killed him with his sword. The samurai told the rural samurai and the lesser retainer to leave and keep their mouths shut. The incident was to be described as if they had not been present. The samurai did this because the interrogation of the two lower-ranking men would have disclosed Sabanoshin's anger and desire, emotions that would have made him to some degree guilty of murder. The samurai themselves went separately to the captains of their units to report the incident. Sabanoshin also sent a report to the commander of Taigo's division and then waited at home for the inspectors to arrive.

Sabanoshin told the inspectors a slightly different story that made it look as if he had not lost his temper. His version was that the three samurai and Taigo had come over to talk, and Sabanoshin had brought out his collection of swords. He then told the inspectors, "At that point, Taigo became rude and said, 'With your stinking arm and rusty sword you couldn't cut my neck!'

" 'Are you totally insane?' I replied.

" 'I am not the least insane.' He thrust out his neck at me, saying, 'You couldn't cut it if you wanted to!'

" 'I could not bear this so I killed him.' "

The inspectors also asked Sabanoshin if he had served sake and if others of Taigo's status were present—to which Sabanoshin replied no. Sake would have made him more culpable for his violence and Taigo less culpable for his words. The other question probably had two implications. First, it was officially frowned on to fraternize outside one's status group. Even though such relations were common, when it led to incidents, the party of higher rank was often deemed at least partially guilty. Second, the inspectors may have worried that the witnesses of lower status might talk. They also asked Sabanoshin if he knew Taigo. He answered vaguely that Taigo had come to his place a few times, leaving out the fact that he had himself stayed at Taigo's house in the country considerably more often than once. It was illegal for a warrior on duty to stay outside the city without permission. Besides, Sabanoshin did not want to admit that he and Taigo were friends, because that would have meant that he should have been more tolerant of the insult. The inspectors had Sabanoshin write down his statement and asked him again if it were wholly true, which he reaffirmed. His own servants were questioned separately and then ordered to dispose of the body properly.

The unit captain then ordered Sabanoshin to suspend his duties and socializing while he awaited judgment. The judgment, which came after two months, was that, although the incident arose because he had been fraternizing with someone below his status and this should cease, Sabanoshin had been right to kill Taigo for his extreme rudeness. The other four samurai present were let off but warned against fraternizing as well.

The rural samurai were incensed at the judgment and began organizing in protest. There were around eight hundred households of rural samurai in Tosa, about a hundred more than the number of full samurai households. Furthermore, they represented the highest rank of retainers beneath samurai. Some were distant descendants of warriors who had served the previous lordly dynasty of the sixteenth century. Unlike the full samurai, however, *gōshi* was a rank that could be bought and sold by commoners. Many *gōshi* were simultaneously rich landlords and members of extended families of business entrepreneurs. Although they did not have the full samurai right of formal audience with the lord, they were permitted to wear two swords and to ride in the most important domain ritual, the annual military parade. Indeed, while many samurai opted out of the parade because they could not afford to keep or rent a horse, it was often noted that the rural samurai rode the finest horses and were dressed in the latest fashions. Yoshiki himself wore an old red jacket and rather plain sword and scabbard when he rode in the parade. His wife remembered how she had once asked him to at least replace his faded jacket, but he made a virtue of frugality, saying, somewhat defensively, "I respect old weapons and armor. . . . Armor is different from what women think!"[9] For reasons such as these, both samurai and rural samurai felt insecure in their status, and conflicts often arose that required adjudication.

In Tosa as in most of the other realms in Japan, enforcing the letter of the law was secondary to maintaining the public peace. In most cases, each side had to expect a judgment that required it to yield a little. Thus, the laws on the books did not have the authority they might appear to have. As for the legal right of a samurai to execute a person of lesser status for rudeness, one might assume that this gave the samurai free rein, but in actuality it did not. It usually led him into deep trouble. Only if his conduct were so spotless and the misconduct of the murdered party so obvious that the survivors would not strongly question the justice of the execution, would a samurai escape punishment. This time, not merely relatives but a whole status group complained of injustice. The gathering storm of protest made the samurai uncomfortable. They started saying that, unlike similar previous situations in which the inspectors had exerted themselves to the utmost, this time the judgment had been made too casually and without taking the opinions of rural samurai into account.

The case thus had to be reconsidered. Within a month a new judgment was announced. The government took away Sabanoshin's substantial fief of 200 koku, demoted him in status from mounted guard to the "equivalent of page," and gave him only a small stipend to live on. This new judgment was ostensibly based on the grounds that Sabanoshin "had been living loosely." It was a concession, but hardly enough to appease the rural samurai, who were incensed at the continued insult to their status. They organized the writing of petitions and lobbied samurai who were friends. "Was not Nonomura Chūemon banished for killing a coatmaker, and Matsui Dōsetsu banished for killing a landless peasant?" they complained. "If such a judgment is given for even a townsman and landless peasant, then the judgment for killing a member of the military should be more severe! . . . Last year, Itasaka Umazaemon was ordered to commit ritual suicide because he had speared to death one of his *wakatō* retainers." At this point, Yoshiki, who had been watching events unfold, became deeply involved in resolving the issue, visiting samurai friends and chief government officials to gain information and offer advice. Many people showed him drafts of petitions they were writing. One samurai wrote five separate drafts and asked Yoshiki for his opinion. They all argued the basic point that the judgment was correct, being based on the need to treat old lineages and new lineages differently. Presumably, the venerable Inoue house needed to be preserved. Although Yoshiki may have let his friend down easy, he confided in his diary that all five versions were "utter nonsense!"

The government then tried to put a spin on the judgment. It issued an official statement that it did not give samurai the right to cut down rural samurai for any rudeness at any time; all cases had special circumstances that must be considered. In this instance, the murdered Taigo had been guilty of much loose living, and the incident should serve as a reminder to all to behave with greater decorum. Rural samurai, whom Yoshiki heard on the subject, responded with, "Is Sabanoshin a person of good character? . . . Had he not spent four or five nights at Taigo's, which is a crime, . . . had they not eaten together and slept under one roof ? . . To kill such a friend who in a state of drunkenness chanced to say rude words is pitiless and shameful. . . . Does this mean that any samurai equal to Sabanoshin in character has the right to slay a rural samurai?"

The official statement satisfied no one. The very next day one of Yoshiki's friends, the respected and venerable Fukutomi Hanjo, came to say that a crisis was looming and that the relevant government officials should resign by way of apology. He wanted Yoshiki to funnel this message to the lord via Shosaburō, one of the three senior administrators. Yoshiki replied that even Shosaburō's own retainers think him "gutless and useless." Therefore, he approached another senior administrator, Moku, with whom he had close ties. Moku took the position that although the idea had merit, "relevant officials" would bring about wide-ranging resignations, including those of the senior administrators, and leave new appointments open to undue influence by the lord's companions. Moku's worries over internal house politics prevented him from acting decisively on this case.

The following days were filled with rumor. Five days later, Yoshiki wrote in his record of this incident, "People are getting extremely agitated, and it burns my heart." Many people suggested that a direct missive from the lord should be issued to forestall a large protest by the rural samurai. One rural samurai assigned to Moku's own division submitted a petition to Moku, stating that if Sabanoshin were not ordered to commit ritual suicide, then the rural samurai would be without honor and hardly have the desire to die in battle for their lord. Yoshiki repeatedly urged Moku to get the lord to make a statement, but Moku continued to talk endlessly with the other administrators, "again resolving nothing," Yoshiki fumed.

Officially submitted petitions by rural samurai came flooding in. One of them stated, "Human life is a precious thing, and so the government orders execution only after a criminal has written a signed confession to the most heinous of crimes. How can the decision to cut down a man who is even a member of the military be left to the understanding of a single samurai? . . . To be treated as less than a criminal or beast takes away all desire to do faithful service." The senior officials endlessly debated whether they should resign, whether the lord should directly issue a judgment, and what the conditions were under which the samurai right of execution should be defended. Meanwhile, more than seventy or eighty rural samurai submitted petitions, and they filled the castle town with their presence. Yoshiki and many of his friends became upset at the inability of the three senior administrators to take action. One of his friends, Chōhei, a house elder of the highest status, complained, "They should take the petitions into account and start making decisions." Yoshiki himself had learned many of the opinions of the rural samurai. On his visit to Chōhei, he laid them out. Chōhei was shocked: "Presented to me like that, I would not know how to respond." They agreed that a judgment was needed soon, as each day the situation was becoming worse. Fights were breaking out at large gatherings, fortunately with no bloodshed, and a major festival was only weeks away. Some samurai dining at an inn had heard rural samurai calling them "executioners."

That same night, Chōhei took Yoshiki around to the important parties and got them all to agree that the domain should not try to defend its position to the rural samurai. Instead, it would send out an announcement that all petitions from rural samurai that had been submitted to lower authorities would be forwarded to the senior administrators so that they could make a judgment. As everyone had finally come to agree that this was the best course of action, they had the lord issue a decree supporting this statement and thanking all his retainers for their loyal service. Within days the many rural samurai who had assembled in town began returning to their homes. Commanders and captains, in reading out the official admonition, repeatedly reminded all their subordinates to behave properly and cause no incidents: "Correct your behavior, and devote your mind to letters and the military arts. . . . Be polite and forbearing so that superior and inferior will trust each other and be in harmony, and make having a heart of merciful love of first importance."

It is interesting that Yoshiki closes his diarylike account of the affair with this admonition issued by the senior councillors on the twenty-fourth day of the sixth month—the true denouement to the three months of disorder caused by Sabanoshin's rash temper and a faulty judgment by the inspectors. No general statement on the rights and wrongs of the samurai privilege of summary execution had been made, but the rural samurai felt that they finally were being heard and given the respect due their status. In terms of the crisis, the final punishment of Sabanoshin was but a postscript. It did not come for three years, in 1801, when he was banished to the western reaches of the domain and all of his income was confiscated.

Yoshiki's key role in the resolution of the crisis earned him the respect of many chief officials in government. In the tenth month of 1797 he was appointed a grand inspector—the chief of investigations in charge of most of the judicial decisions in the domain, a post he shared with two other men.[10] Most senior positions in the domain required three holders simultaneously. The three officials were put on a rotating schedule so that only one was on duty each month. The duty official might consult with the other two on important matters, but mostly he managed his month alone. Normally, only one of the trio would be replaced at a time. This allowed the third member to be integrated into the role by the two experienced officials. This time it was different. The Taigo murder case had shaken the government badly, and many officials had had to take responsibility. Within four months, two of the senior administrators resigned, and all three of the junior administrators were relieved of office. All three grand inspectors had been laid off in a single day—the day that Yoshiki began work with two other fresh recruits.[11]

Yoshiki's duties included sitting in council with the senior administrator and junior administrator to deliberate policy issues for the domain. He clearly relished this role, and his diary is filled with descriptions of these deliberations. He had to investigate and approve all personnel appointments and inheritances. He also judged one case of rural protest in the Toyonaga district of mountain villages. The villagers were suffering from unfair exchange rates set by the domain for rice to cash that effectively increased their tax payments. Eight villages declared that they would refuse their duty to be porters on the lord's alternate attendance trip to Edo. Four hundred of them gathered on a river plain where lower domain officials came out to meet them. The officials explained the domain's position. When the villagers seemed loathe to acquiesce, the officials captured thirteen of the leaders and took at least four of them to judgment in Kōchi. The four were interrogated by the inspector of commoners (*kachi metsuke*), one of Yoshiki's subordinates who handled most of the cases involving only commoners. Here, because of the seriousness of the crime of leading group insubordination, Yoshiki also interrogated them. More than a month later the inspector of commoners recommended that the three villagers who had come to be identified as the leaders of the protest not be executed. Yoshiki asked for his reasons and insisted on a recommendation of the death penalty. He does not explain his decision in the diary, but he probably felt the need to assert domain authority. Later, for the final judgment, he recommended that the chief leader be executed and the others banished to the farthest regions of the domain. He must have felt certain that no subsequent protest would occur to embarrass the government and that it was important to defend the status hierarchy with severity.

That decision did not necessarily mean that commoners could be suppressed with impunity. Each case was to be judged according to its merits. Indeed, as we have seen, the protests of 1787 had brought down the administration and led to a major government reform. The domain had promised not to punish the protesters but later broke its word because, as the village headman had pointed out to Yoshiki during his tour, a viable threat of violence was needed to maintain the unequal social order.

On another occasion in 1798, Yoshiki and his group of administrators decided to defer to the demands of commoners. The domain needed to float lumber it owned down the Kokubu River to the coast in order to ship it to Osaka for sale. This was a serious matter for a domain always strapped for money, but the villagers along the river would not allow it. Logs floated downstream frequently damaged dikes and the irrigation system essential to rice farming. Finally, three senior officials of the domain, including Yoshiki, traveled to one of the villages where the various headmen had gathered. There they promised that if the villagers acquiesced, the domain would promise not to send the logs down during the dangerous times of high water, that it would repair any dike damage at its own expense, and that the villages would be given a special tax break by way of compensation.

In the first month of 1798, Yoshiki was promoted to the office of junior administrator, the highest position in the management of domain government that a person of his status could attain, subordinate only to the senior administrators and the lord himself. As with the other high officials, he served with two other junior administrators on a rotating monthly schedule. In his first month of duty, an incident occurred that revealed how badly the mismanagement of the Taigo incident had shaken the government's confidence.[12] A report had come in that, only one month before the lord's departure for Edo, the rural samurai Nonaka Jōhei had threatened to put gunpowder under the floor of the room where the lord stayed on his trip and "blow up the lord and his companions." One would imagine the government response to be swift and simple, yet the senior administrators, junior administrators, and grand inspectors had to discuss in council what they should do. The inspectors said, "If we investigate this now, then the rural samurai will become agitated. Let's investigate it after the lord has left." They had to remind themselves that "this is different from last year's incident," and that the lord's life might be in danger. Although Yoshiki does not mention this in his record of their deliberations, they probably were most worried about the unrest that might arise if the accusation were to prove false. Would the rural samurai feel slandered? It took them two full days to decide to send out a party to arrest Jōhei. They were relieved when he was captured without incident, and things seemed at first to be as his accuser, Watanabe Sakuta, had claimed. No protest arose, but months of subsequent investigations revealed that the accusation was false. Jōhei was set free. The domain stripped Sakuta of his samurai status and family name, banished him to the western reaches of the domain, and ordered many of his relatives into short periods of house arrest.

In addition to the sort of administrative matters and criminal issues described above, which we might see as properly governmental, many of Yoshiki's most important duties both as grand inspector and as junior administrator involved ritual observances devoted to his lord. This was, after all, an aristocratic government centered upon the person of the lord and his family. On days of prayer for lordly ancestors, Yoshiki had to attend services at their temple, and for such rites of passage as a birth, he had to make the rounds of greetings to the various family members. When one of the lord's family died, then the whole government office would be closed for a week as a sign of respect. All retainers high and low were considered members of the lord's household and were thus bound to carry out family observances. For retainers without government office, these observances were infrequent, and their role was peripheral. The higher that one moved in government, the more frequent the ritual demands became. For example, on New Year's day, all samurai retainers were to have an "audience" with the lord, a symbolic reaffirmation of their promise of service and his care for them. As the youthful head of house with no office in 1791, Yoshiki had been required to line up with his unit on a road in town and stand at attention. The lord appeared to them in the castle above, so that Yoshiki got what he called "a bird's-eye audience."[13] In 1798, by contrast, the first ten days of the new year were devoted to his moving from one audience to another at the residences of the lord and the members of his family.

It was most important that the senior officials in charge of government be constantly reminded in ritual of the centrality of the lord to their existence. Often they were pressed with requests from Yamauchi family members for items that entailed the expenditure of more money. The officials did their best to limit such outlays, but if the lord himself wanted something, there was no saying no. Yoshiki wrote in one of his many memorials, "It would be immoral for someone below to order the lord to cut his own expenses." Nevertheless, there was a basic conflict of interest within the government. On the one hand, it functioned to support the lord and his family so that they could in turn serve the Tokugawa overlord. On the other hand, it had to run the domain and maintain peace. There were even two words for government: *kasei*, which meant "governance of the lord's house," and *kokusei*, or "governance of the domanial country." Both cost money and demanded other resources. Viewed over the long term of the domain's history, the relative importance of the lordly household declined, while that of the domanial country increased. The reason was simple. Local people were more frequently, and from positions of greater power, demanding better government. As in 1787, their protests could shake the domain. The reforms of 1787 had set a clear course of better domanial government, which entailed the conscious decision to provide less money for the lord's family and less service to the Tokugawa. Yet there was a fine line to be walked. If the lord did not serve the Tokugawa well, he might be disenfeoffed. In that event, all his retainers would lose their homes and livelihoods as well.

This political subservience to the Tokugawa order was also expressed in ritual. In the second month of 1798, a gift from the Tokugawa overlord arrived in Kōchi. It was the body of a crane, which had been killed by the head of the Tokugawa house himself and sent to the Yamauchi to make into soup. In all of Japan, only he had the right to hunt the crane. This symbolically asserted his ownership of the whole realm: his to dispense with as he saw fit.[14] When the present arrived, a senior administrator had to meet the messenger on the road as a sign of his lord's inferior status. Then all high governmental officials, including Yoshiki, had to be on hand when the gift was received at the castle in order to show the Tokugawa messenger their proper respect for the overlord and his gift.

In the eighth month of 1798, the domain's senior officials became worried that although their lord had been in Edo for three months, he had yet to be granted an audience by the Tokugawa. This was bad news. Perhaps the local reforms, which had required much belt-tightening and limited the Yamauchi's service to the overlord, had gone too far? They feared some kind of punishment was looming. Wishing to forestall disaster, they proposed that their lord request some construction duty for the benefit of the Tokugawa. Throughout their deliberations they realized this would be costly for the people of the domain—and terribly unpopular. When the Tokugawa assigned such duties, and they often did, the request was impossible to refuse. On the other hand, if news ever leaked out that the leaders of the Tosa government had actually *asked for* such duty, there was no telling what would happen. Still, the administrators' fear of possible Tokugawa anger ultimately led them to make this proposal.[15]

Yoshiki served as junior administrator for three years. He was respected, but much too outspoken for the senior councillors' taste. He had consistently and strongly urged that the domain government cut its expenses so as to be able to reduce the tax burden. One of his proposals was to staff similar posts in the companion regiment and the local domain government simultaneously with one individual in order to save personnel expenses. Given the rivalries between the two units, it is no surprise that the senior administrators kept telling him that nothing so drastic was needed. One day he was called in by the senior administrator on duty. The message was that Yoshiki had received a promotion. He would be guardian of the Young Lord Heir Designate in charge of the upbringing of the future lord and a chief member of the companion regiment. According to the story related by Yoshiki's wife, the senior administrator then offered Yoshiki some soup to celebrate. Yoshiki refused, saying, "It is not such a good place to work, and I do not feel like celebrating!" and went home. Yoshiki's friend Miyaji Harue heard her relate this story and said that this was not the real reason he was upset. Rather, it was that Yoshiki had had disagreements with other officials. Because he was blameless, the only way to rid themselves of him was to promote him. "That they wanted to get rid of him is what really hurt."[16]

After his boost up and out of domanial government in 1801, Yoshiki became a guardian in charge of Yamauchi Toyooki, the eight-year-old heir to Toyokazu. This job he performed faithfully, reputedly taking many opportunities to instruct the young lord in the ways of frugality. Once he is supposed to have told the boy, "These days daimyo lords forget their origins, and take on the airs of high aristocrats. But they are, after all, warriors. When the situation calls for a palanquin, they should ride a horse, and when it calls for riding a horse, they should walk."[17] The young lord needed a bit of work. On his first trip in 1802 from Tosa to Edo, he got sick riding in the swinging palanquin and threw up. Then he could not walk and needed to take a nap. The hundreds of retainers in his retinue had to wait for him to wake up before they could continue on their way. Thanks to this delay, they had to walk late into the night and arrived at their lodgings near dawn. Next, Toyooki started to cry because there was nothing to do on the road in the mountains and he wanted to go home. He got sick again, to everyone's great worry. Yoshiki then carried the nine-year-old boy in his arms for more than a kilometer at one stretch.[18] If the heir were to die, disaster might befall the Yamauchi house, and so the heir was coddled even by Yoshiki. Here was Yoshiki right at the heart of government! His outspoken ways continued both to earn him respect and to lead him into conflict with other officials. As might be predicted, right after the young lord's first return to Kōchi in 1804, Yoshiki was retired and given no new appointment.

Yoshiki lived the remaining three years of his life writing, studying, and socializing with his many friends. In addition to his diaries, which were shown only to a few trusted friends, he left behind a great number of transcriptions of historical records. He compiled over thirty volumes of documents related to Tosa history. A lover of books like his father, he was known to be very generous in lending them. His wife remembered, "When he would hear that a certain child, even a servant's child, liked books he would get very happy and lend them whatever they wished." And a friend, Ban Masaji, said, "When I was young and wanted to get on his good side, I knew that if I asked him for a book, it would put him in good spirits!"[19] Yoshiki's fourth son Masana inherited his father's love of books as well. He later became not only a diarist but also well known as a compiler of biographies.

Most remarkable was Masana's attempt to recapture his father's memory. Yoshiki died in 1807; he was only thirty-nine years old, and Masana only two. Hence, Masana hardly knew his father. Nonetheless, later he read all of Yoshiki's diaries. He excerpted and summarized parts that he compiled into a book. To it, he added the notes he took in 1831, when he gathered together Yoshiki's old friends with Yoshiki's wife so they could recount—and he could write down—the stories they remembered about his father's life. Thanks to Yoshiki's own writings and his son's project, today we can contemplate the world of an officer in a samurai government.

NOTES

1. See p. 40, in Moriguchi Kōji, "Mori Kanzaemon Hirosada Nikki no sekai—Tosa-han jōkyū bushi no nichijō," *Bungaku* 2, no. 3 (Summer 1991): 38–42.

2. See pp. 26 and 36 in Moriguchi Kōji, "Josetsu 'Mori Kanzaemon Hirosada Nikki' kokyū," part 1, *Ōtoyo shidan* 50 (August 30, 1986): 23–41.

3. All information on Hirosada and Umeno comes from Hirosada's personal diary, titled *Nikki*, held in the Kōchi Prefecture Library, Kōchi City.

4. From the lord's official record of all inheriting samurai, a manuscript titled "Osamuraichū senzosho keizuchō," vol. 24, held in the Kōchi Prefecture Library.

5. Mori Yoshiki, *Saigun junken nikki* (Kōchi: Kōchi Chihōshi Kenkyūkai, 1965), 32.

6. Hirao Michio, *Tosa nōmin ikki shi kō* (Kōchi: Kōchi Shiritsu Toshokan, 1953), 59.

7. This office diary is the second half of the personal diary entitled "Nichiroku," vol. 1, held in the Kōchi Prefecture Library.

8. All information about this incident comes from the diarylike record compiled by Mori Yoshiki, a manuscript volume entitled "Ikō shishūki," held in the Kōchi Prefecture Library.

9. From a manuscript volume of friends' reminiscences about Yoshiki, compiled by his son Masana and titled "Sendai gyojō," completed in 1831, a copy of which is held in the Kōchi Prefecture Library.

10. Unless otherwise noted, information for this period of his official life comes from his office diary at the time, a manuscript volume titled "Jibutsu kongen," also held in the Kōchi Prefecture Library.

11. "Oyakuninchō (sono 4)," *Tosa shidan*, no. 48 (September 1934): 155–67.

12. Unless otherwise noted, information for this period of his official life comes from his office diary at the time, a manuscript volume titled "Sansei nichiroku," held in the Kōchi Prefecture Library.

13. From a manuscript volume of his personal diary titled "Nichiroku," vol. 2, held in the Kōchi Prefecture Library.

14. Tsukamoto Manabu, *Shorui o meguru seiji* (Tokyo: Heibonsha, 1993), 97–160.

15. "Sansei nichiroku," vol. 1, 8/4–8/5/1798.

16. "Sendai gyojō."

17. Ibid.

18. Constantine N. Vaporis, "Edo e no michi: Tosa hanshi Mori-ke nikki to ni yoru sankin kōtai no sugata," *Kōtsūshi kenkyū* 34 (December 1994): 52–67.

19. "Sendai gyojō."

SUGGESTED READINGS

One of the best studies of the changing role of violence in samurai masculine identity and its relation to the polity as it evolves over the ages is Eiko Ikegami's *The Taming of the Samurai* (1995). There is also the delightful autobiography of a rascally samurai named Katsu Kokichi, translated by Teruko Craig, *Musui's Story: The Autobiography of a Tokugawa Samurai* (1988). Those interested in the legal system should consult the early chapters of John Haley, *Authority without Power: Law and the Japanese Paradox* (1991). To learn more about the realm of Tosa and to read the biography of a rural samurai, see Marius B. Jansen, *Sakamoto Ryōma and the Meiji Restoration* (1961). For samurai travel between Tosa and Edo, see Constantine Vaporis, "To Edo and Back: Alternate Attendance and Japanese Culture in the Early Modern Period," *Journal of Japanese Studies* (Winter 1997).

PART II

THE MEIJI RESTORATION AND THE TRANSFORMATION OF STATE AND SOCIETY

Into the peaceful if unstable world of Tokugawa Japan came Westerners bringing new demands for diplomatic relations and trade. (Although the Dutch had been allowed to visit Japan on terms set by the shogun since the early seventeenth century, aside from Chinese and Koreans, other outsiders had been excluded.) When European powers made their first appearance in the late-eighteenth and early-nineteenth centuries, the shogunate rebuffed them. By 1853, when Commodore Matthew C. Perry arrived to force Japan to negotiate, its leaders and many literate members of the populace knew that foreigners were dangerous. What to do about them became the subject of intense debate. Should they be driven off lest they pollute the nation's sacred soil with their barbarian presence, even if it meant Japan's destruction? Should they be placated temporarily with the tacit understanding that they would be expelled as soon as Japan had improved its defenses? Some shogunal advisers worried that the long years of peace had so sapped the samurai fighting spirit that resistance was futile. Others shared this fear, but believed that war was the only way to revive the martial ethos. Unable to reach a consensus, the shogun's advisers decided to turn to the emperor to ratify the decision to sign a treaty. When he refused, the shogun found himself losing legitimacy as Japan's chief executive officer.

The ruling class by then had other things to worry about besides foreigners. Their best efforts to increase revenues had foundered in the face of commoner resistance. The erosion of the status system continued apace. Wealthy merchants and peasants clearly enjoyed a higher standard of living than many samurai, leading to arrogance on the part of the former and disgruntlement on the latter's. Learning that had once been the monopoly of the imperial court and samurai scholars percolated down to the lower classes. As we see in Chapter 4, even a village headman might consider himself an expert in Confucianism. Students of Japan's ancient history cast a critical eye on military governments that had usurped the emperor's rightful role as ruler. They argued that all Japanese, including the shogun, had to respect the emperor's wishes and obey his commands. When these included expelling the barbarians, the shogun was in trouble.

The contentious decade between 1858 and 1868 saw the shogun beset on all sides. Acting for the United States, Townsend Harris forced the

Japanese to sign a commercial treaty. Like the treaty imposed by Perry, it gave foreigners certain rights and privileges in Japan that its citizens were not to enjoy abroad. The hallmark of the unequal treaty system was extraterritoriality. Under this provision, foreigners who committed crimes on Japanese soil would be tried by foreign judges and serve time in foreign jails. Needless to say, any Japanese person committing a crime in San Francisco, for instance, would be tried by American judges and end up in an American prison. Chapter 5 alludes to some of the efforts to get these treaties revised.

In the meantime, the shogun had to contend with demands that he accept counsel from outside his hereditary circle of advisers. Even his collateral relative, Tokugawa Nariaki from Mito, demanded to be heard, as we see in Chapter 3. The shogun found himself having to work more closely with the emperor. The fourteenth shogun even married the emperor's younger sister in an effort to unite his military power with the emperor's spiritual authority. This move backfired when the emperor insisted that, in return for his sister, the shogun cleanse Japanese soil of foreign pollution. Daimyo from large domains on the periphery of the Japanese islands, especially Satsuma and Chōshū, started building military machines to resist the foreigners and offered their services to the court, first as mediators with the shogun, later as the court's agents. At the end of a long and complicated struggle, they succeeded in forcing the shogun to return his powers to the court. Early in 1868 sixteen-year-old Emperor Meiji announced that henceforth he would rule Japan.

The Meiji Restoration ultimately revolutionized Japan. Within three years the new government had abolished the domains, erased hereditary status distinctions, and allowed people to change their occupations and move about the country. Ironically for a government that owed its origins to the movement to revere the emperor and expel the barbarians (sonnō jōi), it invited foreigners to educate Japanese in things Western and launched a drive to bring modern industry and a modern military to Japan. Along the way it recast governmental institutions more closely in line with Western models and promulgated a constitution in 1889. The first fruits of its efforts were apparent by 1895, when it defeated China, and in 1905, when it bested Russia.

Nishimiya Hide and Ishizaka Shōkō and his children had no impact on the events of these tumultuous years that shaped their lives. Instead, they were caught by sudden changes in status and opportunity like corks snatched by a tidal wave. Once the wave had passed, they found that they had left their old world behind forever—they were beached on the shores of modernity.

CHAPTER 3

Nishimiya Hide

Turning Palace Arts into Marketable Skills

ANNE WALTHALL*

Two aristocracies shared the political landscape of Tokugawa Japan: one civilian, as we have seen in the life of Shinanomiya, and the other military. Although the two tried to maintain separate identities, women of the imperial court held such cachet as exemplars of beauty and high rank and as arbiters of taste that shogun and daimyo eagerly sought them as wives. The ruler of the Mito domain, Tokugawa Nariaki (1800–1860), married one such lady. When the main Tokugawa line failed to produce an heir, their son became the last shogun in 1866. Many years before this happened, Nariaki had exploited his position as a close shogunal relative to sound the alarm against the foreign threat posed by European and American powers, which he and his retainers perceived as being both military and ideological. They cast cannon to counter the former; they looked to the emperor as the symbol of the national polity to combat the latter. Nariaki's idealistic and uncompromising stance on protecting the purity of Japanese soil from foreigners brought him into direct conflict with more pragmatic shogunal advisers who realized that military resistance was futile. He was forced to live in retirement, as Nishimiya Hide relates in her memoirs, and died before the Meiji Restoration in 1860.

Hide's memoirs reveal what happened to ordinary people caught up in the reverberating public events that set Japan on its modern course. The overthrow of the Tokugawa shogunate in 1867 wrenched Hide, her family, and friends from the security of their inherited status as retainers to a military house. Instead, they now had to scramble to make a living. They had to adapt to transformations in commerce, styles of dress, modes of transportation, forms of government, techniques of control and surveillance, and social relations. People in different situations responded differently to these changes; Hide was one who took full advantage of her social background to cope with the fortuitous opportunities that came her way.

*I am grateful to the National Endowment for the Humanities for a grant in the 2000–2001 academic year that provided me with the time to research and write this piece. Kathryn Ragsdale offered valuable comments.

Anne Walthall teaches Japanese history at the University of California, Irvine. Her books include Social Protest and Popular Culture in Eighteenth-Century Japan *(1986) and* The Weak Body of a Useless Woman: Matsuo Taseko and the Meiji Restoration *(1998). She is one of the editors of* Women and Class in Japanese History *(1999).*

Nishimiya Hide was born into and brought up to lead a genteel life buttressed by the security and stability of an inherited income and ruling-class status. Her father was a low-ranking samurai, known for his research on ancient Japanese history.[1] His devotion to the task of compiling new texts out of old ones brought him a position in the personal retinue of his lord, Tokugawa Nariaki. All her life, Hide remained proud that she had been born inside the Koishikawa compound owned by the Mito domain, now the site for the sports and entertainment center known as Tokyo Dome. When she was born, in 1834, the compound housed Nariaki, his wife Yoshiko, concubines, children, and attendants plus a bevy of support staff and guards.

The conditions of Hide's life were defined by the decisions made by Nariaki. During the devastating famine of 1837, for example, he announced that he was cutting back to two meals per day. His retainers all did likewise. As an act of charity, the Nishimiya family provided employment plus meals for three or four extra maids. With no chores to do, the maids played all day. To celebrate her seventh year, Hide's aunt sent her a splendid long-sleeved silk kimono with embroidery on a light green background. Hide could hardly wait to wear it in paying calls on her relatives. Shortly before visiting day arrived, Nariaki ordered all retainers to demonstrate their commitment to thrift by wearing nothing but cotton. Only within the privacy of the family, then, could Hide parade around in her new robe.

Hide began her schooling at age six. Mornings were spent on reading and writing, while afternoons were devoted to training in etiquette, folding paper to wrap presents, and tying elaborate knots. As a properly brought-up daughter of the samurai, she later studied the tea ceremony, sewing, and how to fight with the Japanese halberd. Still, she had plenty of leisure to go sightseeing and mingle with the crowds at famous temples and shrines.

When she fell ill with influenza at the end of her fourteenth year, Hide's childhood came to an abrupt end. Delirious with fever for over a month, she came to her senses only to learn that her mother had caught the disease from her and died. As soon as she recovered, Hide had to take her mother's place in looking after her father, her younger brother, and her little sister. She was the first person in the household to get up in the morning and the last to go to bed at night. As she wrote in her memoirs, "What I did not do did not get done. When acquaintances came to visit, I had to entertain them, and I had not a moment to myself." In the meantime, her best friend received an appointment to serve Nariaki's wife Yoshiko. "I was really and truly envious. I realized bitterly that if only my mother were alive, I too would be going into service, but there was no help for it."[2] Only her father's remarriage liberated her from the drudgery of household chores.

Hide was then free to apply for a position in Nariaki's household. She had to submit to two interviews, one to gauge her personal appearance and ability to compose a poem, the other to assess her skill at the tea ceremony. Both took place in the presence of Yoshiko, who "was beautiful beyond compare, just like a Kyoto doll." (Yoshiko had been born in Kyoto in 1804, the twelfth daughter of an imperial prince.) Having passed both tests, Hide began her career as attendant to Yoshiko in 1850 at the age of sixteen. She was assigned her own room in the quarters for the female attendants with an adjoining room for her maid: "The fulfillment of my long-held desire made me feel as if I had died and gone to heaven" (p. 15). Hide spent the next nineteen years in service to Yoshiko, refining her social skills and embodying gentility.

In 1844, Nariaki had fallen out of favor with the shogun and his advisers. The whole family left the centrally located Koishikawa compound for the more isolated residence at Komagome. Ordered to refrain from reading books and instead to entertain himself in a manner befitting a high-ranking lady, Nariaki spent much more time in the women's quarters than was customary for a man of his rank. Hide's memoirs recount their mutual participation in feminine pastimes. She, for example, wrote a sycophantic poem for him at an early snowfall. Nariaki was engrossed in caring for a rare singing bird presented to Yoshiko by the shogun. He built a splendid run for this bird in the garden, employed a specialist in raising birds, and talked about it incessantly. Hide helped in tending to its needs.

On one occasion everyone participated in an incense-sniffing competition. By the end of the game, Hide had gotten so dizzy that the different scents all smelled the same. In 1855, when a relative in the Buddhist priesthood came to visit, Nariaki organized a daylong set of events climaxed by a game of polo, which Yoshiko and her attendants watched from behind screens. In the evening, Nariaki brought his guest into the women's quarters for an impromptu concert, the performers being himself, the priest, Yoshiko, and her daughters. Nariaki also sponsored a poetry contest among his children and staff, with members of the two teams seated according to rank. He arranged a fishing and sightseeing expedition that roused everyone before dawn, then kept them up to watch the moon rise. Hide wrote, "While everyone was fishing I felt so indescribably happy that I didn't know whether I was in a dream or the real world" (p. 41). To further stave off boredom, Nariaki supervised the production of pictures painted and embroidered on silk. He even did some of the needlework himself, tying his knots in a distinctive style that was the envy of the ladies.

While serving as Yoshiko's attendant, Hide witnessed her triumphs and trials. In 1853 the main building in the compound burned to the ground. A few months later Nariaki and Yoshiko's eldest son married his first cousin, Yoshiko's niece. Hide raved about the bride's beauty of form and face. At age sixteen the bride, she wrote, looked like "a walking, living doll" (p. 24). She so pleased her husband that she quickly became pregnant, giving birth to a daughter within a year of her marriage.

Hide was washing a puppy's feet in the bathhouse when an earthquake, now estimated to have been at magnitude 6.9 on the Richter scale, struck at 10 P.M. on the second day of the tenth month of 1855. The candlestick fell over and the walls collapsed. Startled by the noise, the puppy tried to escape. Hide grabbed it, wrapped it in a towel and, after waiting out the tremors, took it to Yoshiko. While Nariaki and Yoshiko sought shelter in a garden teahouse, Hide and the other attendants returned to the mansion. There they poured fishbowls of water over the coals used for heating lest they start a fire. "It was too bad about the goldfish and colored carp, but there was no help for it" (p. 28). They packed the household's treasures in long trunks to be carried outside, then joined the lord's family for a long, cold night on the ground. Hide's father had been at Nariaki's side when the earthquake struck. Her stepmother had just gone outside to the toilet when their rooms collapsed with Hide's brother and sister inside. Her brother managed to escape, but her sister was crushed under a beam. She was one of approximately seven thousand people to die in the quake, along with one of Nariaki's chief advisers.

Hide's personal concerns never blinded her to the momentous events to which she bore witness, and she paid close attention to political matters normally considered beyond a woman's purview. Nariaki's forced removal to Komagome had resulted in part from his stockpiling of weapons in defiance of regulations limiting each daimyo to a fixed amount. After the Americans under Commodore Matthew Perry insisted that Japan sign a controversial treaty in 1853, however, he was invited to advise the shogun on foreign policy issues. Nariaki believed that the foreigners should be expelled, and he got his sons appointed to supervise coastal defenses. It appeared that he was returning to a position of favor and influence. He started spending his nights at the Koishikawa mansion, leaving Yoshiko at Komagome. When her mother-in-law fell ill,

Yoshiko too returned to Koishikawa. Hide and two other attendants remained at Komagome to take care of the birds and dogs until Nariaki received official permission to move his household back to Koishikawa in 1855. When the shogun died in 1858, the ensuing succession dispute pitted Nariaki and his seventh son against the shogun's most powerful advisers. When the latter won, Nariaki was once again forced into retirement at Komagome. Rumors circulated that he would be ordered to commit suicide. The retainers flocked to Komagome determined to kill any messenger who dared bring such a command. To ease tensions, the shogun ordered Nariaki to retire to his domain in Mito. Rather than remain behind as a hostage, Yoshiko petitioned to be allowed to accompany him. In this way, for the first time in her life, Hide visited her ancestral home. "We said good-by to parents and siblings as people would in going to a foreign country today" (p. 51).

Life in Mito was anything but uneventful. The accommodations were crude, the gardens withered and full of weeds. Nonetheless, the family tried to continue their refined pastimes of admiring snowscapes, writing poetry, and exchanging visits. The illusion of an aristocratic idyll was shattered late one night when the bell at the front gate rang fiercely. "We could hear the crackle of voices from the guards. What could be the matter?" (p. 53). It turned out that Ii Naosuke, Nariaki's chief enemy in the government, had been killed by Mito retainers. Fortunately, the affair ended without Nariaki's being blamed for what his men had done. Next came the news that in an effort to unify the nation's leadership, the shogun was to marry the emperor's younger sister. Because this plan contravened the wish of the previous shogun that she marry one of Yoshiko's princely relatives, everyone in Mito disapproved. Worn out by his concern for Japan's future and frustrated by his inability to act, Nariaki died suddenly in 1860. The shogun married the princess, then paid the first visit by a shogun to the emperor in Kyoto in over two hundred years. Nariaki's heir accompanied him with Hide's father in his retinue. When the shogun sickened and died in 1866, Nariaki's seventh son, Yoshinobu, became shogun as his father had hoped he would in 1858. Under ordinary circumstances, this would have been a matter of great pride for his mother Yoshiko. Beset by enemies from the moment he took office, he returned the power invested in the shogun to the emperor in 1867 and tried to negotiate a settlement that would leave him and his supporters still alive and in control of their old domains. Instead, he was branded an enemy of the court.

While these momentous events were taking place, Hide continued to wait on Yoshiko. She accompanied Yoshiko on visits to Nariaki's grave; she participated in concerts performed monthly at a local shrine in accordance with Nariaki's wishes. As long as Yoshiko remained in full mourning, she stayed in seclusion at the Mito castle, making only one trip outside to view the cherry blossoms. After the mourning period was over, the house elders urged her to see something of the domain by making a trip to Mito's chief port. Hide went with her and had a delightful time admiring the changing scenery, the demonstration of seine fishing in the harbor, and the sight of women diving for abalone. A later trip to watch salmon being caught found the attendants in quarters too cramped for sleep. "We waited for dawn to break, resting by leaning against pillars and walls. That time in particular we had to endure smells reaching our noses that were really disgusting" (p. 60).

Worse was to come. Unhappy at Yoshinobu's craven attempts to appease opponents fighting in the emperor's name, a radical faction of Mito retainers advocated ambushing the imperial forces. Among them was Hide's younger brother. He was arrested before he could act and was thrown in prison. There he caught fever and died at the end of the third month of 1868, leaving behind three small children. Devastated, their father took to his bed and sent an urgent appeal to Hide to come immediately. On the road she met Nariaki's son and successor, the last time she was to see him, because he died of beriberi immediately upon his arrival at Mito, before an heir could be designated. His younger brother Akitake had been studying in France. Upon learning that the emperor had replaced the shogun as the nation's political ruler, Akitake hurried back to Japan but, without the court's permission, he could not succeed his brother. This placed Yoshiko in the position of being the domain's de facto leader. Almost as soon as Hide arrived at her father's house, a stream of messages came requesting her presence at Yoshiko's side. Despite the fighting that had broken out between supporters of the former shogun and those of the emperor, Hide decided that duty called her back to Mito.

Hide tried to conduct her journey as though it were the kind she had been accustomed to make in Yoshiko's retinue, but she faced dangers unheard of in more peaceful times. She wrote farewell poems to family and friends who had come to see her off and another poem contrasting clear skies and dark thoughts. Then, at the first river ford, she was confronted by imperial troops dressed like foreigners in uniforms instead of armor. They made her wait several hours before a senior officer decided to let her pass. On the other side of the river, she had to walk past imposing rows of cannon and a whole military encampment. "We went on down the road, our hearts constricted at the thought that fighting might break out at any moment" (p. 67). Hide had hoped to hire a palanquin for herself and her maid. None was to be had until they had walked several more miles, and, when they did acquire one, it was too cramped for her liking. After a nervous journey across plains, woods still in the grip of winter, and another, more dangerous ford, she and her attendants reached their inn for the night. Hide enjoyed chatting with the other travelers. Unaccustomed to bedding down with strangers, she found it impossible to sleep. Instead she wrote a poem.

On the following day the next river was too high to be crossed safely. Hide's party had to go upstream to find a ford; then they had to zigzag along the ridges between the rice paddies, slipping and sliding in the mud, before they returned to the main road. The post station there had been destroyed, and its inhabitants scattered. They pressed forward, anxious to reach their own domain. Hide decided to spend the night at the border town even though her attendants cautioned against it, saying it was an entertainment district and noisy. "What do they do by way of entertainment? I asked. If it's that unusual, it won't hurt to spend a night watching it." She enjoyed exchanging cups of sake with the geisha. "As I had been warned, we were encouraged to keep them company all night, which I found most enjoyable" (p. 74).

Even though it was a relief to be safely back in Mito, the road to the castle was marked with sad reminders of the 1864 civil war that had destroyed a number of prominent families. Remembering those difficult days cast a pall over Hide's spirits that was dispelled only when she reached the castle and greeted her old friends. How good it was to sleep in her own chamber!

Hide arrived just in time for the final conflict between the various Mito factions. Fearing that Yoshiko might become hostage to the contending forces, the house elders brought in guns to fend off attackers. Hide and the other attendants wrapped cartridges for bullets. "Even though we put food in our mouths, no one felt like eating. Our eyes glazed over, our legs trembled. We didn't sleep at night, but no one felt sleepy" (p. 78). In the meantime, Yoshinobu, the last shogun, had withdrawn to Mito, where he was detained on his own recognizance. He moved into the domain academy just across the moat from the castle. In deference to the new ruling authorities, he remained in such seclusion that he did not send his mother Yoshiko any sort of message at all. When he left for Shizuoka a few months later, Yoshiko was not allowed to see him off. "We all grumbled that the world had brought such change" (p. 80).

Families such as the Nishimiya who had served a domain lord for generations soon discovered that the new government would force them to abandon the sureties of their old life. In the second month of 1869, Hide became redundant when Yoshiko cut the size of her staff. She returned to her father's lodgings in the old Koishikawa compound. It soon became a burden the domain could no longer afford, so the family had to move to rented quarters. At the age of seventy, her father found a position in the new government as assistant helper in charge of imperial tombs, for which his research into the early history of the Japanese monarchy well qualified him. Hide spent her days helping her stepmother and lending her elegant demeanor and good manners to gatherings of former domain lords.

More changes were yet in store. In 1872 her father retired, with a parting gift of two rolls of bleached cloth. Shortly thereafter, he received an urgent summons to return to Mito, and Hide went with him. There he was told that if he did not settle in Mito permanently, he would be expelled from the ranks of the Mito *shizoku* (a term designating former samurai rank at a time when the previous status distinctions were being abolished). It was a hard decision to make, but his family had served Mito for generations. It would affront his ancestors for him to turn his back on it now, not to mention that he would lose his stipend. Besides, the Westernizing wind sweeping the capital upset a man determined to follow the ancient way. The following year he learned that his stipend was to be cut to forty bags of unhulled rice per year. Since that was not enough to live on, he petitioned for a lump sum.

In the meantime, there was Hide to provide for. Had she remained an attendant till Yoshiko died, she would have cut her hair, retired to a nunnery, and received a pension to support her in her old age. Instead, she was thirty-eight and too old to be placed as a bride in another family, yet in need of insurance for her old age. To solve this problem, her father decided to adopt a son-in-law for her to marry. Hide gave birth to her son Nobutaka in 1873, at an age when most women of her generation would have been expecting grandchildren. Having done his duty, the adopted son-in-law was sent on his way. (Hide's great-granddaughter still owns one half of a pair of ivory chopsticks embossed in silver with the Tokugawa crest; the other half was given to Hide's husband to mark the divorce.)

Hide and her father were not the only former samurai suddenly faced with a need to make a living. Their first venture was supplying rental futons to the flophouses and brothels that had sprung up on the recently filled-in outer moat of Mito castle. At first the business flourished, and Hide and her father were able to make a profit. Of poor quality, however, the futons quickly deteriorated. Hide and her father could not rely on their customers, either. One renter, for example, not only did not pay his fees but also pawned the futons. Hide realized that the business was more than they could handle, and they gave it up. Next, she tried raising chickens, but a fox decimated the flock. What was she to do? Her stepmother was ill, her father old, and Nobutaka a mere babe-in-arms.

Following the advice of an old acquaintance, Hide decided to draw on her carefully honed skills as a social facilitator and arbiter of taste by sinking her savings into a geisha house. Her parents were aghast. None-theless, she found space next to a candy store, thanks to its mistress who had once worked as a drudge for Yoshiko's attendants. Under the old regime, the candy storekeeper would have remained forever subservient to her former superiors; now she was in a position to do them favors. Next, Hide went back to Tokyo to procure geisha, traveling with a woman whose daughter had already entered that profession. In the manner to which she was accustomed in her old life, they stopped at Narita to visit the temple, then made a pilgrimage to the Sakura Sōgorō Shrine erected in memory of a peasant martyr of the seventeenth century. In Tokyo she stayed with relatives who, although they had been the shogun's retain-ers, had not followed Yoshinobu into exile in Shizuoka. Using their con-nections, Hide quickly procured two trained geisha plus one apprentice.

Despite the coming of peace and improvements in transportation, Hide's journey back to Mito proved more eventful than she would have liked. The apprentice geisha's mother was nearly a day late at the meet-ing place, because the men hired to carry her baggage had led her up the wrong road. That night, Hide's rickshaw men decided they did not want to go all the way to Mito. They insisted on returning to Tokyo, assuring her that she would soon find replacements. Of course, she did not. In-stead, she was forced to rent oxen. They had not gone far before one of the geisha fell off and cut her lip. Hide found one rickshaw for the in-jured geisha to ride in, but the latter refused because "who knows where he might take me" (p. 93). Instead, they all decided to walk, keeping one ox to carry the baggage. That evening, Hide pleaded with the innkeeper to find her four rickshaws to carry the party the rest of the way to Mito, no matter what the cost. They finally arrived safely at Hide's parents' house late the next night, to the great relief of everyone there.

It turned out that Hide had a flair for the entertainment business. A number of her acquaintances patronized the establishment, and it soon flourished. "My father was greatly relieved at what his child had accom-plished. My intimate friends were all astonished. People often came to see how I was doing as my business expanded, saying such things as, 'Wow, look at what you've done' " (p. 94). Burned out of one building, Hide quickly reopened for business in another. Within three years she was back in Tokyo to hire more geisha, a trip made this time without incident. Several years later, another fire brought this stage in her career to an end.

Throughout this period, Hide's son Nobutaka had been a constant source of concern. As an infant he had been sent to a wet nurse in the countryside, and she had him stay with that family for a time following the first fire. That prevented the celebration of his third birthday, an important one for a boy. Instead, Hide dressed him in formal wear in the spring of his fourth year and invited friends and relatives to a party. When he was six years old, it was time for him to begin his education. Hide moved him from one school to another, but no matter where he went, he hated it. His grades were terrible. "All he was learning on his own was how to watch plays, sumo, and spectacles" (p. 99). It was something of a scandal for the nine-year-old grandson of a noted scholar and former employee of the Imperial Household Ministry to be hanging out in the red-light district. Already concerned that her business was having a bad effect on his character, Hide saw the second fire as a blessing in disguise. In the spring of 1882 she liquidated her business and moved back in with her father.

Even though Hide had a roof over her head, she still had to find some way to make money and take care of her family. "My father and son didn't think about such things in the least, so I tried to keep my anxieties to myself" (p. 100). A friend she had made through the entertainment business suggested that she try lending small sums of money. While waiting for the interest to come in, she gave a hand wherever friends or relatives needed help. Nobutaka's grades remained poor. Hide's father died at the end of the year, having reached the advanced age of eighty. Hide was then forty-eight; Nobutaka was only nine. Hide did not bother to note when her stepmother died.

Following her father's death, Hide became something of a vagabond. Nobutaka announced that he wanted to learn how to make Western-style shoes, so she took him to Tokyo to be apprenticed to a shoemaker. Given that he came from samurai stock and shoes were made of leather, traditionally a material worked on only by outcasts in Japanese society, his commitment to this form of manual labor demonstrates both the volatility and the opportunities inherent in the new society. Back in Mito and without the responsibilities of either father or child, Hide enjoyed herself thoroughly, visiting friends and going on short excursions around the city. Through an intermediary, she accepted a position in a clothing store. It was not quite the case of a merchant employing a daughter of the samurai, because the arrangement was temporary and Hide received only housing, meals, and pocket money. Her duties consisted of inspecting goods before they were shipped, performing the tea ceremony for the master, and chatting with members of the household in the evening. She helped the family with all the ceremonies involved in the marriage of their son; then, when that was over, she moved out. "There I was, with nothing to do and nothing to entertain me." A geisha asked for Hide's help in getting started, and so she went back to her old haunts for a few months. "Living with her was the easiest thing I ever did" (p. 102).

In 1887, Hide decided to give up being a moneylender and return to Tokyo. She had already had to seek a new position for Nobutaka after his first employer went bankrupt. Nobutaka tried working in a Western-style clothing store, but there he was nothing more than an errand boy with no future. After a few unhappy months, Hide apprenticed him to another shoemaker. She herself moved in with her niece's family, because her niece was expecting a baby. After the birth, Hide rented rooms from a former shogunal retainer. Her nephew Kumeo was a student at that time. Hide proposed that he stay with her for the cost of staying in a rooming house. She tried to teach the tea ceremony, but found no takers. Instead, she acquired three or four other boarders and looked after their needs.

All too soon, Hide discovered that she could not always trust her relatives. In the middle of 1888, Kumeo announced that he was moving to a rooming house closer to his university, but without telling her his new address. The next day he came back, saying he had something to give her. He went back and forth in front of the door, then left abruptly. Later that afternoon his brother arrived with a package bearing Hide's name. It contained the box in which she kept the passbook for her savings account. Three yen that she had put in the box were gone. Worse, 50 yen, worth several hundred dollars in today's terms, had been withdrawn from her account. Hide searched all over town for Kumeo, to no avail. She got her son to take a leave of absence so she could tell him the whole story, she talked to all her friends and relatives, she wrote a letter to the bank asking why it had turned over the money without her seal. The bank responded that Kumeo had reported her seal to have been lost, and so it had issued him a new one. The fact that he was a man, her nephew, and living in her house made it plausible that he would control her finances. After many fruitless efforts, Hide finally caught up with Kumeo in the middle of a busy street. She grabbed onto his sleeve. "It's difficult to talk in the midst of all these passers-by," he said. "In that case, why haven't you been in the places you're supposed to be? Don't you know I've been looking for you?" (p. 107). He pulled his sleeve free and ran off. Hide decided that there was no point in trying to get her money back. Nonetheless, she was so upset that she gave up running a boardinghouse.

In the midst of all her personal turmoil came the most spectacular occasion to mark the new regime. This was the 1889 celebration for the promulgation of the constitution, a document designed to place the government on a firm foundation. Despite the enormous economic and social upheavals experienced by Hide and people like her, her enthusiasm for this, Japan's first modern, national ceremony, was wholehearted. The main event was a procession through the streets of Tokyo by the emperor and empress in a European-style, horse-drawn carriage. The crowds were so vast and Hide so short that she caught a glimpse of no more than the gold phoenix on the roof of the carriage. Even though she was nearly trampled while trying to cross a bridge, she still found it exhilarating to have seen the floats, banners, ceremonial gates, and festival carts and to be in the midst of the citywide festivities. "I had never experienced anything like this since the day I was born. It really showed how much the world had changed" (p. 113).

Hide had left the hilly aristocratic section of her childhood for the lowlands near the bay. Her niece having died, Hide kept house for her niece's husband and his brother until the widower remarried. Hide was delighted with his choice because she treated Hide as a bride should treat her mother-in-law. Hide rented a house where they could all live together. She kept the smallest room for herself and took in laundry and did needlework, a skill learned in her childhood. This happy situation did not last long. The police decided to tighten the regulations governing cohabitation in the wake of an assassination attempt on the minister of foreign affairs in 1889. They summoned Hide to the police station, where they informed her that it was absolutely forbidden for her to have two unrelated people living with her. They would have to leave at once. Without help in paying the rent, Hide had to give up her little house. She worked as a live-in cook for four teachers, then found a position as a personal maid to the wife of a military man, much the same sort of role she had performed in her youth for Nariaki's wife, Yoshiko. Almost every night she slept with the wife and her children. Her robust health and social acumen soon made her indispensable. After the husband died of tuberculosis in 1892, she found herself with offers of other positions.

When Hide's son finished his apprenticeship, they decided to try living together and pooling their resources. Hide borrowed money from Yoshiko, and with the 60 yen as capital, they opened a small shop to make and repair shoes. At first they had no clients whatsoever. In desperation, Hide went to all her friends and acquaintances touting the shoe business. With their help and patronage, Hide and Nobutaka managed to get by.

While Hide and Nobutaka were struggling to succeed in the shoe business, an official whose daughter was to be married begged Hide to help out with the trousseau and wedding preparations and to accompany the bride to her new home. Only she had the training and the breeding to instruct the bride in what to do during the various rituals. Hide rode with her in a horse-drawn carriage painted red and guided her through the ceremonies performed in accordance with the old samurai traditions. When the bride and groom left on their honeymoon, Hide noted the innovation with wonder. She was to stay behind to look after the house, but Nobutaka needed her so badly that she asked to be excused. She had been gone about ten days. In recompense for her trouble, the bride's father gave her enough money to pay the taxes they still owed on the store and to tide them over their immediate difficulties.

At the beginning of 1892, Hide received a postcard announcing that Yoshiko was very ill. Hide hired an expensive rickshaw to rush across town, then hurried to the bedchamber already crowded with relatives and attendants. Soon after she arrived, Yoshiko stopped breathing. Even the highest-ranking people, including her son, the former shogun Yoshinobu, collapsed in grief. Yoshiko's body was placed in a coffin; the coffin was moved to a drawing room soon to be filled with elaborate flower wreaths sent by the emperor and empress as well as by members of the nobility. Hide attended the funeral and bid a final farewell at the train that was to carry Yoshiko back to Mito to be buried with her husband. Along with the relatives and other attendants, Hide received a number of mementos, chiefly little purses elaborately embroidered, which she carefully labeled and handed down to her descendants as proof that she had once served a great household.

Nobutaka was twenty-nine, the proprietor of a struggling business; it was time for him to marry. A go-between found him a bride, Ogawa Teru. Hide was dismayed to think that she might be a burden and wondered if she should find herself a position elsewhere. Nobutaka assured her that he could manage to support both her and a wife.

Five months later, however, Nobutaka was conscripted into the army, leaving Hide and Teru to run the shoestore. Hide was lonely; she was worried about how they would survive: "Spring arrived, but there was no spring in my heart." Her first grandchild, a boy, was born. Occasionally, Nobutaka took leave to visit his family. "The days he had off were the only days I lived for" (p. 121). In the meantime, one of the shop's employees stole some money and escaped by jumping on the express train to his parents' home in Nagano prefecture. Hide borrowed a helper from Nobutaka's former master, but without making sure that both sides had agreed on his responsibilities. Caught between conflicting demands, the helper made Hide furious when he did not do everything she wanted him to. This led to a rift between the two families that was not really smoothed over even after another man arrived from Mito to work at the store. Hide had already started looking for ways to get Nobutaka discharged. Although local officials were sympathetic, the army insisted that it needed him to make boots. When the Sino-Japanese War broke out in 1894, Hide and Teru received special rations each month, just enough to tide them over. Generally speaking, the government did not consider the plight of soldiers' families to be its concern. All must sacrifice for the war effort. At the end of the war, Hide renewed her efforts to get Nobutaka back, calling on influential people she knew from long ago. "Our joy at his return gave us new courage" (p. 125).

By dint of hard work, perseverance, and help from friends, Nobutaka was gradually able to make life easier for his growing family. To earn a little extra money, he also worked at a Western-style clothing store, never taking a day off. The family repaid its loans, then took out new ones to buy sewing machines. Teru gave birth to a second child, a girl. By 1898, Nobutaka felt that he could afford to do something for his mother to make up for all she had suffered during his absence.

The last pages of Hide's memoirs are filled with the trips she made once the shoe business was well established. Nobutaka accompanied her on her first trip to visit her father's grave in Mito. Even though it was Kumeo's responsibility as the family's heir to erect a gravestone, he had not done so. For that reason, the trip to the cemetery was followed by one to a stonecutter. Hide and Nobutaka also called on all the relatives who still resided in Mito. Wined and dined wherever they went, Hide commented, "The food was truly awful and we escaped as quickly as we could" (p. 127). The castle had been torn down leaving only a public park, just one more example of how the world had changed for the worse. Hide remembered the days in the past and wished that they might return. She never set foot in Mito again.

Hide got another chance to travel two years later when the wedding for the crown prince brought Teru's mother to Tokyo along with another woman. When Hide learned that they planned to go on to Nikkō, she wanted to go, too. Nobutaka thought that was a fine idea. This was Hide's first chance to travel by train, a mode of transportation that eliminated all the old hazards of the road as well as reduced the length of the journey from three days to six hours. Her destination was the shrine and temple complex erected to the founders of the Tokugawa regime that had provided a secure livelihood for her ancestors for more than 250 years. The three old women departed at 5 A.M., arrived at their inn at 11:15, ate lunch, hired a guide to take them to every site worth visiting, returned to the inn early in the afternoon, shopped for souvenirs, and took the 3 P.M. train back to Tokyo. Hide described all the buildings and bridges they saw in excruciating detail, always careful to note which daimyo family had donated the lanterns, the stone staircases, and the rest. At the end she felt as if she had had the most wonderful dream.

In the years before her seventieth birthday, Hide made two more trips. The first was to western Japan with Nobutaka and his former master. The group visited Kyoto, Osaka, and the Great Shrine at Ise. Despite visiting a part of the country she had never seen before, Hide included no details in her memoirs. Perhaps she did not enjoy the company. Shortly thereafter she went with her son, grandson, and another man to the resort town of Fujisawa, not far from Tokyo. It was a hot summer day, and they had to stand in a large crowd of people waiting to change trains at Yokohama. Hide nearly fainted. She revived when they arrived at the beach. From there on, she thoroughly enjoyed herself, riding in a rickshaw along the embankment, crossing the channel to Enoshima on a swaying hanging bridge, and picking her way into the cave there to worship the god of good fortune. She played with her grandson on the beach and watched her son and his friend go fishing. Later they had a delicious dinner of grilled shellfish. They stayed up late to watch the moon rise and play a game of chess. The next day they went on to Kamakura, a sightseer's mecca of shrines, temples, and historical landmarks. The night train saw them safely home.

Her memoir ends with an account of how the Russo-Japanese War affected her family. When hostilities broke out in 1904, Nobutaka was once again inducted into the army to supply it with boots. He was discharged two months later, then reinducted at the beginning of 1905. As before, he was absent at the birth of his child, a second daughter. At the end of the war, the citizens of Tokyo rioted in protest at the terms negotiated to end the conflict. They set fire to the prime minister's residence, police boxes, and electric trains. Hide noted that it was the first urban riot in the Meiji era.

Hide lived another seven years after completing her memoir. She died in 1912, the year in which Emperor Meiji also died. She had witnessed vast changes during the course of her life, changes that wrenched her out of the relatively predictable world of her ancestors. To a certain extent, the traditional skills she had learned served her well, but she also had to develop new qualities of adaptability, resiliency, and resourcefulness to thrive in an unstable environment. She survived through forging bonds of mutual dependency with friends and relatives, helping others, and receiving favors in return. Through it all, she maintained her good humor and zest for living. The conclusion to her memoirs suggests that she wanted to be remembered most not as someone who had endured the trials of a rapidly changing society, but as a woman of good breeding who had served the lord of Mito.

NOTES

1. Nishino Nobuaki (who changed his name to Nishimiya after the Meiji Restoration) had a meager stipend of 10 koku plus a four-man allotment in 1840. According to his own diary, he received a tremendous raise in 1867, giving him a stipend of 150 koku. Suzuki Eiichi, "Mito han ni okeru kokugakusha no tachiba: Nishino Nobuaki no baai," *Ibaraki kenshi kenkyū* 22 (March 1972): 25–29.

2. Nishimiya Hide, "Ochiba no nikki," manuscript owned by Futami Miako currently in the archive of the Ibaraki Kenritsu Rekishikan, Mito City, p. 14. All quotations are drawn from this document.

SOURCES AND SUGGESTED READINGS

Information on Nishimiya Hide comes from her unpublished memoirs, "Ochiba no nikki." I am indebted to the reading group Katsura no kai and particularly to Shiba Keiko for providing me with a computer-generated copy of the manuscript. A summary can be found in Shiba Keiko, "Tokugawa Yoshinobu no haha Teihōin Yoshiko to oku jochū Nishimiya Hide," *Edo-ki onna-kō* 9 (1998). Hide's great-granddaughter Futami Miako provided details on the family history in an interview on September 15, 2000, in Tokyo.

For another perspective on the lives of samurai women, see Yamakawa Kikue's *Women of the Mito Domain: Recollections of Samurai Family Life*, translated and with an introduction by Kate Wildman Nakai (1992). Yamakawa points out (p. 144) that following the Meiji Restoration of 1868, the samurai women who had the most difficulty adjusting were not the wives and daughters of provincial samurai, but those from the city who had been raised to lead lives of leisure. The origins of the political infighting that led to the Mito civil war and Tokugawa Nariaki's activities are discussed by J. Victor Koschmann in *The Mito Ideology: Discourse, Reform, and Insurrection in Late Tokugawa Japan, 1790–1864* (1987). See also Ryotaro Shiba, *The Last Shogun: The Life of Tokugawa Yoshinobu* (1998).

On more specific topics, see the first chapter in Anne Walthall, *Peasant Uprisings in Japan: A Critical Anthology of Peasant Histories* (1991), for a history of the peasant martyr Sakura Sōgorō; Takashi Fujitani, *Splendid Monarchy: Power and Pageantry in Modern Japan* (1996), for an analysis of the ceremonies surrounding the promulgation of the Meiji Constitution; and Andrew Gordon, "The Crowd and Politics in Imperial Japan: Tokyo, 1905–1908," *Past and Present: A Journal of Historical Studies* (November 1988), for a depiction of the riots following the end of the Russo-Japanese War.

CHAPTER 4

The Ishizaka of Notsuda

A Family in Transition

M. WILLIAM STEELE

The transformation of politics, society, economy, and culture wrought by the Meiji Restoration uprooted rural Japan. The abolition of most hereditary status distinctions in 1873 allowed people to leave their ancestral villages, find different occupations, get involved in politics, pursue new forms of learning, practice new religions, and develop new identities. Ishizaka Shōkō began his adult life as a village headman, as his forefathers had before him. Unlike them, however, he took advantage of the new political opportunities afforded by the centralizing bureaucratic state to become a politician. He joined a number of political movements that promoted freedom and popular rights, including the short-lived Daidō Danketsu, designed to overcome factional disputes and unite grassroots activism with national political organizations. He ended his career in a position of power and influence unimaginable before 1868. More significant, his writings and deeds demonstrate that it was entirely possible for a man steeped in Confucian training to advocate and practice democratic ideals.

The transition to modernity changed the way people felt and acted, it changed the way men and women behaved toward each other, and it encouraged new values such as freedom, love, and ambition. The lives of Shōkō's children demonstrate the impact of these changes on individual fortunes. Through the eyes of his daughter Mina, we encounter a modern sensibility that frankly expressed love and expected equal relations between the sexes. She and her brother Kōreki seized opportunities to go abroad in search of personal fulfillment. The trajectory of her life brought her back to Japan where she pursued a career in social welfare organizations only created at the turn of the century. Kōreki remained an emigrant, another career that opened up for Japanese in the modern world.

M. William Steele is professor of history at International Christian University in Tokyo. He has written extensively on local politics in the Tokyo hinterland in the 1870s and 1880s. He is the author of Mō hitotsu no kindai: Sokumen kara mita bakumatsu Meiji (Localism and nationalism in modern Japanese history) *(1998).*

Ishizaka Shōkō was born in 1841, the third son of a branch of the wealthiest family in Notsuda, a village located in the Tama region southwest of Tokyo. Seven days after his birth he was adopted into the main family, which had lacked an heir. The Ishizaka were small farmers at the beginning of the Tokugawa period, but by the 1830s they had amassed both political and economic fortunes. They became the largest landowners in the village. In 1839, Shōkō's adoptive father in the main family was recognized for his service both to the local community and to the Tokugawa state by being awarded the privilege of wearing a sword and using a surname.

The Ishizaka family helped to maintain local law and order following the opening of Japan to the West. In 1857, at the age of sixteen, Shōkō succeeded his father as head of the Ishizaka family. At the same time he became village head of Notsuda and chief of a league of thirty-eight villages in the South Tama area. Despite his youth, he proved an able administrator. Developing an interest in Confucian scholarship, he encouraged education and added to the family library, which, by the 1870s, consisted of over ten thousand volumes in Japanese and Chinese. Concerned with local security, in 1863 he invited Kondo Isami, a leading swordsman in the Kanto region, to Notsuda and set up a fencing academy to instruct village youth in the art of self-defense. Later, in 1866, he helped to organize a farmers' militia that held regular training sessions with rifles and one makeshift cannon.

Shōkō took a wife, Yama, in 1864. Little is known about her, except that, at thirteen years of age, she was ten years his junior. She gave birth to three children: Mina, a daughter, was born in 1865; Kōreki, son and prospective heir to the family, was born in 1868; and a second daughter, Toshi, was born in 1870. In 1888, Mina was to shock her family, friends, and community with the passion and frankness of her love affair and eventual marriage to Kitamura Tōkoku, a rising political critic, novelist, and poet. Two years earlier, in 1886, Kōreki had abandoned Japan for the United States in his personal search for liberty, independence, and fortune. Toshi, the second daughter, established herself as an accomplished violinist and instructor in Western-style music. They all led lives radically different from their father's. Nonetheless, his expectations and his goals provided their inspiration, albeit in unexpected ways.

ISHIZAKA SHŌKŌ: FREEDOM FIGHTER

Throughout the 1860s, Shōkō had been a supporter of the old regime, but following its defeat in 1868 he worked to make sure that Notsuda would profit from the new political arrangement. Despite a bewildering array of changes in administrative titles, he remained in control of the village in the years following the Restoration. Moreover, he took the initiative in introducing "civilization and enlightenment" into rural society. In 1869, when he was appointed village head to a new administrative unit that had once consisted of multiple fragmented jurisdictions, he drew up a pledge for the village officials who were in his charge. Among the eighteen points were injunctions to promote agriculture, to give mutual assistance in times of disaster, and to resolve all disputes harmoniously. As preamble to the pledge, he described a new political morality for village officials: "As a result of the restoration of imperial rule, it is fortunate indeed that peace has come to each village. Therefore, even more than before, you are expected to exert yourselves in respecting the notice boards, to uphold loyalty and filial piety and sympathize with the weak, to cast aside all base customs and selfish ideas, to quit any support for partiality or prejudice, to avoid all wasteful expenses, and forever keep in mind that work for the village is of primary importance."[1]

After the eighteen points, Shōkō gave instructions on how village government was to be reformed, calling for assemblies to undertake a thorough examination of existing laws. "Old regulations are to be reviewed. New and old regulations, one by one, shall be subject to exhaustive public discussion. Village regulations based on justice shall be established." His emphasis here on open discussion, justice, and the primacy of village interests foreshadows his later activities as a politician in pursuit of local autonomy and people's rights.

Shōkō was attracted to the People's Rights movement in the early 1870s. He became a local ally of the liberal Kanagawa governor Nakajima Nobuyuki and helped set up a system of village assemblies and representation of local interests at the prefectural level. In 1874, the same year that Itagaki Taisuke and others petitioned on behalf of a "publicly elected national assembly," Nakajima made clear his commitment to more open forms of government: "The government is the government of the people and seeks improvement for the benefit of the people." Shōkō agreed with this philosophy. He helped with the implementation of national military conscription and land-tax reforms, set up new schools, and even encouraged the new, short Western-style haircut in his village. In 1876 he and other local notables set up a study group that discussed and debated political issues. The society sought to bring an end to the politics of hierarchy and to prepare for a new style of politics, based on notions of equality and justice, at local, regional, and national levels.

In 1879, Shōkō was elected to the newly established Kanagawa Prefectural Assembly. In recognition of the leadership he had displayed in local politics, the sitting body of elected representatives voted him chair of the first assembly. By this time Shōkō was known as a leader in the Liberty and People's Rights movement and was on familiar terms with famous men such as Itagaki Taisuke and Gotō Shōjirō. In the three Tama districts, he was often the sponsor for petitions to establish a national assembly and a sought-after speaker at political rallies. Above all, he was able to take advantage of an impressive network of members of the local political, economic, social, and cultural elite to "get things done." His house in Notsuda had become the political nerve center for the Tama districts.

The year 1880 was a landmark one for the People's Rights movement. The first of a series of drafts of proposed national constitutions appeared in January. March saw the founding of the League to Establish a National Assembly and the inauguration of a massive nationwide petition campaign to pressure the government for immediate political reforms. In the southern section of Kanagawa prefecture, for example, a petition was circulated in 559 villages and gathered 23,555 signatures; one out of every three residents in these villages demanded a national political assembly. And in December, Japan's first political party, the Liberal Party (Jiyūtō), was set up. By 1880, People's Rights had become a truly national movement, linking demands at the village level with decision making in the prefectural assemblies and agitation in the national arena.

Thanks to the activities of local freedom fighters such as Shōkō, Kanagawa prefecture became one of the most politically active areas in Japan. During the eight-year period between 1878 and 1886, 102 local political societies are known to have been established. The societies held regular meetings with speeches and organized study groups. Farmers, young and old, gathered to read and discuss translations of Western political texts or to listen to speeches. Scattered over the countryside, even in remote villages, the study, discussion, and debating groups were important agents of politicization. Shōkō was personally responsible for the organization of several. In 1881, for example, he set up the Yūkansha, a study group designed to make people aware of their political rights and responsibilities, foster a spirit of local autonomy, and work for the establishment of a national assembly.

At the same time political societies such as the Yūkansha served as support organizations to mobilize voters for district and prefectural elections. Shōkō joined the national Liberal Party in 1882, and the Yūkansha developed into one of its branch organs. Even after the Liberal Party was disbanded in 1884, Shōkō continued to make preparations for 1890, when elections were to be held for the first national assembly. In October 1886 he was among the guests at a meeting in Tokyo called by Hoshi Tōru. The aim was to regroup the politically concerned in readiness for the upcoming election. Hoshi asked political leaders from throughout the country to "cast aside petty differences and unite around a greater common goal." This was the beginning of the Daidō Danketsu movement. Formal leadership fell to Gotō Shōjirō. In early 1887, Gotō called for a campaign in rural areas, beginning with the Kanto region, to bring local political societies into a national network, thereby creating one central "People's Rights Party." Shōkō took up the work of building a grassroots organization in the Tama districts.

Politically minded young men flocked to his side; never an ideologue, Shōkō used their skills and the support of the Yūkansha to develop a smooth-running machine that could mediate problems, use force if necessary, and get out the vote. He mobilized thugs (*soshi*) to silence the misgivings of local leaders less willing to join hands with politicians at the center. On December 22, 1887, for example, Shōkō and four young men found themselves arrested by the Yokohama police. Their attempts to "recommend" that certain prefectural assemblymen resign their posts had resulted in a drunken brawl; one man was knocked unconscious. Detained for several days following the incident, Shōkō seems to have lost his sanity temporarily. Newspapers reported that on Christmas Day 1887 a crazed Shōkō began to shout and sing at the top of his lungs. In a fit of anger, he banged his head on a pillar, slashed his testicles, and, covered in blood, fought off anyone who tried to get close to him. He recovered his senses after a brief period of convalescence.

Shōkō's combination of a strong local support group and close ties with national politicians ensured his victory in the July 1890 national election. He was elected to the House of Representatives three times, before he took up an appointment as governor of Gumma prefecture in 1896. Beginning his political career as village headman at the age of sixteen, Shōkō had managed to work his way to the top. By the 1890s he had shed much of his early radicalism. When he retired from the political world at the end of the 1890s, Kanagawa citizens looked on him with awe. The local boy who had made good, he won elections because he fought on behalf of local interests; he was appointed as a prefectural governor because he had proven himself loyal to his country and his emperor. At the end of his career, Shōkō was also broke. Proving the old saying—for his time, at least—that politics does not pay, when he died in 1906 "neither the well nor the walls of his house" remained. Now a stone monument marks the site where the People's Rights movement began in Notsuda, but any trace of the Ishizaka house and, indeed, of the Ishizaka family has long since disappeared.

ISHIZAKA MINA: A WOMAN IN LOVE

Mina, or Minako, was born in 1865; her father, Shōkō, was twenty-four years old and her mother, Yama, was only fourteen. Shōkō's adoptive mother, Hayo, who was in her early forties, took charge of Mina's upbringing. Shōkō insisted on a rigorous education. He maintained a vast library in his house and, despite his busy administrative schedule, engaged in the study of Chinese classics and Chinese poetry. Together with other members of the rural elite, he also sought to understand Western society, history, and politics. Although they grew up in a rural and remote village, Mina, Kōreki, and young Toshi had nonetheless been exposed to the major intellectual currents of their day. Their father's passion for scholarship was as contagious as his abiding interest in politics.

Mina began her formal education in the new village public school and proved herself an able student. When she finished her four years of compulsory education in 1877, the Yokohama Mainichi newspaper published her name among those singled out by the Kanagawa prefectural government for academic distinction. In 1877, Mina left the village for Tokyo. At that time only a few schools permitted women to pursue education beyond the primary level. Mina entered the Hio Academy, a private school with roots in the Edo period that first became coeducational and then entirely female. Students lived in dormitories and returned home only during the summer vacation. By emphasizing classical studies, the school reinforced Shōkō's own background and belief in the fundamental importance of Confucianism for proper human behavior at all levels of society. Mina studied Japanese prose and poetry and the Chinese classics. She took classes in calligraphy and etiquette. Again she was an exemplary student. By 1880 she had completed the required curriculum and was asked to stay on as an assistant instructor. She remained at the Hio Academy until 1884; her brilliance seems even to have inspired talk of adopting her into the Hio household.

She was not yet ready to settle down. Like other young men and women of the 1880s, Mina had big dreams. Japan in the 1870s had embarked on a determined drive to catch up with the Western countries. Everywhere, people spoke of the need for reform and change. Her father was no exception. Mina had grown up impressed with Shōkō's insistence on a political and personal morality of autonomy, self-reliance, and independence. In 1885 she decided to continue her education at the Yokohama Women's Academy. The choice was a bold one. The school, founded by Christian missionaries, was demanding; its curriculum was as far removed from the Hio Academy as one could possibly imagine. Mina studied English, Christianity, and Western literature. Her graduation speech, delivered on July 14, 1887, the anniversary of France's Bastille Day, was entitled "Women Too Have the Responsibility to Spread Liberty." Mina had come a long way.

In 1885, home from the Women's Academy for summer vacation, Mina had her first glimpse of the man she would marry three years later. Kitamura Tōkoku, who later gained fame as a romantic poet and novelist, was born in 1868, the eldest son of an impoverished retainer from Odawara domain. He had accompanied his parents to Tokyo in 1881 and transferred to elementary school. Like many other young men and some women at the time, he quickly traded an interest in formal education for a passion for politics. "I resolved to sacrifice my life to freedom. All my ambition became centered now upon this great ideal, which began to command my heart with fearful energy."[2]

In the world of politics, 1881 was an exciting time. Itagaki Taisuke and his followers, men such as Ishizaka Shōkō, had managed to pressure the government into promising that an elected national assembly would be in place by 1890. National political parties were founded, first the Liberal Party in October 1881 and then the Progressive Party in March 1882. Tōkoku had worked for a while as a boy in the Yokohama Grand Hotel and learned English. As a teenager he also took a job as an errand boy for the Kanagawa Prefectural Assembly and caught an unfiltered glimpse into the political world. He entered the Tokyo Senmon Gakkō (the forerunner of Waseda University) to study politics. By 1885, when he first met Mina, at the age of seventeen, he was a true "political youth" with grand ambitions. "I desired . . . to become a great statesman and recoup the failing fortunes of the Orient. I conceived the ardent desire to sacrifice myself entirely for the benefit of the people. Like another Christ, I would consecrate all my energies to politics."

Tōkoku was also a sensitive youth, given to fits of melancholy and wild swings of emotion. In a long letter to Mina, Tōkoku described his upbringing, which he said accounted for his nervousness and his romantic streak:

> My father, though raised under the feudal system, somehow or other managed to grow up without being overly repressed by its strict forms. He was of open disposition and proud, though he was at the same time in certain respects extremely conscientious. When, for example, my grandfather in 1878 became ill, my father immediately resigned his position with the government and returned home. With great filial devotion he watched over him for seven years, sparing no pains whatsoever in his care. The fact that he worried not at all that the small capital he had accumulated was dwindling away is an example of his conscientiousness. My mother was of a nervous temperament and a woman to be reckoned with. She was a general, hard-to-please, who ruled the roost with firm hand and would brook no interference. From my mother I have inherited my defects of extreme

sensitivity and nervousness; and from my father I have inherited my proud and independent spirit.

In the summer of 1885, Tōkoku visited the Ishizaka residence in Notsuda as the guest of Mina's younger brother Kōreki. Both young men, each seventeen years old, were members of a political study group that was using the Ishizaka house as temporary headquarters during the summer. Having just recovered from a bout of depression, Tōkoku was only a reluctant participant in secret talks to join a group of patriotic adventurers and advance the cause of liberty in Korea. Instead, he announced the waning of his political ambitions and his resolve to become a writer. "I determined to become a novelist. I did not as yet desire to become an artist. Rather, like Hugo of France, I longed to wield an eloquent pen in the service of society." Mina usually was unimpressed with the wild, hot-headed young men who gathered around her father and brother, but she did take notice of Tōkoku, who was quiet and spoke more about literature and the plight of the downtrodden.

They would not meet again for two years. During that time, Mina continued her studies at the Women's Academy. Under the spiritual guidance of the school's headmistress, she developed an interest in Christianity and was baptized on November 14, 1886. Many years later, in 1901, while attending college in the United States, Mina wrote out a recollection of her conversion in English:

> According to the custom of heathenism I was taught to worship idols as guardians or gods. My family had every so many gods in home to worship as many as possible, so that we may receive more happiness. We must give the best we have to please them. While I was yet a mere child my loved ones said to me: "Since you are a girl you must choose at least one god for your own god, because women are more sinful than men; and if you do not commence the right way, you will have more trouble in the future. Moreover, the priests often say you will go to hell after you die, and you will have to climb the mountain of projecting a sword and cross the pond of blood." Then I thought that I must trust something. A few years after my mother bought me a little but pretty idol, which represented the human heart, and also called the god of women. And I was told to give special service to it, by offering lighted candles, fruits, flowers, etc. Well, I did it simply to be an obedient girl, not because I had a spirit of service.
>
> I was in a normal school, where I was compelled to worship the Emperor, whose picture on his birthday and on New Year's day was exhibited before the school, for it is the rule of every school in Japan. It did not satisfy my mind, although I did it as an obedient student. Later, I was in a mission school, where I went just to learn the English language. We were required to attend the services morning and evening. One morning the question, "What have you been worshipping?" was asked. I answered, "The worshipping of the sun is the most reasonable service." "Why?" "Because it is our ancestor, and even our Emperor bows his head toward the sun." Then discussion followed quite often until I recognized the Sun of Righteous-

ness. And at last I came to the feet of Christ, where He received me as one of His and gave me peace, joy, true happiness, true rest and hope. But it took me about three years to cast away the old ways and all my many doubts.[3]

Mina and Tōkoku met again after her graduation from the academy in the summer of 1887. Tōkoku thought he had found the perfect woman; he was in love. He lost no time in declaring his intentions. He wrote a series of letters, which have since become classics in a new genre in Japan of love letters. He praised Mina for her discernment, experience, and intelligence; he praised her love of beauty, her high ideals, and her determination to serve society. Sometimes he declared himself unworthy of such a prize, but Mina responded with equally frank expressions of love. As Tōkoku wrote to his father, Mina was no slave to fame and fortune. Tōkoku professed that she dispelled the clouds that covered his spirit; that adrift upon giant waves in a world gone mad, through her he heard only the sound of beautiful music.

They spent much time together in the summer of 1887. In one letter, Tōkoku hints that their relationship was platonic: "My dearest . . . our love stands on something other than mere passion. We love each other's spirits, each other's hopes. . . . Even though we are not one body, we already think as if we were one. Our love is not the usual carnal affection that passes for love in Japan." Although Tōkoku felt unworthy and tried to leave Mina, attempts at separation brought them closer together. She spoke to him of her conversion and urged him to accept the Christian message. By the end of 1887, Tōkoku wrote to his father, telling him that he had also converted to Christianity. He apologized for his lack of filial piety and blamed his personal defects on his lack of faith. Mina, he wrote, had made him aware of the greatness of God and of the need to draw apart from the world of greed and self-aggrandizement.

Tōkoku referred to Mina as his angel. She had restored his hope and changed the way he looked at the world. "God, through the hands and mouth of the one person I love best, has given me an invitation. . . . My angel's words have dispelled completely my foolishness and pride; no longer do I wish to work for the world with my own power alone, but now, rather with the patriotism of one who wishes to be a soldier of truth, with the intention that God's will be done throughout the world; no longer fighting on earth, looking for a reputation and a great name, but fighting now to make known the blessings of God." Tōkoku, the onetime patriot, politician, and poet, now saw his role in society as preacher. He was baptized on March 4, 1888, some months before his marriage to Mina on November 3, the emperor's birthday

Both sets of parents as well as Mina's friends and teachers opposed the marriage. Mina was three years older than Tōkoku; she was from a good family, her father was a well-known politician. His parents lived off the income generated by a tobacco shop run by his mother. Mina had received an education beyond the reach of most Japanese women of her day. For her parents, marriage to a sensitive poet, penniless, and with little prospect of political, let alone economic, success was unthinkable. In any case, the family had already arranged Mina's match to Aoki Yūsuke, a medical student and ally in local Kanagawa politics.

Mina was not dissuaded. Much to her father's distress, she could use his own political creed, the call for autonomy, independence, and self-reliance and the demand for rights and freedom, to stress her own independence from the community and family restraints. In conscious opposition to tradition, Mina and Tōkoku aimed at a new sort of marriage, accepting each other as equal partners. The Christian wedding ceremony itself was simple. It took place in the already-crowded rooms above his mother's tobacco shop. Mina's brother, Kōreki, was already in the United States, and the other members of the family did not attend.

The young couple took up residence with Tōkoku's family. Mina went every day to a girls' school where she helped with instruction. Tōkoku worked as translator, interpreter, and Japanese language teacher to a number of missionaries. Fighting fits of depression, he found it difficult to write, but in the early 1890s his poems and essays began to attract attention. A daughter, Eiko, was born in 1892. In that same year he published an essay on love that marked him as the leader of a literary and cultural movement that would stress the primacy of the inner life in all human beings. At a time when nationalism was on the rise and the Japanese people were being exhorted to offer themselves courageously in service of the emperor, Tōkoku offered a spiritualism that transcended national and ethnic boundaries. "Love," he wrote, "is the key to life. Life comes only after love. What is there to embellish life if love is taken away?" The essay, "The Pessimistic Poet and Women," praised love in a way never seen before in Japanese literature: "He who has not love is like a tree before spring; he stands somehow in a position of loneliness. It is after going through love that each individual may learn something of the art of life. For love had a pellucidity which pierces to the very truth of beauty." Even the word Tōkoku used for love, *ren'ai*, seemed new and fresh. Love, stressed Tōkoku, was nothing dirty or secretive, but the most human and humanizing of all emotions.

But as Tōkoku himself realized, love was also often self-destructive. Love leads to knowledge of self, of society, of nature, but marriage, entered into with such hope, offers little escape from the drudgeries of the real world. Indeed, by 1893, the love that had made them eager to marry had cooled. Burdened by poverty and frequent moves, Tōkoku was easily angered and often depressed. He had seen too much infighting among the missionaries to trust their charity and had quit organized hierarchical religion for Quakerism and, eventually, the transcendentalism of Emerson. With no resources, a baby to care for, and a silent and often absent husband, Mina was herself depressed.

On May 16, 1894, after one failed attempt at suicide, Tōkoku succeeded in hanging himself. The love match had ended in tragedy. Twenty-nine years old when Tōkoku died, Mina left young Eiko in the care of Tōkoku's parents while she devoted herself to evangelism among the poor. Assuming the translation and interpreting duties of her deceased husband, she also worked for the Azabu Christian Church and took up residence, first with the Woodworth family and later with Christina Penrod, all American missionaries. During this time, her father Shōkō continued to advance his political career. Determined to maintain her independence, Mina saw little of him. Her work as a "Bible woman" took her, instead, into the homes of some of the poorer members of Tokyo society.

In 1899 came the chance to further her education. Supported by a church scholarship, Mina accompanied the Woodworth family when they returned to their home in Indiana. There she enrolled in the Union Christian College, graduating in 1904. She decided to continue her studies at Defiance College in Ohio, graduating two years later with a Bachelor of Arts degree. After eight years of study, she arrived back in Japan on January 30, 1909, just seventeen days after her father's death at the age of sixty-five. Mina had dreams of establishing a women's school, but lacked funds. She pursued a career as a teacher of English at the Shinagawa Women's School until she retired at the age of seventy in 1936. Throughout these years she remained self-reliant and financially independent, a forerunner of the highly educated professional career woman who was to fire the aspirations of Japanese women later in the twentieth century. She kept up her Christian duties, including Sunday school teaching, until her death in 1942.

ISHIZAKA KŌREKI: FAILED AMBITIONS

Shōkō's son, Kōreki, was a true child of the Meiji Restoration. Born in 1868, the same year as Kitamura Tōkoku, he grew up in an atmosphere of constant change and expectations of a bright new future. As with Mina, Kōreki was given a first-rate education. In 1881, after four years at the local public primary school, he was sent to Tokyo to continue his studies. This was the same year in which Tōkoku, also at the age of thirteen, arrived in the capital city. Kōreki studied at the Mosai Academy, headed by Konagai Shōshū, a well-known Confucian scholar. Konagai was a former Tokugawa retainer who had joined the first Japanese mission to travel abroad on a Japanese-manned ship, captained by Katsu Kaishū, in

1860. After the Restoration, Konagai opened his own school for the education of youth, stressing a thorough grounding in the Confucian classics. Kōreki spent a total of 420 days under his tutelage.

It was impossible for Kōreki, the son of an active politician, to escape the political excitement of the day. Like Tōkoku, in the early 1880s his every moment seemed devoted to politics. Well aware of his enthusiasm, his father sent him on a study trip to Tosa, the so-called birthplace of liberty, in 1882. In Osaka, Kōreki met Ōi Kentarō, Baba Tatsui, and others in an atmosphere charged by a recent assassination attempt on Itagaki Taisuke. It was on this occasion that Itagaki uttered the immortal phrase: "Itagaki may die, but liberty, never!"

Returning to Notsuda, Kōreki became active in local political youth groups. He entered a dormitory that allowed young men from the village to engage in political debate day and night. The facility was set up by Murano Tsune'emon, a member of the Kanagawa Prefectural Assembly and close associate of Kōreki's father. Political youth clubs were not unusual in the Kanto area. In the South Tama district alone, twelve groups of eager young people debated politics past and present. Wealthy farmers such as Tsune'emon and Shōkō were the patrons of these intensive study groups. The young men read Western authors such as John Stuart Mill, Herbert Spencer, and Alexis de Tocqueville in translation; discussions and debates followed, and what free time remained was devoted to fencing practice.

In 1884, Kōreki returned to Tokyo in order to prepare for exams that would allow him to enter Tokyo University. A short diary surviving from this period provides an amazing record of the aspirations of a sixteen-year-old. Kōreki's first objective was to gain entry into Tokyo University, where he intended to study politics and economics. He expected to study hard for ten years; then, after graduation, he would travel around the world, meet people, and make connections. His second goal was to become a political critic by comparing the gap between theory and reality. He would develop his own great philosophy, publish books, and seek to influence society. Third, he would enter politics at the head of his own party and heroically work for peace, justice, and truth within Japan. His grandiose fourth goal entailed the creation of a new federation of all nations, which would lay the foundations for liberty throughout the world.

Kōreki and his friends formed a reading group, which met nine times between October 1884 and January 1885. During this short period they read an impressive array of books, including Western, Chinese, and Japanese classics. The Western books consisted of some thirty titles in translation. The meetings involved reports, discussion, and debate. Kōreki assumed leadership of the group and was present for all the sessions. Kitamura Tōkoku, who was losing his interest in politics, attended only one.

In June 1885, despite all these preparations, Kōreki failed to gain entry to Tokyo University. A second attempt in 1886 similarly failed, and a frustrated Kōreki hit upon the idea of a sojourn in America. On the one hand, it offered a solution to his family's failing finances: America was the land of opportunity. But America was also the land of liberty, the antithesis of Japan where the government had begun systematically to suppress the liberal movement. Press laws stifled freedom of expression; public speeches were severely curtailed. As members of the government prepared to draft Japan's constitution, the more liberal factions in society were forced into silence. Kōreki and some other politically frustrated youth dreamed of following in the footsteps of Tōkai Sanshi, the peripatetic hero of the 1885 best-selling novel *Strange Encounters with Elegant Females* (*Kagin no kigu*). They would escape to the United States and continue the struggle for freedom's sake. Indeed, the author of *Strange Encounters*, Shiba Shirō, had himself only recently returned from six years of study at Harvard University and the Wharton School of Finance and Commerce at the University of Pennsylvania. On December 12, 1886, Kōreki set sail for the United States with only two hundred dollars in his pocket and a copy of the Confucian Analects. At San Francisco, when asked the purpose of his visit, he wrote: "to study independence, self-support, and politics." Kōreki was not alone; scores of other young men left Japan in 1886, lured by the promise of American liberty, independence, and opportunity.

Kōreki was overwhelmed by what he saw in the United States. Letters back to his family were filled with descriptions of the wonders of Western civilization, including the famous cable cars of San Francisco. He took up residence across the bay in Oakland and immediately joined a group of young men, who, like him, were trying to advance the cause of political liberty in Japan. Five of them, all in their late teens or early twenties, formed the League of Japanese Patriots. They took it upon themselves to publish a Japanese-language newspaper, which they intended to smuggle back into Japan. The first issue of *Shin Nihon*, or *New Japan*, in a run of 250 copies, appeared in December 1888. It carried a level of political criticism directed at the clique-dominated regime that would have been impossible within Japan. Indeed, Kōreki and his colleagues were tried in absentia and sentenced to six months' imprisonment for violating the press laws. Acting through diplomatic channels, the Tokyo government managed to suppress the newspaper, but it was immediately replaced by another title. For six years, between 1888 and 1895, the California expatriots continued to publish their criticism of authoritarian rule in Japan, running through six titles: *New Japan, The Nineteenth Century, Liberty, Revolution, The Patriot,* and *The Nineteenth Century Newspaper.*

Kōreki's life in California was not easy. He received some help from the Methodist church in Oakland, but had to support himself primarily through manual labor. His original plan to study at Antioch College in Ohio never materialized. Instead, he tried various schemes to make his fortune. In 1889, for example, he bought land south of Sacramento and, naming the place New Hope, sought to establish himself as a pioneer in the growing of hops. In 1890 he arranged to import fifty Japanese laborers to work in his hop fields; another seventy workers were brought over in 1891. The New Hope project failed miserably, and in 1892 Kōreki returned briefly to Japan to raise money. Once back in the United States, he continued the life of a wanderer, trying his hand at journalism in Fresno, at farming in Lodi and Modesto, and finally at seasonal work following the fishing boats up and down the Pacific Coast from Alaska and Canada to southern California. He visited Japan once in 1907 when his father died, but returned immediately to California, where he spent the rest of his life. In a rapid reversal of circumstances, the patriot who had come to the United States in search of liberty and independence died in 1944 in a Japanese-American internment camp at Manzanar, in the bleak desert plains of Death Valley, blind and deprived of his civil rights.

CONCLUSION

What happened to the Ishizaka family of Notsuda was not unusual. For generations it had occupied pride of place in village society. Although change was not unknown in the years before 1853, the opening of the country to foreign intercourse introduced a bewildering series of reforms along with wanted or unwanted changes that fundamentally transformed the Ishizaka family—and Japanese society as a whole. No one escaped the process of what some scholars have termed "modernization." New values and new lifestyles emerged as did new tensions between men and women, husbands and wives, and young and old. How could anyone in the 1860s have imagined what lay ahead for the Ishizaka family? The father was a farmer from rural and remote Notsuda elected to the National Diet and appointed governor of Gumma prefecture. His daughter married for love against her family's wishes; his son abandoned not only his family but also his country in a tragic search for freedom and fortune. His younger daughter mastered the violin and became a teacher of Western classical music. She married into another family soon after Kōreki left Japan and died in 1938, never having shown any interest in politics. When Ishizaka Shōkō died in 1907, he was penniless and heirless. The house in Notsuda had been sold to pay debts, and his son in America had failed to marry. The Ishizaka family of Notsuda was no more.

It was Shōkō, the Confucian, who was initially attracted to Western ideas of rights, liberty, and independence. As a responsible political leader, he saw therein possibilities to increase the well-being of people under his charge. From village through national society, he would strike down private interests and champion the public. The next generation appropriated these political rights and added to them civil liberties. The love affair between Ishizaka Mina and Kitamura Tōkoku consciously challenged allegiance to the chain of generations and responsibility to the community. Kōreki gave filial piety scant attention; he had succeeded to the Ishizaka family headship at the age of eight, but he devoted his life to making his own way outside Japan. Even Toshi, with her violin, had left the old world behind. All three children had converted to Christianity; this was unusual, but not so their exaltation of personal happiness and self-development. Like their father, they sought freedom, but their goals were more personal in nature: freedom to develop their own personalities and freedom to realize their own ambitions. Their goals were often frustrated, but these very frustrations were symbolic of the changes taking place in Japanese society during the Meiji period.

NOTES

1. Biographical information on Ishizaka Shōkō is taken from Watanabe Susumu and Tsumaki Takao, *Ishizaka Shōkō to sono jidai* (Machida: Jaanaru Publishers, 1997). For the eighteen-point village regulations, see pp. 54–55.

2. This and other quotations from Tōkoku's letters come from Francis Malthy, "Kitamura Tōkoku—the Early Years," *Monumenta Nipponica* 18:1 (1963): 1–44.

3. Quoted in Michael Brownstein, "Kitamura Tōkoku and Christian Missionaries," *Gakushuin Daigaku Bungakubu Kenkyū Nenpo* 36 (1989): 61–62.

SUGGESTED READINGS

See Carol Gluck, *Japan's Modern Myths: Ideology in the Late Meiji Period* (1985), for a good introduction to the social and intellectual history of the Meiji period and especially the development of popular nationalism. Irokawa Daikichi, in *The Culture of the Meiji Period* (1985), examines rural political society with emphasis on the role played by wealthy farmers. Irokawa stresses the indigenous origins of Japanese democratic thought and practice. On the Liberty and People's Rights movement, see Roger Bower, *Rebellion and Democracy in the Meiji Period* (1980). This book focuses on the series of violent incidents, such as those of Chichibu and Kabasan, that marked the early 1880s. A more general treatment of the People's Rights movement is Nobutake Ike, *The Beginnings of Political Democracy in Japan* (1950). On political developments in the Tama districts, see M. William Steele, "Political Localism in Meiji Japan: The Case of Yoshino Taizō," *Asian Cultural Studies* 18 (1992). (Yoshino Taizō was a rival of Ishizaka Shōkō active in North Tama.) Neil Waters, in *Japan's Local Pragmatists: The Transition from Bakumatsu to Meiji in the Kawasaki Region* (1983), looks at early political developments in the area. In Japanese, see Ōhata Satoshi, *Jiyū Minken Undō to Kanagawa* (1987), for a general account of the People's Rights movement in the Kanagawa area.

For material on Ishizaka Shōkō in Japanese, see Watanabe Susumu and Tsumaki Takao, *Ishizaka Shōkō to sono jidai* (1997). Ishizaka Shōkō's papers are held in the archives of the Machida City Jiyū Minken Museum, where the permanent exhibition gives an excellent overview of his life. On his daughter Mina, see Esashi Akiko, *Ishizaka Minako no shōgai, Tōkoku no tsuma* (1995). The standard biography of Kitamura Tōkoku is by Irokawa Daikichi, *Kitamura Tōkoku* (1994). In English, see the section on Tōkoku in Masataka Kōsaku, *Japanese Thought in the Meiji Period* (1958), and the article by Francis Malthy, "Kitamura Tōkoku—the Early Years," *Monumenta Nipponica* 18 (1963). See also Michael Brownstein, "Kitamura Tōkoku and Christian Missionaries," *Gakushuin Daigaku Bungakubu Kenkyū Nenpo* 36 (1989). For a study of the experience of Christians in the Meiji period, see Irwin Scheiner, *Christian Converts and Social Protest in Meiji Japan* (1970). Koiyama Rui has written a study of the role of American women missionaries in Meiji Japan, *Amerika fujin senkyōshi* (1992). *Haru* (Spring), a novel by Shimazaki Tōson published in 1908, is based on the tragic marriage of Mina and Tōkoku; Tōson was a close friend of Tōkoku's.

Irokawa Daikichi has written extensively about Ishizaka Kōreki. In his *Zōhō Meiji Seishin-shi* (1968), he covers Kōreki's early life and political ambitions. In *Shinpen Meiji Seishinshi* (1973), he gives more detailed coverage of Kōreki's experiences in California. His general book on the People's Rights movement, *Jiyū Minken* (1981), gives additional information on Kōreki's antigovernment journalism in Oakland. For information on Shiba Shirō and his novel, *Strange Encounters with Elegant Females*, see George Sansom, *The Western World and Japan* (1949), and M. William Steele, "The American Revolution in Meiji Japan," *Journal of Social Sciences* 27 (1989).

PART III

BUILDING THE MODERN STATE

Emperor Meiji's advisers, the men who ruled in his name, inherited a system of government that was decentralized, an economy still rooted in an agrarian regime, a society structured according to a vertical hierarchy of rank and privilege, and a vibrant cultural sphere in which access to education was unequal. The problems that had beset the Tokugawa regime—disgruntled samurai, uppity commoners, and rebellious peasants—still remained. In confrontations with the Western powers, Japan looked weak indeed.

Building a strong centralized state required more than simply dismantling the old domains and substituting prefectures. New institutions had to be created to set policy, see that it was carried out, and gain, if not the support of the populace, at least its acquiescence. The boundaries to the nation had to be established and guarded against all other nations. As we see in Chapter 6, this had particularly unfortunate consequences for Okinawa. The 1870s saw a variety of efforts to rule Japan made through trial and error. During the 1880s the highest decision-making body became the cabinet headed by a prime minister (1885); ministers were appointed to head bureaucracies in charge of education, finance, public works, and so forth. A national police force maintained law and order. Its responsibilities expanded under the Peace Preservation Laws to include the suppression of antigovernment speech and publications. Criminal codes were revised to conform more closely to Western standards in hopes of eliminating the need for extraterritoriality. In 1890, Japan's national assembly, the Diet, opened its doors. For the first time commoners had the opportunity to debate matters of state, within carefully delineated limits. By the early twentieth century the Diet was dominated by politicians belonging to two major parties and determined to promote their own interests.

It was not enough to transform the government; the people also had to be trained in line with state goals, the economy had to become competitive with the West, and customs deemed disgusting in Western eyes had to be reformed. The slogan became "*Bunmei kaika*" (Civilization and enlightenment). Men cut their hair Western-style and started wearing trousers. Education could no longer be left to the vagaries of individual teachers and private academies. Instead, the government ordered that every child in Japan, boy and girl alike, learn reading, writing, and mathematics. Now that careers in government were open to any young man of talent and ability, aspiring candidates crowded into the small number of institutions for higher learning. Both Jahana Noboru (Chapter 6) and Kinoshita Yoshio (Chapter 7) took the path opened by education to better themselves. Like Hatoyama Haruko, even a woman could take advantage of new educational opportunities to pursue a career, albeit not at the same level as a man (Chapter 5).

To compete with the West, Japan's leaders reorganized the military and promoted industrialization. The slogan that epitomized this goal was *Fukoku kyōhei* (Rich country, strong army). In place of the samurai warriors, conscription filled the ranks of the new military machine. Clothing soldiers in Western-style uniforms and arming them with rifles, the military enhanced Japan's interests abroad and provided an advanced education in patriotism for every young man who served his country. Government ministries took over the munitions factories developed by a few domains before the fall of the Tokugawa shogunate, added more, and cast about for ways to earn foreign currency while providing jobs. The government settled on the textile industry, which already employed countless workers, chiefly women, in spinning and weaving. By 1905, 40 percent of Japan's income from exports came from the sale of silk.

The government also took the lead in developing more advanced means of transportation and communication, both for security reasons and for the promotion of industrialization. It inaugurated a nationwide telegraph service to tie the country together. In addition to building bridges and widening, smoothing, and macadamizing highways, it started building railroads to haul freight and passengers, as we see in Chapter 7.

Thus, rather than identifying primarily with a village and tangentially with a region or a domain, people had to learn to see themselves as fellow citizens of an entity that stretched from Okinawa to Hokkaido, united under an emperor descended from the gods. This ideological imperative relied not only on the new educational system and conscription but also on printed materials. The famous Imperial Rescript on Education issued in 1890 is often seen as indicating an end to the extremes of Westernization that had marked the previous decades, because it signaled a return to Confucian values, and yet its dissemination relied on modern printing presses. These same presses churned out newspapers, journals, and books for an increasingly literate audience. Although their content sometimes reinforced the government's message, Chapter 5 shows how access to the printed word also made it possible for different segments of the Japanese population to explore new subjectivities.

The individuals who figure in the next chapters coped with the challenges posed by the coming of modernity with varying degrees of success. Hatoyama Haruko became an advocate for a new definition of womanhood while experiencing some difficulty herself in conforming to all of its dictates. Jahana Noboru earned the reputation of being an early and constant champion for Okinawan rights, although at great personal cost. Kinoshita Yoshio took full advantage of the new opportunities that opened up for men in the twentieth century to make a concrete contribution to Japan's industrialization. His success and his fate speak to the lives of Japanese white-collar workers today.

CHAPTER 5

Hatoyama Haruko

Ambitious Woman

SALLY A. HASTINGS

The creation of a centralized state drew people to Tokyo who would otherwise have spent their lives in the provinces. Tokyo took the lead in the strong Westernizing trend known as Bunmei kaika *(Civilization and enlightenment). This movement encompassed education, dress, behavior, and relations with the world outside Japan. The Meiji government launched numerous attempts to revise the unequal treaties with Western powers. Some involved changing Japanese civil and criminal codes to conform to Western standards; others meant doing away with customs that Westerners considered barbaric. In the 1880s the foreign minister promoted dance parties and charity bazaars at which Japanese citizens could mingle with foreigners in Western-style settings. Because foreigners expected their wives to attend such affairs, Japanese women, too, had to learn the intricacies of Western etiquette. Hatoyama Haruko (1861–1938) prepared herself first, and then other women, for a life that combined a new notion of domesticity with the ability to function easily on a variety of occasions. She epitomized the* ryōsai kenbo *(good wife, wise mother) who defined conventional womanhood in modern Japan.*

Although born before the fall of the Tokugawa shogunate, Haruko was a thoroughly modern woman. In the areas of education, family relations, child-rearing practices, and career paths, her life-course trajectory differed dramatically from Shinanomiya's and Nishimiya Hide's. Owing to her advantages of birth and marriage, she enjoyed a much higher standard of living than did Ishizaka Mina; nonetheless, both these women shared the opportunities brought by modernity to discover new avenues of self-fulfillment.

Sally A. Hastings is associate professor of history at Purdue University. She is the author of Neighborhood and Nation in Tokyo, 1905–1937 *(1995), and she is an editor-in-chief for* U.S.–Japan Women's Journal. *This article draws from her current research on political women in modern Japan.*

"*Boys*, be ambitious!" These are the words with which the American educator William Smith Clark (1826–1886) inspired his students at the

Sapporo Agricultural College, where he taught in 1876. Many of the students at Sapporo took him at his word. Nitobe Inazō (1862–1933), who earned a doctorate at Johns Hopkins University, became a noted scholar, educator, and civil servant. Uchimura Kanzō (1861–1930) also studied in the United States, earning degrees from Amherst College and the Hartford Seminary; he is noted in Japanese history as the founder of a nonchurch movement within Christianity.

As far as we know, no educator, Japanese or Western, had told Japanese girls to be ambitious. Hatoyama Haruko, however, who was born in the same year as Uchimura and a year after Nitobe, led her life as if she had heard and heeded Clark's message. Because she was a woman, she did not have the opportunity to study in the United States and she certainly never held public office. Nevertheless, like Nitobe and Uchimura, she became a noted educator, writer, and organizer. Through these roles, she was highly influential in constructing the definition of woman in the modern Japanese state.

Haruko was born March 23, 1861, in the city of Matsumoto, in what is now Nagano prefecture. Her samurai father Tsutomu changed his original family name of Watanabe to Taga on the occasion of the Meiji Restoration (1868). She was the youngest of seven children, five girls and two boys. One brother died in infancy, her three older sisters left the house as brides, and her only surviving brother went to Tokyo to be educated. Consequently, Haruko grew up in a relatively small household with only her next-older sister as a companion.

At first glance, this would not seem to be a household that would foster ambitious plans for a woman's life. In keeping with the custom in the domain in which her father was a samurai, Haruko's family maintained a strong tradition of "honoring men and despising women." Her mother deferred to her father, and the children did the same. Within the household, her mother was busy with a variety of tasks: raising silkworms, spinning, weaving, and sewing. Haruko learned these skills at her mother's side.

Haruko's literary education gave shape to her ambition. Although her schooling began at home and her mother was her first teacher, Haruko's education differed from that of her sisters, for she was allowed to pursue the same curriculum as a boy. Once she could read and write, she studied by herself in the cold season from first dawn to the evening lighting of the lamps. Her mother's instruction was supplemented by lessons from local teachers of the Chinese classics, who were all the more available because of the upheavals of the Meiji Restoration. Haruko's memory of her tutorial in Chinese was that all the other students were boys, but that she herself was always the best student.

Ironically, it was the opening of a school in Matsumoto specifically for girls that gave Haruko the opportunity to continue her education in Tokyo. Haruko was one of the first students to enroll when the school opened in a local temple in 1873, but her level of Chinese learning was already much higher than that of the other students. Her father thus determined to take her with him to Tokyo.

In Tokyo, her father's excellent political connections enabled Haruko to obtain the best possible education then available to women. In 1872 the government had opened Takebashi Girls' School to train female teachers and interpreters. Through a friend from Matsumoto, Haruko's father secured an introduction to the head of the school and a place there for Haruko. The curriculum included zoology, botany, physics, chemistry, and handicrafts as well as Chinese and Japanese literature. Part of the day was spent on Japanese studies, part on English. The English classes were taught by foreign instructors, the first of whom was the wife of an American missionary.

The fact that part of the instruction was in English was a huge shock to Haruko, who had had no exposure to Western languages in Matsumoto. She studied hard, even during the summer vacation. With the help of a distant relative who had gained a Western education, she read *Self Help* by the American voluntarist Samuel Smiles and several other books. Her father also made arrangements for her to study with a scholar of Chinese. Soon, Haruko was in the most advanced class, even in English. Consequently, she was sorely disappointed when the government closed the school in 1877.

Haruko's experience at Takebashi shaped her life in several respects. If she had stayed in Matsumoto, she might have continued her education with Chinese teachers and have enjoyed the kind of active participation in predominantly male literary gatherings that was possible for exceptional women in Tokugawa Japan. Exclusively female schools, such as Takebashi, were an innovation of the new Meiji era, and Haruko's enrollment foreshadowed her leadership in the separate sphere of women-only educational institutions, women's clubs, and women's magazines. Her tutelage under American faculty members was her first experience with female teachers. That her first women teachers were Westerners meant that her understanding of the proper role for women in the modern world was shaped by Western views. Last, but by no means least significant, Haruko's study of English with native speakers gave her expertise on which she would draw for the rest of her life.

After the closing of Takebashi Girls' School, the Education Ministry transferred Haruko and her classmates to a newly established English section within the Tokyo Women's Normal School. Haruko was unhappy that there were no foreign teachers at this school, and for a time she withdrew to take private lessons with Mrs. Wycoff, the wife of an American educator. Some of her classmates from Takebashi joined her in these lessons. When Mrs. Wycoff had to return to the States, however, Haruko and her friends rejoined their classmates and graduated from the English section in 1878.

In 1878 there were very few educational opportunities for Japanese women. Haruko decided to continue her education by enrolling as a regular student in the Tokyo Women's Normal School. The highlight of her years there was her selection as one of three students chosen by the Ministry of Education to study in America in 1879. In preparation for her anticipated trip, she studied English intensively with the wife of an American teacher. The greatest disappointment of Haruko's life was the cancellation of this trip. In the midst of her disappointment, she had to study especially hard to catch up in the regular Normal School subjects that she had neglected for the sake of English. Algebra and geometry caused her particular pain, so she defied the dormitory monitors by studying late into the night. In later years, she wondered whether her weak eyesight and heart trouble originated in the stress of her studies.

Haruko graduated from Tokyo Women's Normal School in July 1881. She joined the faculty briefly, but resigned when she married in November of that year. Her marriage was an arranged one, and it does not figure in her life as the culmination of a long romance. On the other hand, neither did she ever suggest that it had impeded her career. In one sense, her marriage to Hatoyama Kazuo (1856-1911) represented a fitting climax to her education, for she had been selected precisely because she had studied modern subjects. Moreover, her marriage launched her into public life. First, her husband was one of the best known and most admired men in Japan. In an 1885 newspaper contest to identify Japan's ten most outstanding men, Hatoyama Kazuo ranked fourth.[1] Moreover, he was happy to have his wife engage in activities outside the home.

The discussions that led to Haruko's marriage to Hatoyama were initiated by Kōzu Senzaburō, a history instructor at Tokyo Women's Normal School. Kōzu had studied in the United States from 1875 to 1878. He thus had shared experience with Hatoyama Kazuo, who had studied law at Columbia and Yale. Hatoyama had explained to Kōzu that because he enjoyed speaking English more than he enjoyed speaking Japanese, he wanted a wife who understood English. Might there not be a woman at the Normal School who spoke excellent English? Kōzu recommended Haruko and, after further discussions with Hatoyama, approached Haruko's father. Hatoyama Kazuo and Haruko were married November 16, 1881, shortly after he passed the bar examination. The ceremony took place in the house that he had purchased on returning from abroad.

With her marriage, Haruko embarked on a modern life in the company of Kazuo and his friends, many of them high-ranking government officials. Two weeks after their wedding, Kazuo and Haruko hosted a banquet to announce their marriage to their friends, an occasion that Haruko termed the first Western-style marriage announcement banquet in Japan. The guests included Kurino Shinichirō (1851–1937), later ambassador to the United States, Mexico, Italy, France, Spain, and Russia, and Furuichi Kōi (1854–1934), a prominent civil engineer in charge of many public works projects. The entertainment ranged from U.S. Civil War songs to Nō chants.

Ambitious as she was in pursuit of knowledge, Haruko nevertheless accepted the idea of separate spheres and separate functions for men and women. She simply assumed that most women would and should become mothers. At the same time, she in no way acknowledged that men were superior to women and she was supremely confident of her own intelligence and learning. When she wrote about the home or motherhood or women's education, she invoked both the Chinese classics and the latest foreign publications with authority. She identified herself as a modern woman, able to serve as a companion to her husband and a teacher to her sons. She publicized her own life, presenting it as a model of modern womanhood.

Japanese brides usually began their married lives as daughters-in-law, and Haruko was no exception. For the first few months of their marriage, Haruko and Kazuo lived with Kazuo's mother Kikuko; she also lived with them in Koishikawa where they moved in 1892 and accompanied them on summer vacations. She died only a short time before her son. Given that they were women of two very different worlds, mother and daughter-in-law got along remarkably well. Self-sacrificing and diligent, Kikuko embodied the traditional virtues of Japanese women. She had a reputation for holding others to a high standard. Even before Kazuo married, however, he had impressed his own views upon her. Thus, by the time that Haruko arrived as a bride, the mother-in-law who had such a reputation for being difficult was so undemanding that Haruko felt sorry for her.

Haruko's behavior deviated considerably from that of the typical bride of the period. First of all, she continued to carry out professional responsibilities of her own. Although she had resigned from her faculty position at the Normal School, at the request of the school she continued to teach until a suitable successor was found. In addition, she was also engaged in translating legal documents. Her light household duties allowed her to study English and Chinese in her spare time and to read selected works with her older sister. With Kazuo's encouragement, she spent time with her friends. When her husband was free during the day, she relaxed with him. Although Haruko enjoyed the support of her husband in her relatively independent life, it is clear from her memoirs that she occasionally chafed at her mother-in-law's disapproval of her English lessons and at her obligation to entertain Kikuko's guests.

The image Haruko projected of her modern marriage was an attractive one. As a newlywed, Kazuo was preparing to open his own law practice. Haruko helped him by copying over his scrawled translations and providing clean copy of his legal opinions. The young couple also knew how to relax. Haruko treasured memories of playing the poem card game *Hyakunin-isshu* during their first New Year's holiday together as a married couple. Kazuo, who enjoyed Tennyson's poetry, would also read some of the passages aloud to his wife.

Although Haruko was occasionally in conflict with the varying expectations society had of wives, she was unambiguously anxious to be a good mother. Despite a little morning sickness during her pregnancy, she continued to exert herself. Because they considered their present location in the middle of the city unhealthy, Kazuo and Haruko decided to move. After spending many Sundays looking at houses, they bought one slightly farther out in Ushigome and moved immediately. Haruko believed that it was important to keep both mind and body active during pregnancy. When the weather was fair, she walked along a riverbank. Other pursuits included yet more study of English and sewing baby clothes.

Haruko gave birth to her first son, Ichirō, on January 1, 1883. Although tradition called for a long bed rest after the birth of a first child, by the third day Haruko was sitting up in bed knitting. Her obstetrician, much freer from the old ways than a midwife would have been, even allowed her that same day to go into the next room to sit next to the charcoal brazier. By the seventh day, she was able to handle the baby by herself. She anticipated the infant's needs so skillfully that, even as an infant, Ichirō did not wet or soil his clothing.

Haruko did not find it easy to balance her responsibilities as the wife of a modern official with her role as a nursing mother. When Ichirō was only a month old, Kazuo and Haruko accepted (with her doctor's permission) an invitation to a ball at the official residence of the governor of Tokyo prefecture. Haruko did not attend this gala for her own pleasure. Rather, she felt that it was not right for her to cease all social intercourse just because she had a child. The problems of maintaining a social life, however, were daunting. Sometimes when it was time to leave for an affair, Ichirō would be nursing. At other times he would wake up in an irritable state. Even though he cried, he would refuse to drink his mother's milk because he had become accustomed to a bottle. This rejection was, of course, very painful for Haruko.

The second son, Hideo, born February 7, 1884, proved to be an even greater challenge. Right after he was born, he developed sores in his mouth that kept him from sucking properly. She had to feed him with a spoon day and night, without any sleep herself. Although Hideo recovered, his growth did not equal that of his brother. Ichirō could walk from the time he was a year old, but Hideo could not. Through middle school, Hideo was always the smallest pupil in his class. He had a spurt of growth in high school, however, and by his university days he had reached average height.

Despite Hideo's health problems, Haruko returned to teaching at the Tokyo Women's Normal School shortly after his birth. In order to secure revision of the unequal treaties with the Western powers (especially to expunge extraterritoriality), the Japanese government was struggling in the 1880s to win recognition as a civilized country. The principal of the Normal School invited Haruko to return to the faculty to assist in the national effort to wipe out every trace of customs oppressive to women. In June 1884, with her husband's approval, she agreed to return to teaching. Although she was given a great deal of leeway in her schedule, she was nevertheless at the school virtually every day. One of her motivations in returning to teaching was to continue her study of English, something her mother-in-law regarded as an unnecessary luxury.

Moreover, Haruko never entirely relinquished her identity as an educator. In 1886, when the Education Ministry decided to merge the Women's Normal School with the men's, some of the faculty at the women's school, Haruko among them, resigned to found a women's vocational school, Kyōritsu Women's School. Haruko maintained that affiliation, serving in various capacities, even as a member of the board of directors. On the other hand, her identity as a talented married woman who could contribute to national development did not include the idea of economic self-sufficiency. On the contrary, she carefully distinguished herself from unmarried teachers or from Normal School students who pursued their educations in order to get a job.

In Haruko's recollections of how she brought up her sons, we can see what Jordan Sand has termed the invention of Japanese domesticity. Although Haruko had a mother-in-law, her emphasis was always on her relationship with her husband and her sons. Her considerable responsibilities for balancing the domestic budget and educating her sons reflected the separation of work from home, for Kazuo was often absent. Haruko constructed an orderly home life that provided a refuge from the world at the same time that it provided a building block for the nation. When her husband was at home, she was at his side, caring for him. Whereas earlier generations of Japanese had dined from individual tray tables at random hours, the Hatoyama family sat down to dinner together at 6:00 P.M. and then talked together in the living room for the next hour. Afterward, Haruko and Kazuo played billiards or looked at foreign magazines while their children studied.

One dimension of Haruko's identity as a modern mother was her assumption of responsibility for the education of her sons. She never scolded them. When they misbehaved, she made them apologize to their father. In teaching them English, she was particularly concerned with correct pronunciation and their facility in understanding spoken English. In teaching them mathematics, she never let them be aware of her own dislike for the subject. While they were in school, she rose daily at 3:30 A.M. to help them review their lessons. She took charge of her sons' studies so that they could enjoy their time with their father, taking the position that he was in charge of play. She, however, took pride in their knowing how to play well. Their skills included gardening, piano, singing, calisthenics, croquet, tennis, rowing, and swimming, often pursued during the family's summers. While the boys were young, they went to places on the seashore such as Oiso, but later the family built a summerhouse in Hokkaido. The house was so far out in the country that Haruko and her mother-in-law were carried there in baskets, while Kazuo and the boys rode horseback. Haruko especially remembered the Chinese millet and the delicious soybeans they ate there.

Ichirō records in his autobiography that when he qualified, in 1900, to enter the First Higher School, Haruko approached the headmaster to ask whether her son could live at home instead of in the dormitory.[2] Her request was denied. Lest we read too much overprotectiveness into Haruko's plea, we should note that a year and a half later, she and Kazuo left for a trip abroad, leaving both boys behind.

After Kazuo opened his own law practice in 1884, he continued to lecture at the Law School of Tokyo University. In April 1885, at the request of Minister Inoue Kaoru, he also became an employee of the Foreign Ministry, a responsibility he maintained until 1890 and resumed in 1898. From 1890 to 1907, he was president of Tokyo Senmon Gakkō, the forerunner to Waseda University. Haruko became even more actively involved in Kazuo's life when he decided to enter politics. His political career began in the Tokyo Prefecture Assembly to which he was first elected in 1882. He became its head the same year and was reelected in 1884. When the first elections for the National Diet were held in 1890, the head of Ushigome ward, where the Hatoyama family lived and where Kazuo had his law office, nominated Hatoyama Kazuo. The Koishikawa, Ushigome, and Yotsuya wards constituted an election district for one seat in the Diet. The newspapers reported that there were three candidates, one from each ward. No one from the Hatoyama family, however, did any campaigning, and on the day of the election, Kazuo was away in Sendai on business connected with his law firm. He lost to the candidate from Koishikawa.

Haruko's first involvement in political campaigning came in another contest that Kazuo lost. Shortly after the 1890 election, the village heads of Kita Toyoshima-gun in the Tokyo suburbs approached Kazuo. The Diet representative from their district had been convicted of a crime in a preliminary hearing and would have to resign his seat. Kazuo agreed to run on the understanding that he could continue his legal practice. Because his opponent was campaigning vigorously, Kazuo's supporters asked if Haruko might not campaign in his place. She complied, on the condition that it be in the evening, so as not to interfere with her teaching obligations. She went from house to house, visiting the powerful leaders of the district. As the election approached, supporters of Kazuo's opponent maligned Haruko in the press and employed thugs to frighten voters away from the polls. The village heads who had supported Kazuo ended up hiding in rice bins and under Shintō altars. With about a thousand votes cast, Kazuo lost by fifteen. This dramatic defeat should not obscure the fact that Kazuo won a number of elections to the Diet later. He served in the lower house from his election in February 1892 until his death, winning reelection in March 1894, September 1894, March 1898, August 1898, August 1902, March 1903, March 1904, and May 1908. In 1896 he became Speaker of the House. Having learned his lesson in 1890, he waged an effective campaign for every election thereafter.

During Kazuo's lifetime, suffrage in Japan was limited to a small percentage of the male population, and the primary method of campaigning was house-to-house. Haruko undoubtedly engaged in such campaigning in regular elections in the Tokyo district where they lived just as she had done in the unsuccessful by-election of 1891. When she was asked as a politician's wife why politicians needed domestic support, she replied that wives should distance themselves from their husbands' political battles and, short of capitulation or flattery, try to conciliate their husbands' opponents. In addition, wives should refrain from unnecessary expenditures on clothing or theater tickets. From accounts written after her husband's death, we can see that her exhortation to economize was an oblique reference to her own major role in providing funds for her husband's election campaigns. Kazuo, who valued time more than money, was perfectly prepared to borrow. Haruko avoided that trap by investing the money Kazuo gave her for clothes when he had received a particularly large legal fee.

As the wife of a prominent man, Haruko finally got the trip to America she had wanted so much as a Normal School student. Yale University invited Kazuo to come to New Haven to receive an honorary degree on the occasion of the two hundredth anniversary of the university's founding. Kazuo and Haruko set sail from Yokohama on September 4, 1901, reaching Seattle on September 18. The Japanese consul in Seattle, whose wife had been a student of Haruko's at Kyōritsu Women's School, met them with a horse-drawn carriage. The Japanese community in Seattle held a reception in their honor. In Chicago, they stayed for four days in the home of a wealthy philanthropist and were feted at dinner parties in other homes. When they toured the University of Chicago, they were duly impressed with John D. Rockefeller's munificence. They also had an interview with its president, William Rainey Harper. Their next stop was Niagara Falls and then a tour of an exposition in Buffalo. In New York City they stopped briefly to write letters and send telegrams and then took a late night train to Washington, DC.

When they arrived in Washington early the next morning, Ambassador Takashima and his staff were at the station to greet them. Takashima invited them to dinner and at the same time informed them that Kazuo had received the unusual honor of a dinner invitation from President Theodore Roosevelt. Kazuo immediately accepted, but he never got to attend. Roosevelt had not been aware that Kazuo was accompanied by his wife. If Haruko were to come to dinner, then Mrs. Roosevelt would have to be present as well. The city was in mourning for President William McKinley, who had been assassinated just days before the Hatoyamas arrived in Seattle, so it would not have been proper to have an elaborate dinner party. The engagement was therefore changed to a luncheon. Knowing nothing of this, Kazuo and Haruko were out sight-seeing, visiting the Library of Congress and the Treasury Department. They did not return until long after lunchtime, and all of Ambassador Takashima's efforts to find them failed. The next morning, as had been previously arranged, Takashima took them to the White House for a meeting with the president. Despite the crush of people waiting for interviews, Haruko was immediately taken to a separate room where Mrs. Roosevelt served her tea and cakes. Haruko had her photograph taken with the president's wife and daughter. After a tour of the White House, Kazuo and Haruko left the same day for Philadelphia.

In the City of Brotherly Love, Kazuo and Haruko toured Independence Hall and attended a dinner party. Their tour of the suburban Bryn Mawr College for women included an interview with its president, M. Carey Thomas. A letter in the Bryn Mawr archives from Tsuda Umeko, also the founder and president of a women's college, introducing her friends Dr. and Mrs. Hatoyama, shows us that this trip was planned well in advance.[3] Returning to New York, they stayed at the Waldorf-Astoria. A Civil War general gave a reception for them at the Century Club, and their days were filled with sight-seeing and shopping.

In New Haven, they spent sixteen days at the home of George Trumbull Ladd, a Yale professor who had lectured in Japan in 1892 and 1899. For ten days, Kazuo gave a two-hour lecture daily. More than seventy women attended the tea that Mrs. Ladd gave for Haruko. Helen Hadley, the wife of Yale President Arthur Twining Hadley, entertained Haruko at a luncheon at the country club, where she first saw golf being played. Kazuo's former classmates and professors invited the couple to numerous luncheons and dinners.

Haruko and Kazuo met many well-known educators and politicians. On October 14 they went to Northampton, Massachusetts, to tour Smith College because a friend from New York had sent a letter of introduction to Laurenus Clark Seelye, the longtime president. The women's college had set aside a room for them overnight, but they returned to New Haven the same day. On October 21, President Hadley held a large reception that included President Roosevelt; the two men stood for a long time greeting guests. Taking a lesson from President McKinley's assassination in a receiving line, however, they refrained from shaking hands. At this reception, President Roosevelt exchanged a few words with Haruko.

While Haruko and Kazuo were in New Haven, the eminent statesman Itō Hirobumi joined them at the Ladds' house. On the evening of October 22, they gathered in Itō's room to share some drinks provided by a mutual friend. The three stayed up late while Itō held forth on the virtues of American women, their easygoing grace and their capacity for friendship. He encouraged Haruko to speak freely with him on future occasions in Japan. The event clearly made a deep impression on Haruko, who had never enjoyed such frank discussions with her husband's other colleagues.

On October 23, Yale bestowed honorary degrees on both Hatoyama Kazuo and Itō Hirobumi. The next day, Kazuo and Haruko left New Haven for New York, where Kazuo had promised to give a lecture at the Brooklyn Club. That night they stayed at the home of a prosperous Columbia classmate of Kazuo's. On October 25 they returned to Manhattan, where their last full day in the United States included a dinner party and attendance at a campaign rally for the New York City elections. The next day they boarded a steamship for Liverpool, England. In their cabin they found candy, fruit, and flowers from their American friends. Having recognized Kazuo as the recent recipient of honors from Yale, representatives of the shipping company moved them to a larger and more luxurious cabin.

Their visit of just over five weeks in the United States was a far cry from the extended stay Haruko had looked forward to as a Normal School student. Her account conveys an impression of haste and missed opportunities: the lunch they never ate at the White House, a room they never slept in at Smith College. Nevertheless, this trip was one of the major events of her life, an experience that she referred to repeatedly in her writing. The visits to Bryn Mawr and Smith bear testimony to her strong self-consciousness as an educator of women. Her many social engagements with statesmen, university presidents, and illustrious women convinced her more than ever of how important it was that Japanese women be trained to conduct themselves with dignity in international social settings.

Soon after arriving in foggy London, Haruko and Kazuo left for Paris. Inoue Kinjirō, a Japanese businessman, showed them the sights, most memorably, Versailles. In Germany, Mrs. Itō and Mrs. Nabeshima were their guides to places such as the Parliament and the palaces in Berlin and Potsdam. They returned to England via Brussels. During their ten-day stay in London they went to the theater and enjoyed more sightseeing and dinner parties. Sailing home via the Indian Ocean, they reached Nagasaki on January 4, 1902.

Prior to her visit to the United States, during which she attended dinner parties, receptions, and even had tea with the First Lady, Haruko had engaged in many activities in Japan that had prepared her for such events. In the mid-1880s, Kazuo's boss, Foreign Minister Inoue Kaoru, put on balls and dinner parties at which he hoped the Japanese elite would demonstrate to the diplomatic community the high level of civilization in Japan. Haruko attended the first of these balls in the company of the education minister, Mori Arinori, who invited Kazuo to bring her on many subsequent occasions. At first she wore Japanese clothing, but later she and the other women guests switched to Western dress. Haruko had joined others in taking lessons from a German woman in how to behave appropriately at such functions. Whereas Haruko's language study had begun as self-cultivation in pursuit of knowledge, her training in Western manners was part of a project of national representation. The majority of foreigners, she said, "see the geisha and think that she represents Japanese womanhood."[4]

Over the next two decades, Haruko participated in several women's groups that were, in some respects, a continuation of these lessons in how Japanese women should behave at Western-style social functions. One group that met in the late 1880s was sponsored by Miss Prince, a teacher at the Tokyo Girls' School, and included Tsuda Umeko, Ōyama Sutematsu, and Uryū Shigeko, the three women who had gone to the United States as government-sponsored students in 1871 and remained there for a decade. Other members of the group were Imamura Junko, a graduate of the women's higher normal school and the wife of an insurance executive, and Gotō Kazuko, the wife of the powerful bureaucrat, Gotō Shinpei. At the monthly meetings, Miss Prince answered questions that members had written on slips of paper and placed in a box. Under Haruko's leadership, the meetings continued even after Miss Prince left Japan because of illness. Some years later, in 1897, Haruko was involved in another organization for English-speaking women, the Monday Club, which included aristocrats such as Ōyama Sutematsu and Nabeshima Nagako and court ladies such as Kagawa Shihoko and Kitajima Itoko. The women gathered at one another's houses , only disbanding at the time of the Russo-Japanese War. Yet another women's gathering in which Haruko participated was the reading group under the sponsorship of the Oxford-educated Miss Weston. This group ceased to exist after Miss Weston fell ill and returned to Great Britain.

In addition to these social and educational gatherings, Haruko was active in formal women's organizations, most of them created through some type of semiofficial government leadership. In 1895 she was a founding member of the Japanese Women's Academic Society (Dai Nihon jogakkai), and in 1901 of the Patriotic Women's Society. She was also a member of the Japan Women's Hygiene Association. These organizations held meetings and published magazines. Haruko was a frequent contributor to *Onna* (Women), the publication of the Women's Academic Society. Her attendance at meetings seems to have varied considerably from organization to organization. Other groups were formed on a smaller scale, for instance, the alumnae of the Takebashi Girls' School and the Women's Normal School. The Hoshin Women's Club was associated with Kyōritsu Women's Vocational School. It was one of the groups that participated in the annual *"Hana no hi"*(flower day), on which women sold flowers to raise money for charity. Haruko never allowed any such obligation to interfere with her being home when her husband was there. If the Women's Hygiene Association or the Normal School alumnae held meetings on Sunday, Haruko simply did not attend.

When some Japanese men invoked the women's liberation movement in Western countries to argue that Japanese women should not be allowed to go out to meetings, Haruko was quick to defend women's organizations. She claimed that women broadened their horizons by getting out of the home, and thus, in moderation, their engagement in outside activities contributed to the peace and happiness of the home. To be sure, in her defense of Japanese women's right to attend meetings, Haruko pronounced the women's liberation movement a danger. "As long as our country has the custom that women exercise self-denial and patience in their self-sacrifice for the peace and happiness of the home," she assured her readers, "the number of single women will not rise as in Western countries." Moreover, "women's liberation will not occur in Japan."[5] She cited Mrs. Ladd of New Haven as an example of the model wife, who, although she belonged to women's organizations, was always home when her husband returned from work. To Haruko in 1911, the women's liberation movement was an unfortunate development for the West but one that brought into relief the native virtues of Japan. By the 1920s, however, she had moderated her views to the extent that, when a group of younger women formed the Women's Suffrage League, she lent her support.

As a young wife, Haruko had prided herself on being a wife chosen by her husband rather than by her mother-in-law, and she extended the same independence to her sons. When her older son Ichirō was named a cabinet minister, she emphasized her view of motherhood as a temporary role. "Mothers bring up children," she said, "but children are not babies forever. When they leave school and go out in the world, they must become responsible for their own development."[6] By her own standard, Haruko's work as a mother, into which she had poured her being for more than twenty years, drew to a close around 1908. Ichirō graduated from Tokyo University in 1907 and Hideo in 1908. On September 18, 1908, Ichirō married Kaoru, one of Haruko's relatives and the adopted daughter of Terada Sakae, a Diet member. Hideo married Kikuike Chiyo soon thereafter. Around this same time, Haruko's mother-in-law entered her final illness, and Haruko herself was diagnosed with an enlarged heart.

Before Haruko had much opportunity to redefine herself as a mother-in-law and grandmother, Kazuo's health failed. Caring for him required all her time. We learn of this period in Haruko's life from an article that she wrote for the women's magazine *Fujin sekai* (Woman's world) shortly after his death. The New Year's Day celebration for 1911 marked the divide between normal days and days of illness. In December 1910, when they had heard that a friend of Kazuo's was deathly ill with stomach cancer, Kazuo had blurted out, "Perhaps I have stomach cancer." But when Haruko questioned him about his health, he dismissed the remark as a joke.

Soon, however, it became clear that Kazuo was not in good health. Their New Year's trip to Oiso was cut short so that he could consult his doctors, as was their April trip to Izu. Always Kazuo's companion in both work and recreation, Haruko was instrumental in securing both diagnosis and treatment for her husband. Once it was determined that he was suffering from incurable cancer, she secured painkillers for him. From April on, she took full responsibility for feeding, bathing, and grooming him, and she sacrificed her own sleep to care for him.

Kazuo's death on October 3, 1911, left Haruko a widow at the relatively young age of fifty. During the months of Kazuo's illness, she had cut herself off from her usual obligations in order to remain at his side. With his death, she was freed from her duties as a wife. On the occasion of her sons' marriages, she had made it abundantly clear that she had fulfilled her responsibilities as a mother and had no intention of interfering in her sons' lives, although she did share a home with Ichirō and Kaoru.

Haruko's decision to become head of the newly created home economics department at Kyōritsu Women's School made national headlines. She told reporters of the *Tokyo nichinichi* that she wanted to nurture students who would become "good wives and wise mothers." Haruko used this expression—one that in postwar Japan has come to stand for everything repressive about customs toward women—to describe what she considered to be a new type of Japanese woman, one who would be able to stand on her own, not deriving her strength from her husband. She assumed that everywhere in the world women would exercise their autonomy within the home. She explained that the purpose of home economics, the invention of which she credited to the city of Boston, was to provide graduates of girls' higher schools with sufficient knowledge of sewing, laundry, cooking, and etiquette to run a household. Once again distancing herself from women who supported themselves by teaching, Haruko went out of her way to emphasize that she was not accepting the position because she needed a salary. Her formal duties were indeed light—two hour-long lectures per week, one on morality and one on the home.

In December 1922, Haruko became principal of the Kyōritsu Women's School, a position she held until her death. Soon after taking office, she faced a formidable challenge. In the Kantō earthquake of September 1923, the entire campus burned to the ground, and some sixty faculty members and students perished. Haruko took a leading role in the fund-raising that allowed the school to start rebuilding on the old site by March 16, 1924.

From 1912, then, Haruko's educational endeavors constituted her primary identity. Prior to her husband's death, she had been listed in the pages of the women's magazines in which her articles appeared simply as "Hatoyama Haruko" or as "the wife of Diet member Hatoyama Kazuo." The one exception occurred when she was identified as a member of a society in whose journal she was publishing. From 1922 on, she was routinely referred to as the principal of Kyōritsu Women's School. References to her as the mother of Diet member Hatoyama Ichirō were the exception rather than the rule. When she died, the school conducted her funeral on its premises.

Until at least 1931, Haruko continued to be an active member of women's organizations and a prolific writer. She not only maintained her membership in older organizations such as the Japan Women's Hygiene Association and the Women's Patriotic Association, but she also appeared at the opening ceremonies of newly formed groups such as the Japan League of Women's Associations.

In her essays for various magazines, one of her recurring themes was the importance of raising the level of women's education in Japan. For instance, when asked whether women should be admitted to men's universities, she answered in the affirmative but also used the question to press for making girls' higher school education (three years beyond the mandatory six years of primary schooling) more widely available. She made two compelling arguments for women's higher education. The first spoke to the needs of the family: without adequate preparation, women would be unable to fulfill their proper function as "good wives and wise mothers." The second argument invoked the needs of the nation, which ought not to deprive itself of the abilities of unusually talented women.

Even in her seventies, Haruko maintained a presence in women's magazines. She wrote essays with titles such as "Building Character for Chastity" and "Education Centered on Motherhood." In addition, she answered reporters' queries on topics such as going away for the summer and her own home cooking. She also wrote short essays for occasions such as the thirty-fifth anniversary of the magazine *Fujo shinbun* and the death of the noted educator Shimoda Utako. She produced most of her autobiographical writings in the years after her husband died.

In those years, Haruko also received a number of awards. Her work on behalf of women's education was recognized not only by the Imperial Household Ministry, the Tokyo prefecture, and Tokyo City but also by local organizations such as the Tokyo League of Women's Associations and the Koishikawa Young Women's Association. Ad hoc committees for special celebrations, such as the accession ceremonies for the Shōwa emperor in 1928 and the festivities in 1930 in honor of the restoration of the capital following the devastation of the earthquake, also brought her awards.

News reports inform us that she was in ill health for about two years before she died, but that she continued to work even in the last months of her life. *Fujo shinbun* reported on January 24, 1937, that Hatoyama Haruko had been at home since the end of the previous year suffering from kidney disease, but that she seemed to be getting better. On April 16, 1938, *Asahi shinbun* reported that she had fainted in her office at Kyōritsu. When she died at home on July 12, 1938, the newspapers gave arteriosclerosis as the cause of death.

The young Taga Haruko had had many ambitions. Her early promise as a scholar was fulfilled in her years as a teacher, writer, and school
principal. Her sons may even have exceeded her expectations. Her
younger son Hideo (1884–1946) graduated from Tokyo University in
1908 and served on the faculty there from 1910 until 1926. He was elected
to the lower house of the Diet in 1932. Her older son Ichirō (1883–
1959) won election to the Diet in 1915 and became education minister
in 1931. Long after his mother's death, in 1954 he became prime minister. In the short run, Haruko's desire that Japan be freed from the unequal treaties with the West was realized by 1911. She could never have
imagined the economic prosperity of the nation today.

Although Hatoyama Haruko was known far beyond her family and
local community, her story has not been incorporated into Japanese
women's history. This history has usually been presented as one of struggle
against externally imposed restraints. In contrast to the writers for
Seitō, the feminist journal that began publication in the year that she was
widowed, Haruko had little interest in women's individual freedom. She
regarded the strength of women in the face of adversity to be one of the
pillars of modern Japan.

Haruko's ambition for Japanese women, that their general level of
education be raised so that they could be good companions to their husbands and skillful teachers of their children, has largely been realized.
Graduation from high school is nearly universal among them and the
pursuit of college education common. Her life story reminds us that
Japanese domesticity is not simply the result of male oppression. Haruko
actively appropriated Western ideals of domesticity, articulated them to
the reading public, and inculcated her own values in the next generation. Her vision of the ideal housewife did not limit women to the home
but rather promoted social interaction with other women, philanthropy,
and patriotic activities. Every society accepts trade-offs between individual rights and the needs of the greater community. If we record only
the lives of Japanese women who fought for individual freedom, we ignore the contributions of other women to Japan's postwar prosperity
and order.

NOTES

1. Cited in James L. Huffman, *Creating a Public: People and Press in Meiji Japan*
(Honolulu: University of Hawaii Press, 1997), 180.

2. Donald T. Roden, *Schooldays in Imperial Japan: A Study in the Culture of a
Student Elite* (Berkeley: University of California Press, 1980), 133–35.

3. Cited in Barbara Rose, *Tsuda Umeko and Women's Education in Japan* (New
Haven: Yale University Press, 1992), 181 n.35.

4. Hatoyama Haruko, "Watakushi no mitaru Nabeshima Kōshaku fujin," *Fujin sekai* 3, no. 1 (January 1908): 35.

5. Hatoyama Haruko, "Nihon ni naze ni fujin kaihō mondai ga okoraruka," *Fujin sekai* 6, no. 2 (February 1911): 33–35.

6. Hatoyama Haruko, "Wagako o monbu daijin ni sodateru michi," *Fujin sekai* 27, no. 2 (February 1, 1932): 3.

SUGGESTED READINGS

Hatoyama Haruko wrote extensively about herself. Autobiographical writings serialized in the journal *Shin katei* (New home) from 1916 to 1918 were published in 1929 as an autobiography, *Waga jijoden* (reprint, 1997). Over a period of more than three decades, Haruko published numerous articles, many about her own life, in women's magazines such as *Fujin eisei zasshi, Fujinkai, Fujin kurabu, Fujin mondai, Fujin no tomo, Fujin sekai, Fujin shūkan, Fujo shinbun, Fusen, Jogaku sekai, Katei, Kyōiku josei, Murasaki, Onna,* and *Shojo no tomo.* She is mentioned in her son's autobiography, *Hatoyama Ichirō kaikoroku* (1957), and in magazine articles by her daughter-in-law Kaoru. In addition, Haruko's name frequently appeared in the news columns of women's magazines and even in daily newspapers.

Three books that provide perspectives on upper-class women's activities in the Meiji period are Sharon L. Sievers, *Flowers in Salt: The Beginning of Feminist Consciousness in Modern Japan* (1983); Gail Lee Bernstein, ed., *Recreating Japanese Women, 1600–1945* (1991); and Barbara Rose, *Tsuda Umeko and Women's Education in Japan* (1992). On the development of domesticity in the Meiji era, see Jordan Sand, "At Home in the Meiji Period: Inventing Japanese Domesticity," in *Mirror of Modernity: Invented Traditions of Modern Japan,* ed. Stephen Vlastos (1998). On the elite higher school that both her sons attended, see Donald T. Roden, *Schooldays in Imperial Japan: A Study in the Culture of a Student Elite* (1980). On the Meiji press, see James L. Huffman, *Creating a Public: People and Press in Meiji Japan* (1997).

CHAPTER 6

Jahana Noboru

Okinawan Activist and Scholar

GREGORY SMITS

The slogan "Civilization and Enlightenment" took on peculiar overtones when extended from Tokyo to Japan's periphery in Okinawa. There, too, the slogan had held out the promise of success through education, although only for a few and only in certain largely technical fields. On the mainland, commoners had been castigated for lascivious behavior during festivals, mixed bathing, and casual dress that Westerners considered barbaric. Okinawan customs were deemed uncivilized in the eyes of other Japanese.

Okinawa also suffered peculiar political disabilities. The builders of the new Japan came overwhelmingly from two former domains, Satsuma and Chōshū, that had taken the lead in defeating the last Tokugawa shogun. In the eyes of many men excluded from positions of power and responsibility because they had been born in a different region of Japan, these self-styled statesmen constituted nothing more than a Sat-chō clique. Through the historical accident that Satsuma had originally asserted Japanese suzerainty over the kingdom of the Ryukyus in the seventeenth century, men from Satsuma dominated the bureaucracy that replaced the Ryukyuan aristocracy centered on the old capital of Shuri, now a suburb of Naha. Renamed Okinawa, the islands became incorporated into a centralized administrative system, its people becoming Japanese citizens. Nonetheless, the discrimination they experienced under Japanese rule undercut the illusion of homogeneity promoted by government leaders in their drive to construct a strong modern state.

Like Hatoyama Haruko, Jahana Noboru was ambitious. He exemplifies the possibility of going from rags to riches opened up by the modern educational system and exposes the vicissitudes awaiting the self-made man. While lacunae and contradictions in the historical record make it impossible to learn precisely what he did and what really happened to him, his story can still be read as a commentary on the torturous relations between Okinawa and the mainland.

Assistant professor of history at Pennsylvania State University, Gregory J. Smits wrote his first book on the history of the Ryukyu Kingdom, Visions of Ryukyu: Identity and Ideology in Early Modern Thought and Politics *(1999). He is currently planning a book on the history of modern Okinawa.*

On July 25, 1901, the *Ryūkyū Shinpō*, Okinawa's first daily newspaper, printed a brief message from Jahana Noboru (1865–1908), stating that he had completely recovered from the illness the same paper had described the previous month as "a nervous disorder" likely caused by "the vicissitudes of constant rising and falling, praise and censure."[1] In fact, Jahana had lost his mind, and, the notice in the newspaper notwithstanding, he would never recover it. He led the remaining seven years of his life in pain and poverty, dying where he was born, in the small rural village of Kochinda, in the southern part of the island of Okinawa. Jahana's affliction came on suddenly in May 1901 while he was standing on a platform waiting for a train at Kobe Station. He had spent most of his short life battling various interest groups in Okinawa. Even though he won some of these battles, they left him increasingly isolated. In the end, he had nowhere to go but back to the obscure village that had made him famous.

"Kuchinda Jahana" was Jahana's nickname when his career was in its ascendancy, Kuchinda being the Okinawan pronunciation of what in Japanese would be "Kochinda."[2] He got this name because he rose from rural Kochinda to prominence as a high official in the Okinawan prefectural administration. By so doing, he became a symbol of the self-made man who had climbed above his humble social origins. But this success weighed heavily on him, for, among other reasons, he was the only example among Okinawans of such a dramatic rise in status. This is not to say that Jahana was the only prominent Okinawan at that time, but that he was the only prominent one of commoner background. There was, unfortunately, no place for someone like him in the Okinawa of his day. His high-powered education forever removed him from the ranks of the island's peasants, but it did not gain him acceptance from its traditional elite or from the mainland Japanese who governed the country's newest prefecture.

The Meiji government forced the creation of Okinawa prefecture in April 1879 by dispatching soldiers and police to bring an end to the Ryukyu Kingdom. Early in the fifteenth century a strong monarchy had asserted its rule over Okinawa and gradually extended its authority to the other Ryukyu islands. At this time, the kingdom prospered as a trading center, with Ryukyuan ships buying and selling goods all the way from the eastern coast of the Indian subcontinent to East Asia. Ryukyu developed a particularly strong diplomatic and trade relationship with China. In 1609 the powerful southernmost Japanese domain of Satsuma (present-day Kagoshima prefecture) sought to gain access to the China trade by invading the Ryukyu Kingdom. Satsuma's invasion resulted in the Ryukyu monarch's agreement to serve and assist the ruler of Satsuma. By way of its connection with Satsuma, Ryukyu also began regular diplomatic relations with the Tokugawa shogunate in Edo. Ryukyu kept its connections with Japan secret when dealing with China for fear that, if they were revealed, China might sever its connections with the small kingdom. In fact, China was vaguely aware that Ryukyu maintained close ties with Japan, but chose to ignore them.

From 1609 to 1879 the status of the Ryukyu Kingdom was ambiguous, at least by modern reckoning. Was it a sovereign state, a subordinate of China, or a subordinate of Japan? The answer is that Ryukyu was all three at once. Most premodern East Asians saw relations among states as an extension of Confucian-style family and social relations, which is why, for example, the Board of Rites oversaw foreign relations in China. It was therefore normal for a relatively small and weak country like Ryukyu to acknowledge the cultural and economic superiority of its larger neighbors.

By the early 1870s, however, Japan had reorganized itself into a centralized state, and its leaders were well aware of the power of the major Western countries. They knew that were Japan to avoid the fate of many parts of Asia then succumbing to imperialist aggression, it would have to play by the rules of "international law" as defined by the Western powers. In this conception of international relations, sovereign states with clearly defined boundaries interact by means of contractual agreements, that is, treaties. For this reason Ryukyu became an issue in the 1870s when Japan's new government tried to clarify the boundaries of the Japanese state. Realizing that Ryukyu's location was of strategic importance, that Ryukyu's government was militarily weak, and that China or an imperialist Western power might lay claim to it, Japan's leaders decided to act first.

By 1874 the Meiji government was making the claim that Ryukyu had long been an integral part of Japan. More ominously for Ryukyu's fate, Japan managed to persuade France, Holland, and the United States—the three Western countries that had signed treaties with Ryukyu—to agree to Japanese sovereignty over the islands. Although they tried for several years to convince Ryukyu's king and government officials to agree to become part of Japan, in the face of stiff resistance from the Okinawan court, the Meiji leaders eventually used coercion to force the issue. It was only after Japan formally annexed Ryukyu in 1879 that China made any serious attempt to intervene diplomatically, but by then it was too late to save the kingdom.

Because of Meiji claims that Ryukyu had always been a part of Japan, the newly gotten territory was immediately designated a prefecture and named Okinawa. The prefectural title did not mean that the former Ryukyu Kingdom received the same treatment as the rest of Japan. Indeed, during its early decades of existence, the Okinawa prefecture was treated much like a foreign colony. Its people struggled under the highest per capita tax burden of any prefecture and received the lowest per capita expenditure of money from Tokyo. In a successful move to buy the cooperation of the Ryukyuan aristocracy, the Meiji state agreed to maintain the stipends and many of the privileges of these elites, pursuing into the early years of the twentieth century what it called a policy of "preserving old customs." In this arrangement, the king went to reside in Tokyo and was granted the title of Marquis in the new peerage system. The kingdom's former aristocracy, however, did not fare so well, for they received no such titles. Instead, in return for their acquiescence to Japanese rule, the upper echelons were paid approximately the same stipends that they had received as officials of the kingdom. The funds for these stipends came from Okinawa's prefectural government, not from Tokyo. The lower-ranking former aristocrats were given no such payments. They typically sought work as schoolteachers, interpreters, clerks, and petty bureaucrats. Such positions were relatively few in number, and many former aristocrats sank rapidly into dire poverty.

Replacing the king in this new order was a governor, always a mainlander and always appointed by Tokyo until 1945. Although he usually required approval from Tokyo to institute major policy changes, the governor possessed supreme authority in the day-to-day management of the prefecture's bureaucracy. The higher ranks of government and education officials were overwhelmingly non-Okinawans. Furthermore and somewhat distressingly for the Okinawans, a disproportionately large number of the top officials in prewar Okinawa came from Kagoshima, the former domain of Satsuma that had invaded Ryukyu in 1609.

LIFE AND TIMES

Jahana Noboru grew up in this Okinawa, theoretically a prefecture of Japan but actually more like a quasi colony. The early governors of Okinawa put a high priority on disseminating basic education, which consisted mainly of Japanese language training. Jahana first benefited from this top-down promotion of education by being selected in 1881 to attend Okinawa's teacher-training school for elementary schoolteachers. The next year, for the first time, the prefecture selected five outstanding students to pursue advanced education in Tokyo at government expense. Jahana was one of them. The four other students were all of aristocratic background. They included Ōta Chōfu, later to become editor of the *Ryūkyū Shinpō*, and the two men who would become Okinawa's first members of the lower house of the Diet, Takamine Chōkyō and Iwamoto Gashō.

The prefectural authorities thought it most appropriate that Jahana study agricultural subjects because he was of peasant origin. He began by studying forestry at the Tokyo School of Forestry and then transferred to the Imperial College of Agricultural Science, the most prestigious institution of its kind in Japan. He graduated in 1891 with what in today's terms would be a graduate degree in agricultural science. His graduation thesis was a study of the history and circumstances of sugar production in Sanuki (present-day Kagawa prefecture in Shikoku). Much of his study consisted of a detailed chemical analysis of various types of fertilizers and fertilizing methods. He argued that the quality and quantity of fertilizer was the most significant factor in sugarcane yields. Nonetheless, sugarcane growers often wasted cash on commercial fertilizer preparations that ended up being less effective than the careful use of the by-products of agricultural processes. Five years later, he would produce a similar study on the conditions of sugar production in Okinawa and make many of the same points. His graduation thesis about Sanuki was in effect a methodological trial run in preparation for his masterful writing about the same issues in Okinawa. Indeed, the development of the island's sugar industry was a constant concern of Jahana's throughout his short career, for he thought that its revitalization would be the basis of a general improvement in Okinawa's economy.

In the year of his graduation, Jahana returned to Okinawa amid much fanfare. "Kuchinda Jahana" had proven that an ordinary Okinawan could succeed in the new Japan. Commensurate with his high-powered education, he joined the upper levels of the prefectural administration in the capacity of prefectural engineer. He was the only one among his cohort of Okinawans who had studied in Tokyo to be appointed to such high office so early in his career.

Almost a year after Jahana's triumphant return, Narahara Shigeru (1834–1918) of Kagoshima (formerly Satsuma) was appointed governor of Okinawa, a post he held for the unusually long period of sixteen years. Although Jahana and Narahara eventually became political adversaries, in the early years of the Narahara administration, Jahana advanced in civil service rank and seems not to have had any major differences with the governor. Narahara was well connected with government and business leaders. He was an activist governor with a strong interest in practical affairs, and his mandate from the central government was to carry out fundamental reforms of Okinawan society. He ruled with such a firm hand that he earned the nickname "King of Ryukyu."

One of the pressing problems of that time was the pitiful state of former low-ranking members of the urban aristocracy. In the days of the kingdom, impoverished low-ranking aristocrats had been encouraged to take up commerce or skilled manufacturing, and, when all else failed, to set up agricultural villages and farm tax-free. The problem of poverty among these aristocrats, in other words, was not new, but by the 1890s it had become especially severe. To make matters worse, little or no untilled farmland remained for them to occupy and work. Jahana and Narahara both endorsed a plan to clear selected forests, turn them into farms, and offer them to unstipended former aristocrats at a low cost.

One legacy of the former kingdom was the presence of extensive tracts of forest land with a special status, known as *somayama*. This term indicates forest land managed and harvested in a controlled manner by the nearby peasant villages, with local officials from the villages themselves and government administrators overseeing the process. In 1893, Jahana formally proposed that select areas of *somayama* with the potential to make good farmland be cleared for the relief of unstipended former aristocrats. He explained that some land labeled as "*somayama*" was not really *somayama*—in other words, not true forest land that could be used for lumber and fuel. On such land, typically, dense underbrush grew but few trees. These pockets of so-called *somayama* were effectively wasteland and hence should be brought under cultivation. In his proposal, Jahana stressed that under no circumstances should such land clearance be permitted to an extent that would disrupt or harm the way rural villagers made their living.

Governor Narahara accepted Jahana's proposal and appointed him to put it into practice. The peasants living in the vicinities of the proposed clearance areas, however, protested vigorously. Jahana visited the forests of northern Okinawa to inspect their condition personally and to meet with village leaders. Although he tried repeatedly to assure the local peasants that they would suffer no harm from the project, he was unsuccessful in securing their cooperation. Indeed, their opposition was so strong in some areas that they levied a small tax on themselves to send a delegation to Naha, the capital, to petition the prefectural government directly.

The documentary evidence concerning these events is not always clear about who stood where and why, and there is disagreement among historians regarding Jahana's stance. The standard line usually found in general histories of Okinawa is that Jahana sided with the peasants, championed their interests within the prefectural government, and thus clashed with Governor Narahara, who had advocated widespread clearing of *somayama* lands. Furthermore, it suggests that the governor was not really interested in resettling impoverished ex-aristocrats. While pretending to help them, he instead sought to put as much cleared land as possible into the hands of entrepreneurs from outside Okinawa and of high-ranking former aristocrats such as the royal family. When Jahana used his position as head of the project to try to block such moves, Narahara fired him.

Some historians, however, have expressed serious doubt about this scenario, which casts Jahana in the role of tragic, idealistic hero and Narahara as the corrupt, worldly villain. Jahana was indeed relieved of his duties as head of the land-reclamation bureau in 1894, but the reason is unclear. A close examination of Jahana's writings and actions, from the time of his proposing the reclamation plan to the time of his removal as its head, indicates that he regarded the peasant opposition as misguided and ignorant. As historian Arakawa Akira has pointed out, the Jahana of 1894 was a headstrong young technocrat who vigorously countered the peasant opposition that dared question his expertise. Furthermore, an inspection of the statistics for land clearance and sales indicates that the transactions for approximately two-thirds of the land that went to former high-ranking aristocrats and for over half the land that went to people from outside Okinawa prefecture took place while Jahana was in charge. If Narahara fired Jahana to clear the way for such land sales, why did they decline after Jahana left his post?

Jahana's dismissal from the land-clearance project does not seem to have had an immediately detrimental effect on his career. He continued to advance in civil service rank, he remained prefectural engineer, and he participated in other projects connected with land reform. Eventually, he did become a critic of Narahara and his policies, but there is no strong evidence for such a stance in the early 1890s. As we shall see, the circumstances contributing to Jahana's frustrations and eventual downfall were more complex than the simple ill will of an evil governor.

The first well-documented conflict between Jahana and Narahara began in the last month of 1897, when Jahana was appointed to devise a plan for the disposition of all remaining *somayama* land. He and Narahara clashed repeatedly over the fundamental issue of ownership. Narahara advocated government ownership but with the peasants having the right to harvest trees from the land, an arrangement that would have caused no fundamental change in the current situation. Jahana advocated peasant ownership of the land, despite the administrative difficulties entailed in parceling out the plots. For Jahana, government ownership was simply too dangerous, the potential for abuse and corruption too great. Peasant opinion was solidly behind Jahana's plan. It is at this point that Jahana clearly emerges as an advocate for the peasantry against the interests of the Narahara administration. Largely as a result of his refusal to yield to Narahara, pressure on Jahana to step down increased. In December 1898 he resigned from government service.

Jahana's conflict with Narahara, however, was not his only battle at the time. During the decade of the 1890s, the former high-ranking aristocrats from the days of the kingdom vigorously sought to reassert dominance in the governance of Okinawa. One milestone in this process was the establishment of the *Ryūkyū Shinpō* by a group of former aristocrats headed by Ōta Chōfu. Recall that Ōta and Jahana had both gone to study in Tokyo in the same year. By the time Jahana resigned from government, Ōta had become one of his most vocal critics. Significantly, Ōta spoke for the whole group of Shuri-Naha former elites in denouncing Jahana.

Jahana's alienation from Okinawa's former aristocrats was not simply the result of their prejudice against his humble origins. More important, Jahana had energetically and publicly opposed the goals of their political union, the Kōdōkai. Its founding in 1896 represents, among other things, an effort by the former high-ranking elites to set aside past factional differences and work together toward the goal of a return to some semblance of political power. They included many of Okinawa's most influential and wealthy residents. The Kōdōkai proposed a plan for Okinawa's revitalization that began with the premise that the prefecture's unique circumstances called for a special political arrangement. Specifically, the former king, Shō Tai, or a member of his family was to be appointed as a long-term governor. The king-turned-governor would head a government designed to meet the special needs of Okinawa and guide its people through a transitional phase toward the goal of eventual political, cultural, and institutional union with the rest of Japan. The plan assumed that "the people" of Okinawa would rally around the leadership of the Shō family, thus resulting in spiritual unity and mobilization. At the same time, the Kōdōkai was careful to emphasize that the advancement of Okinawa would contribute to the advancement of the Japanese Empire.

The Kōdōkai embodied a paradox. On the one hand, it was obviously anachronistic and reactionary. On the other hand, however, it enjoyed widespread support from Okinawa's leading progressive intellectuals, mostly young men such as Ōta Chōfu, Takamine Chōkyō, and Tomigusuku Seiwa. Men like Ōta had come to the realization that no matter how well educated or talented they might be, as Okinawans they would always face disparagement and discrimination from the many mainlanders who ran the prefectural government. Thus, they made common cause with those who sought, at least in part, to restore past institutions.

The Kōdōkai's proposal attracted substantial support, garnering approximately seventy-three thousand signatures for a petition to be delivered to the Diet and leading officials in Tokyo. The opponents of the proposal labeled it subversive, a move to restore Okinawan independence. It found few supporters outside Okinawa, and even on the island there was vigorous opposition. Interestingly enough, a small number of former Ryukyuan elites opposed it because it called for an eventual merging with Japan. These opponents wanted Okinawa to have nothing to do with Japan. The majority of opponents, however, with Jahana in the vanguard, saw the proposal as reactionary. Furthermore, there had been great suffering in the final years of the kingdom because the Okinawan court had squeezed the peasants as hard as it could to extract the resources it needed to survive. For Okinawans of Jahana's background, the days of the kingdom held no nostalgic appeal. Although Jahana suffered from the same discrimination as did Ōta, he argued that the Kōdōkai proposal would do nothing but make the situation worse.

On the surface, Jahana and the other opponents of the Kōdōkai won their fight. The central government refused even to receive the Kōdōkai's petition and threatened its leaders with criminal prosecution should they continue their efforts. The Kōdōkai collapsed immediately. Frustrated in their effort to garner direct political power, its supporters quickly adopted a new strategy of close cooperation with the Narahara regime. For Jahana, the results of this new alignment were to prove disastrous.

By the time of his resignation, Jahana had become isolated from much of Okinawan society. He was a pariah in the eyes of both the prefectural government officials and the former rulers of the kingdom. Having amassed moderate wealth, he and a small group of supporters founded the Okinawa Club, which set up headquarters in Naha. The core members of the club were, like Jahana, relatively young men from rural backgrounds. They also founded the Nan'yōsha (Southern sun company), a trading firm, to provide the economic foundation for their main function of publishing a periodical, *Okinawa jiron*. A forum for essays on timely political topics, *Okinawa jiron* served as a mouthpiece through which the Okinawa Club advocated broadening participation in the political process and an equitable resolution to land problems, especially the disposition of *somayama*. The club's periodical also served as a platform from which to criticize Governor Narahara.

Jahana's activities at this time closely resemble those of Ishizaka Shōkō and other leaders of the People's Rights movement on the mainland during the 1880s, for which reason he is usually regarded as the central figure in a comparable, if much smaller, Okinawan version of that movement. Overt and covert hostility from the prefectural government hampered him and his supporters at every turn. A decisive showdown took place over the Okinawa Agricultural Bank.

This bank had been established in each prefecture by order of the central government (albeit, in Okinawa's case, several years later than in all the other prefectures). Its purpose was to preserve and promote agriculture by offering loans to small farmers who might have difficulty securing financing from other sources. Jahana had worked hard for the establishment of the bank while he was prefectural engineer. The bank was inaugurated just before he resigned from government, and at that time he was its largest shareholder and a member of the three-person board of directors. Through the Okinawa Club and his position with the bank, Jahana sought to continue his fight to improve conditions on the island.

Although Jahana was the single largest shareholder, his isolation left him vulnerable. Shareholders connected with the prefectural administration and the former Okinawan political elite of Shuri and Naha became allies in an attempt to oust him and his rural supporters from the bank's board of directors. At a stockholders' meeting of January 18, 1900, Jahana proposed a restructuring of the bank's board, increasing its membership from three to five, and specifying that one member would come from each of the following geographic entities: Shuri, Naha, Shimajiri, Nakagami, and Kunigami. The first two were urban centers; the last three were large districts covering the rest of Okinawa. Jahana's proposal, in other words, would have diluted the power of the Shuri-Naha former aristocrats in determining bank policy.

Governor Narahara saw the proposal as particularly dangerous because if Jahana's Okinawa Club could dominate the governance of the bank, its members would have an ideal vehicle by which to enhance their popularity among Okinawa's farmers. He put the resources of his office at the disposal of the Shuri and Naha shareholders, who set about forging alliances with prominent local leaders in rural areas. Once formed, this alliance began to purchase as much stock as it could. Using access to the police, the anti-Jahana forces also tried to intimidate some of the voting stockholders and otherwise interfere with the election process. When the votes were in, Jahana and every other candidate from the Okinawa Club had been resoundingly defeated. Jahana declared the election void owing to improper practices, which threw the matter into court. The court battle lasted four months and resulted in Jahana's defeat. The election results stood.

Although the months immediately after his defeat in the bank election were undoubtedly hard ones for Jahana, he does not seem to have been totally despondent. The loss had devastated the Okinawa Club, however, and it soon disbanded. Furthermore, Jahana had sunk nearly all of his personal wealth into the club, the election campaign, and the court battle—all in vain. Nonetheless, he wrote a detailed article on the effect of taxation on the sugar industry, which he published in a major agricultural journal. Recall that he regarded the sugar industry as the key to any overall improvement in Okinawa's economy. From this article, it is also clear that three things had become linked in Jahana's mind: the sugar industry, Okinawa, and a "regard for what is native" (*tochaku no nenryo*). Yet having devoted his entire career to improving Okinawa through his research into sugar production, through his work as prefectural engineer, and through his activities in the Okinawa Club and the Agricultural Bank, in the end Jahana was forced to recognize that it had all come to nothing.

Broke and isolated, Jahana realized that he would have to seek work on the mainland. He obtained a position in Yamaguchi prefecture as an engineering assistant—much lower in importance and prestige than the posts he had held before. An optimist to that point, the bitter reality of the failure to accomplish any of his goals in Okinawa and the need to start his career over in a place to which he had no emotional attachment suddenly crushed him psychologically. Perhaps he became unable to bear taking the final step in the process of moving to this new, rather unappealing job in a strange place. En route, on the train platform in Kobe, he snapped, never to recover. The last years of his life "were spent in a permanently crippled state, resembling that of a living corpse." He gave up the ghost completely in 1908, while muttering over and over, "Vermin that are devouring Okinawa have now arrived. Drive them out!"[3] He was forty-four years old.

BROADER REFLECTIONS ON JAHANA'S LIFE

Despite his talent, high-powered education, and hard work, it may not be too rash to claim that Jahana ended his life as a de facto alien in the land of his birth. In other words, Japanese society in 1900 had no place for him in which to fit comfortably. As an Okinawan, a *rikijin* (corruption of *Ryūkyūjin* [Ryukyuan]) in the derogatory mainland slang of the time, he would never be accepted as a full-fledged citizen of Japan. This prejudice against Okinawans was no less intense within the prefectural government where Jahana spent much of his career. As long as he was a good "company man," he rose through the ranks of the civil service, but he remained an anomaly.

And Jahana's experience was typical. As Ōta Chōfu finally came to the painful realization that most mainlanders would long relegate Okinawans to the status of second-class citizens, even within their own homeland, he criticized this arrogance in the strongest possible terms from his platform as a public intellectual. For example, an industrial exposition in Osaka in 1903 featured a "hall of peoples" (*jinruikan*) in which a man with a whip presided over a display of Ainu (indigenous people of northern Japan), Koreans, and two Okinawan women depicted as prostitutes. As visitors came through, he pointed with his whip at the people in question and explained some of the exotic objects associated with them in this quasi-anthropological show of "primitive" peoples. Ōta expressed his rage at the exhibit in a series of editorials. Although he described the display of Okinawans as being no different from one of exotic animals, he did not object to the display of primitive peoples in principle. His outrage was that Okinawans, "real Japanese," were included along with Koreans and "barbaric Ainu."[4]

Ōta could and did derive a substantial part of his identity as a descendant of the Ryukyuan aristocracy even while expressing outrage at mainland prejudices. Jahana, on the other hand, had no particular attachment to the former kingdom and its aristocrats. He was the classic modern man who put his trust in the rational principles of science, only to be beaten down by the forces of ethnic prejudice, class prejudice, and factional politics. With this understanding, that he lost his mind in the end is not surprising. As a man who had stepped out of his "place" in the social scheme of things, there was no social niche that he could comfortably inhabit. In the end, his alienation was total.

Jahana's life can serve as an excellent window through which to view a "Japan" with fuzzy boundaries and uncertain membership. The remarkably persistent image of Japan as a land that has long had a homogenous culture is revealed as manifestly inaccurate when we take a close look at the northern (Hokkaido and, later, Sakhalin) and southern border zones. In this broad context, Jahana's alienation was but a particularly severe case of the dilemmas of identity faced by nearly all Okinawans in the late-nineteenth and early-twentieth centuries. Some Okinawan intellectuals such as Ōta Chōfu or Iha Fuyū could, with difficulty, fashion narratives of Okinawan identity that partook of a noble past and yet pointed to a promising future as Japanese. But the masses of Okinawan laborers seeking work in mainland coal mines and factories or in the plantations of Hawai'i and South America faced a situation more akin to that of Jahana. They often had no past to which they could return, literally or figuratively, but their future as "Japanese" provided little promise of social acceptance or economic prosperity.

One difference between the masses of ordinary Okinawans and Jahana is that he became a famous symbol during his lifetime and beyond. Throughout most of his adult life, "Kuchinda Jahana" represented the self-made man in the best sense. Reminiscent of Ninomiya Sontoku, the peasant lad in Japanese elementary school readers who studied by the light of the moon and fireflies after working all day in the fields, Jahana had broken out of his commoner status and made it into the ranks of the elite through hard work and a devotion to learning. If he could do it, so, too, could others like him. And, this line of thinking continued, those who failed to achieve even modest fortune or fame, as was the case with most Okinawans, must have failed owing to laziness or some other character defect.

This "logic" typified the thinking of most of the mainland government and educational officials in the prefecture when they discussed conditions in Okinawa. More specifically, they consistently blamed the island's poverty on alleged cultural and character deficiencies. In a speech in 1913, for example, Governor Takahashi blamed Okinawa's problems in part on the improper and immodest clothing habits of its women:

> Because from now on, things must change in accordance with the world's progress, we must reform what should be reformed and stop adhering stubbornly to outmoded ways. In this place, women do not fasten belts around their robes. . . . No matter where one might go around here, there are women without fastened belts as well as women who do not wear underwear. . . . Even in Korea, women wear underwear. . . . Try going to the mainland in your present state of dress. Not only will people laugh at you, they will hold you in contempt. However impressive and learned you may be, others will regard you as idiots.[5]

Had Jahana been alive to hear this speech, he surely could have provided an alternative analysis of the causes of Okinawan poverty. It would very likely have included such structural factors as excessive taxes on sugar production, the heaviest overall tax burden of any prefecture, and the lack of opportunities for higher education.

Caught between the rock of harsh economic and structural disadvantages and the hard place of officials obsessed with alleged cultural deficiencies, many Okinawans had no choice but to leave their homeland. It was Jahana who first proposed to Governor Narahara that Okinawan poverty might in part be alleviated by encouraging immigration to Hawai'i. Initially, the governor declared the idea ridiculous on cultural grounds. It would be an embarrassment to Japan for Okinawans, who could not even speak Japanese, to be seen in foreign countries. Eventually, after much persuasion by Jahana, Narahara did agree to allow Okinawan immigration abroad.

Jahana's willingness to oppose Narahara or the Okinawan elites and press for what he genuinely regarded as best for Okinawa became the basis for hero-making after his death. In *The Nobility of Failure: Tragic Heroes in the History of Japan*, Ivan Morris adumbrates a theory of Japanese heroism based on tragic failure. More specifically, the ideal hero is a sincere, uncompromising idealist who fights the good fight against the worldly forces of corruption and politics, even though he is doomed to fail. Indeed, it is because he pushes through to inevitable defeat that he is immortalized as a hero for later generations. The typical portrayal of Jahana's life makes him out to be a hero in much the same mold as the figures Morris examines, but with one significant difference: an optimist to a fault, Jahana does not seem to have foreseen that his efforts would end in failure.

One result of the tendency of later generations of Okinawans to make Jahana into a tragic hero, specifically a man who championed the cause of Okinawa's oppressed peasants, is insufficient critical attention to the parts of his life that may not fit the image. We have seen, for example, that early in his career, Jahana opposed all attempts by the peasants of northern Okinawa to stop the conversion of certain *somayama* lands to farmland. Similarly, recent biographies of Jahana commonly repeat colorful details about his life that emphasize his tragic heroism despite a lack of reliable supporting evidence. For example, nearly every one of them claims that, while a student in Tokyo, he associated with people such as Kōtoku Shūsui who would become heroes, at least to some Japanese, for their opposition to the imperial system. More interesting is the legendary tale of Jahana's having determined to kill Governor Narahara with a concealed knife should he refuse yet again to allow Okinawan immigration to Hawai'i. Perhaps sensing the desperation in Jahana's appeal, the evil governor unexpectedly gave in and agreed to the proposal.

Such tales are part of the contemporary, heroic legend of Jahana. Although there is certainly a basis for portraying him this way, the relatively simple narrative of the idealistic hero opposing the evil governor undoubtedly functions to obscure some of the complexity, contradictions, and shifting alliances of late-nineteenth-century Okinawan politics. In the larger picture, the story of Jahana's life and the vexing problems besetting almost all Okinawans of his day enable us to detect the underside of the Meiji state's drive to fashion the Japanese islands (broadly defined) into a homogenous nation.

NOTES

1. Isa Shin'ichi, ed., *Jahana Noboru shū* (Tokyo: Misuzu shobo, 1998), 239.

2. Many personal and place-names from the Ryukyu Islands have both a Japanese and one or more Ryukyuan pronunciations. The languages of the Ryukyu Islands are different from standard Japanese or any of its mainland dialects, although today, the vast majority of Okinawans speak standard Japanese. When writing about Ryukyuan history in Japanese, the problem of pronunciation is easier to avoid, because one simply writes the Chinese characters without normally having to indicate how these characters are to be pronounced. When writing in English, however, a clear choice is always necessary, and, following what has become standard convention, I generally use the Japanese pronunciation.

3. Quoted in Shinzato Keiji, Taminato Tomoaki, and Kinjo Seitoku, *Okinawa-ken no rekishi* (Tokyo: Yamakawa Shuppansha, 1972; reprint, 1983), 186.

4. Hiyane Teruo and Isa Shin'ichi, comps. and eds., *Ōta Chofu senshu*, vol. 2 (Tokyo: Daiichi shobo, 1995), 211–16.

5. Quoted in Naha-shiyakusho, comp. and ed., *Naha-shi shi Shiryo-hen*, vol. 2, no. 3 (Kumamoto, Japan: Shirono Insatsu, 1970), 348.

SUGGESTED READINGS

There is no English-language literature on Jahana Noboru, and even George H. Kerr's history of Okinawa, *Okinawa: The History of an Island People* (1958), mentions Jahana only in passing in one footnote—a type of omission common throughout Kerr's book. All general histories of Okinawa in Japanese devote from several pages to a subsection of a chapter to Jahana; the majority of such accounts portray him as a tragic hero battling for the interests of the peasants throughout his career. The classic biography of Jahana is Ōzato Yasunaga's *Gijin, Jahana Noboru* (Jahana Noboru, a righteous man, 1938), later republished as *Jahana Noboru den* (Biography of Jahana Noboru, 1957), and finally republished a second time as *Okinawa no jiyū minken undō senkūsha Jahana Noboru no shisō to kōdō* (The thought and actions of Jahana Noboru, pioneer of the Liberty and People's Rights movement in Okinawa, 1969). Many of Jahana's writings have long been available in various archives. In recent years, Isa Shin'ichi has discovered several hitherto unknown essays by Jahana and compiled what appears to be a complete collection of Jahana's extant writings, scholarly, official, and private. The resulting volume, *Jahana Noboru shū* (1998) is a major contribution to Jahana Noboru studies. For an example of scholarship that makes good use of the materials Isa has brought to light, see Tasato Osamu, "Kochinda Jahana," in *Shin-Ryūkyūshi, kindai/gendai hen* (1992).

CHAPTER 7

Kinoshita Yoshio

Revolutionizing Service on Japan's National Railroads

STEVEN J. ERICSON*

In addition to promoting education to achieve the goal of "Civilization and Enlightenment," the new Meiji government sought to make Japan strong by building a modern military and encouraging industrialization. "Fukoku kyōhei" (Rich country, strong army) was the slogan of the day. The military took advantage of conscripted soldiers, weapons of mass destruction, and modern organizational techniques to build an impressive war machine. To make the country rich required industry, and industry needed infrastructure. The government took the lead in building railroads, but it soon fell behind private companies in extending the rail network. Thereafter it sometimes went head-to-head in competing with the private railroads; at other times it colluded with them in setting fares; and in 1906–07, it nationalized them. Under Kinoshita Yoshio's direction, it started the process of transforming trains into the speedy, efficient, and comfortable system we know today.

When historians write about the men of Meiji (1868–1912) who built modern Japan, they generally focus on entrepreneurs or statesmen who led the way in promoting modern industries and creating institutions such as the cabinet, constitution, bureaucracy, and national assembly (Diet), or the financial and industrial combines known as zaibatsu. *Even historians of the twentieth century are most likely to examine the deeds of politicians who put together parties in the Diet to promote their own agendas. Seldom do they delve into the middle ranks of the bureaucracy to find the men responsible for making things work. Kinoshita was such a man. His life provides yet another perspective on the opportunities afforded by the modern educational system and by travel abroad to become self-made, and the impact that such individuals had on Japan's development as a modern state.*

Steven J. Ericson, associate professor of Japanese history at Dartmouth College, is the author of The Sound of the Whistle: Railroads and the State in Meiji Japan *(1996).*

*I wish to thank Sylvie Liberman for her excellent research assistance under the Presidential Scholars Program at Dartmouth College.

𝒦inoshita Yoshio (1874–1923) was an elite central-government bureaucrat in the early twentieth century who revolutionized customer service on the Japanese state railways. Unlike more celebrated government railroad officials such as Gotō Shinpei, who headed the national railways in addition to holding a number of other stellar offices, Kinoshita never rose to a position higher than division chief. Nonetheless, by following the lead of Western railroads and progressive private rail companies in Japan, he exerted such a huge and lasting impact on railway service that he earned its title of "father of operations."

Kinoshita was born in northern Kyoto prefecture, the second son of a locally prominent sake brewer. Early on he displayed the drive that would carry him to the upper reaches of railway officialdom when, at age twelve, he left home to learn English at a private school in Kyoto. After moving along the elite higher-school track, he enrolled in the Engineering College of Tokyo Imperial University, graduating in 1898 with a degree in civil engineering. He then stayed on at the university to pursue graduate studies in law and economics. In 1899 he entered the government's Railway Operations Bureau as an assistant engineer and thus embarked on a career in railroads that would last until 1920 and mark the intervening decades as the "Kinoshita age" in the history of the state railway enterprise.

Japan's railway system at the turn of the century was just beginning to experience the problems of relative maturity. The state and private railroads having completed most of the trunk lines, emphasis had shifted to the operation and maintenance of these arteries as well as the building of unprofitable branch lines—problems that had long beset the more developed networks of Europe and North America. To learn from Western precedent and deal with such problems, Kinoshita had an ideal set of qualifications: fluency in English combined with a solid academic background in engineering, law, and economics. No wonder he became a personal favorite of Railway Commissioner Matsumoto Sōichirō, who placed his young protégé squarely on the fast track in the railroad bureaucracy.

After accompanying Matsumoto on an inspection tour of European and American railroads in 1900 and 1901, Kinoshita entered the Traffic Division upon his return to Japan. In April 1902, at the age of twenty-eight, he became head of the Passenger Office. In that position, he strove to bring about a fundamental change in state railway policy toward users, replacing the bureaucratic "suffer-the-passenger-to-ride" arrogance of the past with a new Western, customer-first attitude. Kinoshita drove home the importance of providing "human service," by which he meant courteous and impartial treatment of customers, and he initiated a wholesale modernization of passenger operations along the lines of what he had observed in the West.

Kinoshita's opening salvo came even before his appointment as passenger director. No sooner had he returned from Europe and America than he fired off a proposal for the introduction of dining cars on the state railways' express trains. His plan, however, ran into stiff opposition from motive-power people, who insisted that the locomotives could not pull any more cars, as well as from passenger officials, who refused to allow the displacement of passenger carriages. Arguing that every self-respecting railroad in the West now attached dining cars to its long-distance passenger trains, by the end of 1901 Kinoshita had come up with a complicated solution. On the Tokaido express run, the government railways would alternately add one or two dining cars for the three relatively level stretches and remove such cars for the two intervening sections with steep grades. Once installed as chief of passenger operations, Kinoshita stepped up his campaign for Western-style innovations and improvements, drawing criticism from conservative colleagues for being too *haikara* (literally, "high collar," as in Western-style, starched-collar shirts), or foppishly Westernized, and even earning the nickname "Otowa-ya," the stage family name of the famous kabuki actor Onoe Kikugorō V (1844–1903), who had been producing plays that depicted the new Westernized customs and ideas of the Meiji era.

Kinoshita fully realized that promoting ridership by modernizing the passenger service was vital to the state railways, for unlike contemporary Western railroads, those in Japan catered mainly to passenger traffic. In Japan, riders consistently brought in more revenue than did freight, a pattern that, with the exception of a few years during World War I, has persisted to this day. In the decades prior to Kinoshita's entry into the state railways, the number of passengers had risen steadily. In 1872, the first year of railway operation, nearly 0.5 million passengers —mostly bureaucrats, businessmen, and foreigners—rode Japan's initial line, which ran from Shinbashi (in Tokyo) to Yokohama. As the railways added more lines and reduced fares, more people, especially ordinary people, took the train. The most dramatic increase occurred between 1890 and 1900, when Japan's total population rose from about 40 million to 45 million, but the number of rail passengers leaped from 23 million to 114 million.

The government's Tokaido line, opened in 1889, accounted for well over a third of all the train riders in its first year of operation. For such long distances—the Tokaido extended 376 miles from Shinbashi to Kobe—the impact of the railroad on travel was revolutionary. In the Tokugawa period, going the length of the Tokaido by foot or palanquin had taken twelve to fourteen days. Beginning in 1881, the horse-drawn omnibus cut this time in half, while the steamship could make the trip in only a few days. But the train outdid them all, covering the distance in just twenty hours. Traveling from the Tokyo area to the Kansai by rickshaw or other means of overland transport cost anywhere from 9 to 11 yen. By contrast, third-class passengers on the Tokaido line paid less than 4 yen, besides saving on hotel fees along the way. On March 17, 1889, the *Chōya* newspaper had heralded the impending completion of the Tokaido railway by trumpeting, "How convenient! From Shinbashi to Kobe within a day!"—and for only a few yen, no less—adding hyperbolically that a "person of taste" would soon be able to "view the cherry blossoms along the Sumida River [in Tokyo] in the morning and take a walk in Arashiyama [on the outskirts of Kyoto] in the evening."

Until the turn of the century, however, the railroads seemed to be doing their level best to discourage passengers with their generally shoddy facilities and imperious attitudes. Most of the early railroads were notoriously laggard in providing amenities for travelers, even though passenger income on average accounted for three-quarters of their total revenue as late as the 1890s. They mainly employed British-style "matchbox" carriages divided into compartments furnished with wooden benches. Once inside, passengers found themselves literally confined to their compartments, for they had no way to pass through the car; and shortly before departure, a railroad employee would lock all the doors from the outside "in the approved paternal government style," as an American tourist put it in 1891.[1] To top it off, the third-class carriages had not a shred of upholstery or heat. And none of the early cars had lavatories, which made for a mad scramble for platform facilities at train stops and forced the government, ever eager to present a civilized front to the West, to impose stiff fines of up to 10 yen for passengers caught urinating from the windows en route and a prorated 5 yen for those caught breaking wind therefrom. As a comic song of early Meiji put it, in a play on homonyms: "Passing water from the window of the train, that makes twice I've put out my *chin* (fare/prick)."

Riders began to find on-board relief only in 1889, when the state lines had the distinction of introducing the first passenger cars equipped with toilets. What prompted this innovation was a tragic accident that occurred on the Tokaido line that year. On April 27 a prominent official in the Imperial Household Ministry by the name of Hida Hamagorō got off his train during a brief stop at Fujieda station to use the facilities. When he emerged from the station restroom, his train was already pulling away from the platform. Hida frantically tried to reboard the moving train, but slipped and fell to his death between the first- and second-class cars. The contemporary Japanese press treated his demise as a major scandal—the *Jiji shinpō* describing him on April 29 as "the victim of the lack of toilets on trains"—and pressed the authorities to remedy the situation. The state railways took heed; within a month of the accident, newspapers were already reporting the unveiling of third-class carriages equipped with central toilets accessible to the compartments on either side. In an article on May 26 the *Jiji shinpō* explained that these cars would ease restroom traffic at station stops for first- and second-class passengers, but cautioned third-class riders "to refrain from using [the on-board lavatories] while at stations and to do their business when farthest away from human habitation."

Until late in the Meiji period, trains also had poor interior lighting. As evening approached, railroad employees would clamber onto the tops of the carriages at a station stop and suspend oil lamps through holes in the roof. With the feeble light thus generated, one could barely make out the presence of fellow passengers. The resulting ambiance, as the mystery writer Emi Suiin put it in his 1901 novel *Kisha no taizoku* (The notorious train robber), was like "the inside of the catacombs in the ancient city of Rome." The railroads began to install electric lighting in the late 1890s, but this innovation was slow to catch on. As a Westerner summed up his train-riding experience in a *Japan Weekly Mail* article of December 14, 1898, "The miserable oil lamps of ancient days still defy the traveler to read by their light, and the carriages present an unaltered aspect of conservative comfortlessness."

Not surprisingly, the railroads were late in developing a sense of service toward the traveling public. On the national railways, in the pre-Kinoshita age, employees had sold tickets "as though they were doing the passenger a great favor," but, for their part, passengers had "often stood up for their rights, some even going so far as to haggle over the fare."[2] Upon actually boarding the train, however, customers had tended to bow submissively to the overbearing station workers; and, should they encounter the prestigious stationmaster with his glittering uniform and lofty social status, they had bent over almost to the point of prostration.

In the late nineteenth century, the press began to voice the growing discontent of passengers over their shabby treatment on the state railways. In the aftermath of Hida's death, several journals, including the *Tōkyō keizai zasshi* in an article on July 20, 1889, called on the railway authorities to "treat passengers as customers" by taking such measures as instructing employees to be considerate of riders and having passenger trains stop at the larger stations for fifteen minutes to facilitate visits to the food stand and restroom. Such importunities seem to have had little effect. Almost a decade later, in a December 1897 petition to the Home

Ministry, the Nagano Prefectural Assembly was still accusing station workers on the government's Shin'etsu line of being "arrogant toward passengers."[3]

In fairness to Japanese railroads, one should note that in terms of passenger amenities, they lagged just slightly behind their Western counterparts. In the United States, sleeping cars did not come into general use until after the Civil War, and the trains of one of the industry leaders, the Pennsylvania Railroad, began to feature sanitary facilities only in 1878, diners in 1882, steam heating in 1885, and electric lighting in 1902. On the British railroads, these amenities had all made their appearance by the early 1890s, but they did not become widespread until a decade later. And in class-conscious Britain, where cheaper-fare passengers had originally ridden in open freight cars, railway company attitudes toward customer service resembled those on the more conservative of the Japanese railroads. In 1892 the Great Western put into service the first British train with a corridor running its entire length; this gave third-class passengers access to lavatories, "a startling innovation on the Great Western, which never forgot that they were the 'lower orders.' " When this firm added dining cars in 1896, it restricted their use to first-class passengers, "a rule that was only gradually relaxed from 1900 onwards."[4]

Thus, even in the 1890s, Japanese railroads may actually have been not so far behind those in the West in terms of customer accommodations, but the perception that they *were* behind had become more prevalent. As early as July 20, 1889, an article in the *Tōkyō keizai zasshi* contrasted the "inconvenience and discomfort" of Japanese railroads with "the joys of travel" on American trains, whose special advantages could be summed up by " 'the three W's': warmth, water, and water-closets." A decade later, people were still grousing about the poor facilities not only on the generally undercapitalized private lines but also on the more solidly built state railways. In their December 1897 petition to the Home Ministry, for instance, members of the Nagano Prefectural Assembly exhorted the central authorities to make badly needed improvements on the government's Shin'etsu line, punctuating their request with a long list of grievances about "incomplete" facilities, "cramped" stations, and "squalid" passenger cars.

Yet, despite the inconveniences, people rode the trains in ever-increasing numbers while songwriters and poets continued to sing the praises of rail travel. The growing use and the continued acclaim both reflected the fact that, for all its discomforts, the train was still much faster and far more convenient than any alternative. In addition, however, the surge in ridership coincided with the start of some positive developments in railroad policy that pointed to a more service-oriented future, with private railroads leading the way. In the early 1890s the

Nippon Railway Company introduced discounts for student groups, commuter passes on part of what is now the Yamanote line encircling Tokyo, and special excursion trains to the sight-seeing mecca of Nikkō. Spreading from the Nippon to other railroads, these marketing practices all contributed to the rapid increase in rail use.

The Nippon Railway thus pioneered certain forms of customer service in Japan, but in terms of amenities and attitudes toward passengers, the most progressive railroad was the San'yō Railway Company, followed by the Kansai Railway. Underlying the forward-looking behavior of these two firms was the fact that they probably faced greater competition for customers than did any other railroad during the Meiji period. For the San'yō, the competition came from steamship companies whose vessels plied the Inland Sea routes adjacent to the course of the railroad; for the Kansai, it was initially from a multitude of local private railroads, most of which the company eventually bought out, and later from the parallel state line between Osaka and Nagoya, which put up the fiercest competition. Such rivalry put pressure on both firms to cut rates and improve facilities and thereby acted as a powerful stimulus for innovation. The San'yō had the added impetus of having an ownership dominated by the fledgling Mitsubishi *zaibatsu*, which promoted enterprising career managers committed to expanding the business.

Under the direction of such managers, the San'yō Railway led the industry in introducing a variety of customer services and amenities. In 1895 it began operating express trains pulled by the latest American locomotives; the trains all featured American-style cars with bogies, or four-wheeled swiveling trucks, supporting them and corridors running their length. The company installed redcaps to handle luggage at principal stations in 1896 and porters on through trains in 1898. That same year the railroad initiated an express package-delivery service, and in 1899 it adopted electric lighting for all classes of passenger carriages. The firm also pioneered the use of dining cars in 1899 and sleeping cars in 1900, and opened Japan's first station hotel, at Shimonoseki, in 1902. The following year, it inaugurated the country's first limited express train.

The San'yō's chief of transportation epitomized the spirit underlying these improvements. Sent overseas in 1899 to observe Western railroads, this official was particularly struck by the politeness of ticket agents on one British line who invariably said "thank you" when handing tickets or change to customers. After returning to Japan, he immediately set about enforcing this practice among San'yō agents in the hopes that their "attitude of doing passengers the favor of selling them tickets will thereby unconsciously change to a sense of receiving the favor of having them buy tickets."[5] These and other innovations made the San'yō far and away the country's most modern and progressive railroad at the turn of the century. As a Western observer noted in the *Japan Weekly Mail* on September 3, 1898, "Its cars [are] incomparably the best appointed in Japan, as its service is the best organized."

The Kansai Railway Company made its greatest contribution to customer services from 1902 through 1904, when it waged a furious rate war with the parallel state line and, in doing so, accelerated the government railways' adoption of the "user-friendly" policy that Kinoshita had started to push in 1901. The Kansai had set the stage for this conflict in 1900 by establishing a direct route between Osaka and Nagoya, one that was considerably shorter than the more circuitous route of the state railways (see map). The opening round came in early August 1902, when the Kansai slashed its roundtrip passenger fares, prompting Kinoshita to retaliate in kind.

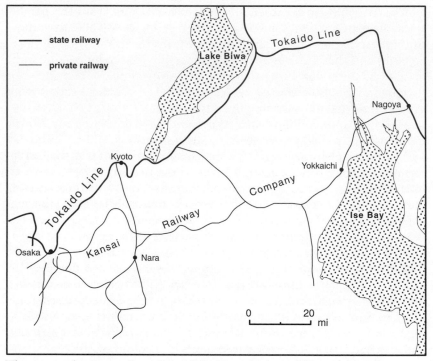

The state and private railway network between Osaka and Nagoya in 1902.

Barely four months on the job, the new Passenger Office chief seized the occasion of this rate war to propel the state railways in a service-oriented direction. Upon matching the Kansai's discounted fares, Kinoshita issued a remarkable statement of policy, proclaiming his long-term intention of competing in services rather than rates:

Even a government railroad is nothing but a commercial enterprise. Since we have already invested huge amounts of fixed capital and begun operations, we are obliged to take measures to defend our earnings, and we cannot submit carelessly to the competition of other lines and let matters take their own course. Therefore, although we do not seek a fight of our own accord, now that the other party has come out with such measures, we are forced to take countermeasures in self-defense, and if necessary we are determined to make even further reductions in the future. To be sure, rate competition in passenger transport has many disadvantages and few benefits from the standpoint both of individual businesses and of society and the economy at large, so as the authorities concerned we wish to avoid rate competition and instead compete in passenger service, train accommodations, and the like. Yet, because rate competition is a route that every country has passed at least once in its railroad history, the present phenomenon should be viewed as one step in the progress of our nation's railroad sector, nay, its economic sector as a whole. However, as long as we both recognize those disadvantages, we should naturally move in the direction of [competing in] general accommodations; so at this time we in the Operations Bureau are prepared to seek even more facilities for the general public in terms of passenger treatment, station and carriage accommodations, operating methods, and various other facilities.[6]

Putting his words into action, Kinoshita at once had his staff distribute written invitations to ride the state railway, to which they appended timetables and discount schedules. In these notices, the Passenger Office boasted that along the route of the government's line, "there are many places rich in scenery. In particular, since it is said that the sweeping view of Lake Biwa is enough to dispel the sweltering heat, travelers taking this route do not in the least feel tired, and it is therefore a most convenient way to travel between these two great cities that are the center of our nation's commerce and industry."[7]

The conversational language of these notices represented a striking change from the previous command style of official bulletins. Similarly, the *Japan Weekly Mail* reported on August 9, 1902, that, when the Passenger Office had recently announced a fare reduction of 20 percent for passengers intending to climb Mount Fuji, the Japanese press had applauded this announcement as further evidence that the state railway authorities had "descended from their eminence of official magnificence and consented to address their customers in polite phraseology."

As if to take up Kinoshita's challenge to compete in both services and rates, and to capitalize on the Bon festival in mid-August, the Kansai Railway proceeded to cut its fares in half and to run extra trains for those desiring to "enjoy the evening cool." It even provided passengers with onboard musical entertainment, presented them with garish paper fans and other souvenirs, and invited them to a restaurant and beer hall it had set up in Nara Park.

In September, the two sides tentatively put an end to the rate war by agreeing to adopt the same fare schedules, to secure the other's consent before offering discounts, and to avoid "unusual methods" of attracting business. Either party could, however, dissolve the agreement by giving thirty days' notice to that effect. In accordance with these terms, the Kansai Railway applied for a rate reduction in October 1903 and, when the state authorities denied this request, went ahead and lowered its rates anyway, after giving the required notice. The upshot was renewed competition for passenger and freight business alike.

Around this time, sumo wrestlers from Tokyo and the Kansai area held a joint exhibition tournament in Nagoya. As they prepared to move their show to Osaka, the Kansai and state railways jostled for the privilege and the publicity windfall of transporting them. In choosing between the two carriers, the wrestlers divided along regional lines. The Tokyo troupe decided to take the government line, reportedly for fear that otherwise the state railway might refuse to give its members passage home from Nagoya. Meanwhile, the Kansai wrestlers displayed their regional pride by opting for the Kansai line. The Kansai Railway put a brass band on board as well as festive decorations on the outside of the cars and scheduled its "sumo train" to reach Osaka twenty minutes before the arrival of the Tokyo troupe.

Fresh from this publicity stunt, in January 1904 the Kansai unveiled yet another innovation in customer service when it began offering passengers free box lunches. By that time, the company's discount had reached the point where roundtrip and one-way fares were virtually identical. This development had the predictable result that enterprising customers sought to recoup their fare by purchasing roundtrip tickets and selling the return portion upon arriving at their destination.

Although presumably benefiting from the bargain rates, the local business community was concerned about the negative effects of the rate war. The instability in charges inconvenienced freight transport, and rolling stock tended to concentrate excessively in the Kansai area. In late January 1904 the Nagoya Chamber of Commerce cited these and other related problems in appealing to the communications minister to bring an end to the competition once and for all. Finally, in April, with the governor of Osaka and two Diet members serving as mediators, the Kansai and state railways agreed once again to institute the same fares. This time the agreement held; with the outbreak of the Russo-Japanese War in February, the government was not about to let such rivalry interfere with orderly military transport.

Even as the rate war with the Kansai was raging, Kinoshita pressed for service improvements throughout the state railways. Following the lead of the private railroads, he introduced special excursion trains leaving Shinbashi for viewing the maple leaves in November 1902 and for paying the first temple visit of the new year in January 1903. Then, in February 1903, his office began making books of tickets available in smaller blocks, "so as to bring them within reach of a wider circle of travelers," and reducing the minimum time limit on commuter passes from three months to one. The upshot of these changes, the *Japan Weekly Mail* predicted on February 28, 1903, "will be to extend the privilege of cheaper and easier travel to the lower orders, whereas it has hitherto been limited to first- and second-class travelers." In November 1903 the Passenger Office took yet another step to provide better service by hiring female ticket agents who, the authorities assumed, would be less likely to "issue a ticket and throw in a scolding as an extra." The four teenagers who began selling tickets at Shinbashi station that month were the first of many women to work in the ticket offices at major national railway terminals. As the *Tōkyō nichinichi* newspaper reported on November 18, 1903, their initial appearance caused a sensation; and with the crush of curious onlookers threatening to obstruct services, the authorities had to "strictly forbid peering into the ticket windows."

Kinoshita thus seemed well on his way to a successful career in government railroad operations. In the course of his baptism by fire in the Kansai rate war, however, he must have come to the conclusion that he needed a more thorough immersion in the theory and practice of advanced railway management in the West. As soon as the competition with the Kansai ended, he applied for a leave of absence to study in the United States. Among the subjects he wanted to investigate were the principles of rate-setting, the operation of ancillary enterprises such as station hotels and restaurants, and the establishment of connecting service between different railroads. Unlike many other government departments, the Railway Operations Bureau had no overseas study program. The proposal Kinoshita made to study abroad at his own expense apparently shamed the railway authorities into setting up such a program and naming him their first official overseas student.

Leaving Japan in September 1904, Kinoshita would spend a full three years studying at universities and inspecting railroads in the United States and Europe. First he went to the University of Wisconsin to audit graduate classes taught by Balthasar Meyer, a young professor of political economy and author of *Railway Legislation in the United States* (1903), who had developed one of the earliest comprehensive courses in transportation in the country. Kinoshita spent his first Christmas holiday in Philadelphia at the home of Joseph Crawford, assistant to the vice president of the Pennsylvania Railroad. Crawford had worked for the Japanese government in supervising construction of the first railroad in Hokkaido from 1878 to 1881, and since then had continued to serve as a consultant to the Japanese state railways. Probably at Crawford's suggestion, early in 1905, Kinoshita transferred to the Wharton School of Finance and Commerce, the first undergraduate business school in the United States, which the University of Pennsylvania had established in 1881. There he found his American guru in Emory R. Johnson, the first academic in the country to offer a separate course in transportation and the first to hold a professorship in transportation and commerce.

Though Johnson was only forty years old when Kinoshita enrolled as a part-time student at the Wharton School, he was already establishing an international reputation as a pioneer and authority in the field of transportation economics. His *American Railway Transportation*, the first textbook on the subject, had just appeared in 1903 and was on its way to becoming a best-seller in university classrooms and railroad offices alike. A number of its passages would have resonated with Kinoshita's prior experience in the Passenger Office, particularly in regard to the Kansai rate war:

> There are two general methods of inducing people to use the railroads more frequently: one is the reduction of fares, the other is the improvement of the service. The American railroads, generally speaking, have been inclined to follow the latter plan. . . . Greater dependence has been placed upon speed and comfort than upon cheap fares to attract travel. (pp. 148–49)
>
> The railroads . . . have frequently connived with [ticket scalpers] by letting them have blocks of tickets to be sold at cut rates. The purpose of the companies doing this was to secure traffic that would otherwise have gone to rival lines, and the practice was one of the results of unregulated competition. (p. 152)
>
> Unbridled competition is intolerable alike to the railroad companies and to the public, and must of necessity be checked. Whatever is ruinous to all parties must be stopped, and if the ruinous practices have no natural limits, an artificial one must be established. (p. 224)

Johnson had a great impact on his first Japanese student, to the point where Kinoshita's biographer claims that Japanese railroad operations subsequently took on a "Johnson style."

Johnson's influence outlived Kinoshita's career. The translation his protégé later made of the book Johnson coauthored with Thurman Van Metre, *Principles of Railroad Transportation* (1916; translated as *Tetsudō un'yu genron*, 1920), became a bible for railway administrators in interwar Japan. Moreover, at Kinoshita's urging, the national railways later sent two or three junior officials per year to study under his American mentor. Johnson continued to teach at the Wharton School until 1941, but as early as 1926, on a trip to visit alumni in Tokyo, he received formal recognition of his service to Japan when the emperor conferred on him the Order of the Rising Sun, Third Rank. Yet, in view of the policies that

Kinoshita had previously adopted in Japan, Johnson's major contribution there may have been simply to confirm the direction in which the chief of Passenger Operations had already been moving the Japanese government railways.

After studying with Johnson for a semester, Kinoshita devoted the rest of his overseas tour to practical training and observation. In May 1905 he served as one of three Japanese delegates to the Seventh International Railway Congress held in Washington, DC. Then he also interned at the Chicago, Rock Island & Pacific Railroad Company, one of the great railway empire-builders of the late-nineteenth and early-twentieth centuries. Through the good offices of the general manager, H. Miller, he was able to work at the company's headquarters and interact with its top executives. Kinoshita undoubtedly pored over the latest rules and regulations of the Rock Island's Operating Department, issued under Miller's name in 1904. These included directives that would have struck a chord with Kinoshita's customer-first orientation, such as "the service demands the faithful, intelligent and courteous discharge of duty," and station masters and train conductors must "attend courteously to the comfort and wants of passengers."[8]

Kinoshita then went on to Europe. In England he interned at the North Eastern Railway Company, whose combined operation of rail and automotive transport services he correctly foresaw as the wave of the future. He also took an inspection tour of various continental countries, comparing their facilities for attracting foreign tourists with an eye to introducing such facilities in Japan. The Tokyo government later sent him to St. Petersburg in 1907 to assist in preliminary negotiations for establishing connecting service between Japanese and Russian railroads in East Asia. When it finally came about in 1910, that connection would form a major link in his program for promoting foreign tourism in Japan.

Kinoshita returned home in October 1907, just as the government was completing the nationalization of the leading domestic private railroads, a move driven in part by a series of financial panics around the turn of the century. In November 1908 he resumed his position as head of Passenger Service, but now in a vastly expanded Imperial Railway Department; the following month he switched to the directorship of the Operations Section. Then, in July 1914, the Railway Department promoted him to chief of the Traffic Division, with oversight of the two sections he had successively headed since 1908. He held that appointment—the pinnacle of his career—until 1918.

That decade up to 1918 represented the heyday of Kinoshita's influence on Japanese railroads. During that time he was czar of operations for all but a small fraction of the nation's railway system, instead of less than a third, as he had been in the prenationalization years from 1902 to 1904. Invigorated by his studies abroad, he had come back more determined than ever, as he put it, "to meet the public's expectations by improving the facilities of the national railways and providing cordial service to customers."[9] Accordingly, he redoubled his efforts to institutionalize such user-friendly practices as running special trains for seasonal excursions and offering discounts for group travel by factory workers, students, and pilgrims alike. He also moved aggressively to upgrade facilities for shippers, introducing, for example, refrigerated cars and express-delivery trains on long-distance freight runs. In all these activities, Kinoshita received assistance from the talented group of experts he had assembled from the old Railway Operations Bureau as well as from the recently nationalized private rail companies. He especially depended on his subordinates from the private railroads who, unlike most of the career bureaucrats in the state railways, brimmed with business sense and experience in innovative management techniques.

As Chief of Operations, Kinoshita focused much of his attention on promoting foreign tourism to Japan. Reflecting his own cosmopolitanism and idealism, he championed such tourism as a vehicle for furthering international goodwill and understanding. Kinoshita was troubled by foreign criticism of Japan as an uncivilized "warlike nation" in the aftermath of the Sino-Japanese and Russo-Japanese conflicts that sandwiched the turn of the century. He had encountered such criticism firsthand while vacationing in northern New York at the time of the 1905 Portsmouth Peace Conference, which sealed Japan's victory over Russia. As he later explained, he had decided that getting foreigners to visit Japan, besides having the economic benefits of tourist spending and free advertising for potential Japanese exports, was the best way "to demonstrate the falsehood" of the country's bellicose image. Moreover, it would "introduce to foreigners the fact that our people are by nature peace-loving, threats to our national existence having compelled us to take up arms in the past two major wars, and that our compatriots are a very friendly race, ever hospitable to visitors from afar." Encouraging such face-to-face contact was "not to be overlooked from the standpoint of national diplomacy at a time when communication between East and West is becoming more frequent everyday."[10]

Accordingly, Kinoshita launched a multifaceted program to raise the standards of tourist accommodations on the national railways to Western levels and thereby attract foreign visitors. Believing mistakenly that Russia would have to pay Japan a colossal war indemnity, he petitioned his government to set aside 0.5 billion yen from the expected windfall for investment in tourist facilities. When, to his disappointment, the peace treaty provided for no indemnity whatsoever, Kinoshita took his campaign to promote tourism directly to state and business leaders. Upon his return to Japan in 1907, he succeeded in lining up a formidable array of supporters, including the director of the national railways and the elite of the business world.

The first goal of his campaign was to make it easier for foreigners to reach Japan, especially by rail. In 1910 the government sent him back to St. Petersburg to conclude the negotiations that he had helped initiate in 1907 to establish Japan's first international railway connections. Kinoshita successfully reached an agreement for connecting service with Russia's Chinese Eastern Railway at Dairen in Manchuria and by ship at Vladivostok. Then in 1912 he made arrangements for Japan's inclusion in round-the-world excursion tickets, with westbound travelers coming to Japan by steamer from Canada or the United States and eastbound ones arriving from Europe via the Trans-Siberian Railway.

While facilitating international travel connections, Kinoshita tackled the equally pressing job of upgrading services and facilities for foreigners within Japan. In 1908 he had founded a language institute for teaching English to a select group of conductors who would serve on trains catering to foreign travelers. To his more insular bureaucratic colleagues, this novel step only reinforced his reputation as a *haikara* official. Personally heading the institute, Kinoshita hired a number of skilled British and American instructors who had graduated from elite universities in their home countries. He also imposed a strict English-language pledge—not one word of Japanese in the classroom or on field trips—a practice he himself observed at home, where he had conversed with his wife exclusively in English from early in their marriage. The graduates of this institute went on to become head conductors on limited express trains, which Kinoshita introduced in June 1912 with a view to accommodating foreign travelers. Pulled by powerful new locomotives that the government had just imported from the West, these trains, featuring parlor cars and other plush amenities, covered the 710 miles between Shinbashi and Shimonoseki in about twenty-five hours.

Kinoshita made his greatest contribution to the development of tourism by proposing the establishment of the Japan Tourist Bureau, which the Railway Department founded in March 1912. This organization was the nation's first travel agency. As the Japan Travel Bureau Incorporated—its formal name and status since 1945—it remains the largest such agency today. As Kinoshita explained to the national railway employees who would staff the bureau, its main purposes were "to introduce the sights of Japan to foreign countries as well as to make available to foreigners various kinds of information necessary for travel" and "to enhance travel facilities for foreign tourists in our country and at the same time to correct bad habits on the part of the businesses concerned."[11] In line with these objectives, the agency set up branch offices not only throughout Japan and its colonies but also in the major cities of Europe and North America. These branches distributed English-language schedules and guidebooks and issued railway and steamer tickets and travelers' checks and insurance. A typical brochure for the national railway handed out by the offices promised foreign visitors "splendid and cozy staterooms," noting that "no efforts have been spared to introduce all the improvements taught by science and experience."[12] Contrary to its founders' intentions, however, the Japan Tourist Bureau in fact ended up doing business overwhelmingly with Japanese rather than foreign customers, testimony to the growing popularity of domestic recreational travel that Kinoshita had played such an important role in promoting since early in the twentieth century.

By 1918 the Traffic Division chief seemed well on his way to becoming a top leader in the national railways. Kinoshita himself thought he would advance at least to the position of vice director-general of the railways. He undoubtedly would have had the support of the Army Ministry, which appreciated his service in overseeing railroad operations on the continent at the start of the Allies' Siberian Intervention in 1918. Army authorities also liked his advocacy of the rebuilding of Japan's narrow-gauge railroads to the standard or "broad" gauge as a way to increase the speed and carrying capacity of trains. The state railways had adopted the narrow gauge in 1870 on the advice of their myopic (both literally and figuratively) British engineer-in-chief, who felt that Japan's mountainous terrain and shortage of capital dictated use of the 3'6" gauge that predominated in Britain's overseas empire. Over the years Japanese authorities had periodically proposed conversion to the 4'8 1/2" "international standard," but had gotten nowhere because of the extraordinary outlay it would have required. The drive to switch gauges, however, appeared to pick up steam after Gotō Shinpei became director-general of the Railway Department in 1908 and, to the delight of Kinoshita, began pushing wide-gauge conversion, electrification, and other basic improvements to the mainline network.

Unfortunately for Kinoshita's career as well as the gauge issue, the Seiyūkai, the majority party in the Diet for all but two years between 1900 and 1924, adamantly opposed renovation of existing trunk lines, including their reconstruction to the standard gauge. The party did so on the grounds that the huge cost of such a project would delay expansion of the network, especially to the local constituencies of Seiyūkai members. Every time the Seiyūkai gained control of the cabinet between 1911 and 1918, a new administration would replace Gotō, who served three separate times as director-general of the state railways, and shelve his plan for broad-gauge conversion.

As a supporter of Gotō's program and an opponent of what he would later call "the reckless building of new lines," Kinoshita also became a casualty of this politicization of railway planning. To the bitter end, he devoted himself wholeheartedly to his work and paid little attention to ensuring his own advancement by developing a personal clique or forging an alliance with a political party. No sooner had the president of the Seiyūkai formed the first genuine party cabinet in 1918 than he demoted Kinoshita for his resistance to the party's pork-barrel construction policy, exiling him to a local field post as head of the Chūbu Railway Office. Yet Kinoshita was too valuable to be kept out of the limelight for long. In 1920 the new Railway Ministry called him back to the center as chief of the Tokyo Railway Office. His workaholic ways apparently caught up with him, however, for, suffering from tuberculosis, he resigned later that year. He died from that disease in 1923, right after the great Kanto earthquake, at the age of forty-eight.

In his posthumous work, *Kokuyū tetsudō no shōrai* (The future of the national railways, 1924), Kinoshita waxed prophetic in setting forth his critique of the Seiyūkai's railway policy and his own prescription for railroad management. In the early 1920s, he noted, the national railways were recording a rate of return "unparalleled in the world, . . . but with the reckless building of new lines, the profit rate will gradually decline." The railways faced the urgent necessity of making enormous investments to renovate existing lines so that they might cope with growing domestic demand for transportation. Nevertheless, the Diet in 1922 had just approved the laying of over six thousand miles of new lines at a projected cost of several billion yen. "If we carry out the plan of works for our national railways as presently constituted," Kinoshita warned, "we will encounter untold difficulties in the future, . . . and in the end the railway account will inevitably go bankrupt." Instead, "we ought to improve existing railroads and either double- or triple-track or change the gauge for sections with heavy traffic." Furthermore, since "the majority of the new lines slated for construction have little in the way of goods or passengers along their projected routes," the preferable course of action in such cases would be to substitute more economical automotive transportation.[13] Just as Kinoshita predicted, the "reckless" building of nonpaying local lines that the Seiyūkai accelerated in the 1920s proved a huge financial drain on the state railway system, contributing to its massive debt by the 1970s. With the privatization of the Japanese National Railways in 1987, the authorities eliminated many of those local lines, replacing them, as Kinoshita had recommended in the first place, with bus and other automotive services.

Despite his relatively brief career, Kinoshita had made a lasting mark on railway operations in Japan. Though he clearly borrowed from progressive managers of the private railroads, he was without question the most innovative of career bureaucrats in the state railways. His successors as Traffic Division chief in the 1920s and 1930s continued the customer-oriented practices he had introduced, as did their counterparts in the postwar Japanese National Railways and, even more so, in the privatized Japanese Railways after 1987. In addition, Kinoshita was unusually prescient in his call for the combined operation of railway and automotive transport. Even his advocacy of broad-gauge conversion foreshadowed the eventual construction of the Bullet Train network to the standard gauge from the 1960s on. Similarly, his idealistic encouragement of face-to-face contact between Japanese citizens and visiting foreign tourists anticipated in part the official internationalization drive of recent decades.

Devoted husband and family man, teetotaler, near-native English speaker—*haikara* Kinoshita may well have felt out of place in his own country. Rarely attending official banquets, he once startled his colleagues by showing up at a geisha party for foreign visitors wearing a tuxedo adorned with the medals he had received at home and abroad. On one score, at least, he fit into the Japanese scene very well and, in the end, tragically so: He constantly drew praise for his total dedication to his studies and work. Emory Johnson, for example, reminisced on his visit to Japan in 1926 that his recently deceased protégé "was indeed a remarkably diligent student, and often while we would go hiking together, he would be absorbed in reading a book."[14] Kinoshita's boundless work ethic, combined with pressures on the job, may well have contributed to his contracting tuberculosis, a disease of epidemic proportions in Japan during the first half of the twentieth century. According to official records alone, it killed nearly six million people during that time, a figure equivalent to 7 percent of the nation's total population in 1950. One might well see Kinoshita's succumbing to that affliction as a precursor of another phenomenon of recent notoriety—*karōshi*, or death from overwork.

NOTES

1. Percival Lowell, *Noto: An Unexplored Corner of Japan* (Boston: Houghton Mifflin, 1891), 36.

2. *Tōkyō shin hanjō ki* [A record of Tokyo's new prosperity] (1874), quoted in *Japanese Life and Culture in the Meiji Era*, comp. and ed. Shibusawa Keizō and trans. Charles S. Terry (Tokyo: Ōbunsha, 1958), 223–24.

3. *Nagano kensei shi* [History of constitutional government in Nagano], 4 vols. (Nagano: Nagano-ken, 1971–73), 1: 459.

4. Jack Simmons, *The Railways of Britain: An Historical Introduction* (London: Routledge & Kegan Paul, 1961), 147.

5. *Nihon kokuyū tetsudō hyaku nen shi* [Centennial history of the Japanese National Railways], 14 vols. (Tokyo: Nihon kokuyū tetsudō, 1969–74), 4: 425.

6. Aoki Kaizō and Yamanaka Tadao, *Kokutetsu kōryū jidai: Kinoshita un'yu nijū nen* [The golden age of the national railways: Twenty years of transportation under Kinoshita] (Tokyo: Nihon kōtsū kyōkai, 1957), 19–20.

7. Ibid., 21.

8. Chicago, Rock Island & Pacific Railroad Company, *Rules and Regulations for the Government of Employees of the Operating Department* (1904).

9. Harada Katsumasa and Aoki Eiichi, *Nihon no tetsudō: Hyaku nen no ayumi kara* [Japanese railroads: A century of progress] (Tokyo: Sanseidō, 1973), 142.

10. *Nihon kokuyū tetsudō hyaku nen shi: Tsū shi* [Centennial history of the Japanese National Railways: General survey] (Tokyo: Nihon kokuyū tetsudō, 1974), 191.

11. Ibid.

12. Dallas Finn, *Meiji Revisited: The Sites of Victorian Japan* (New York: Weatherhill, 1995), 145.

13. Noda Masaho et al., eds., *Nihon no tetsudō: Seiritsu to tenkai* [Japanese railroads: Formation and development] (Tokyo: Nihon keizai hyōronsha, 1986), 181–82.

14. Aoki and Yamanaka, *Kokutetsu kōryū jidai*, 2.

SUGGESTED READINGS

Sources on Kinoshita's life include Aoki Kaizō and Yamanaka Tadao, *Kokutetsu kōryū jidai: Kinoshita un'yu nijū nen* [The golden age of the national railways: Twenty years of transportation under Kinoshita] (1957); Aoki Kaizō, *Jinbutsu kokutetsu hyaku nen* [Hundred years of people in the national railways] (1969); and *Tetsudō senjin roku* [Records on railway predecessors], edited by Nihon teishajō kabushiki kaisha (1972). On Kinoshita's American mentor, see Emory R. Johnson, *Life of a University Professor: An Autobiography* (1943). For more on the disease that killed Kinoshita, refer to William Johnston, *The Modern Epidemic: A History of Tuberculosis in Japan* (1995).

Among publications in English dealing with the history of Japanese railroads are Steven J. Ericson, *The Sound of the Whistle: Railroads and the State in Meiji Japan* (1996); Dallas Finn, *Meiji Revisited: The Sites of Victorian Japan* (1995), esp. 45–50, 138–45, and 246–51; Tokihiko Tanaka, "Meiji Government and the Introduction of Railways," *Contemporary Japan* 28 (May 1966, May 1967); Masaru Inouye, "Japanese Communications: Railroads," in *Fifty Years of New Japan*, compiled by Shigenobu Okuma and edited by Marcus B. Huish (1909); Toshiharu Watarai, *Nationalization of Railways in Japan* (1915); and Hirofumi Yamamoto, ed., *Technological Innovation and the Development of Transportation in Japan* (1993).

PART IV

TWENTIETH-CENTURY VICISSITUDES

From the first Sino-Japanese War that started in 1894 to the end of World War II in 1945, war or its avoidance dominated Japan's foreign policy. Japan fought Russia in 1904–05; it joined Britain and France against Germany in World War I (albeit only in limited operations in the Pacific and China); it participated in the Siberian Intervention launched by the United States in 1918; its army took over Manchuria in 1931, a deed that precipitated the China conflict in 1937; and it finally declared war on the United States in 1941.

In the meantime, by 1910, Taiwan and Korea had become official parts of Japan, with their people expected to serve the emperor as loyal, if second-class, subjects. At the same time, Japan moved to develop its leaseholds for railways and mines in Manchuria. In 1931, Manchuria became Japan's new frontier. With government encouragement, farmers and shopkeepers migrated there to build a new Japanese homeland regardless of the indigenous inhabitants. Opportunities for Japanese professionals to live and work abroad also expanded (Chapter 8).

The early twentieth century saw Japan's emergence as an industrial power. By the end of World War I, heavy industries in steel and machinery had become firmly entrenched, although agriculture and small businesses continued to dominate the economy as a whole and employed the most workers. Japan never experienced the booming good times of the late 1920s that brought a short-lived affluence to the United States and Europe before the Great Depression, yet factories attracted workers both male and female. The problem was that weekly wages hardly made up for horrible working conditions. While the heads of the industrial combines known as *zaibatsu* and their chief managers enjoyed luxuries never before imagined in Japan, the degradation wrought by wage-labor exploitation and poverty became increasingly evident. The inequities inherent in capitalist development sorely vexed Takahashi Masao (Chapter 10).

Industrialization led to the creation of a new urban middle class of salaried, white-collar workers and their families. Unlike the old middle class of shopkeepers and landlords based on family enterprises, salaried workers kept regular hours, never did any manual labor, and enjoyed secure, steady incomes. In the ideal situation, their wives did not work outside the house, leading to a bifurcation between work space and family space unknown to the old middle class. Chapter 8 shows how this new lifestyle held such appeal that it lured those who could afford the entry fee of higher education even from Japan's most isolated rural back-waters.

As society became increasingly complex in the early twentieth century, new space opened up for professionals of various types. In addition, the spread of literacy and the growth of the publishing industry made it possible for popular writers such as Yoshiya Nobuko (Chapter 9) to become specialized and professionalized. The 1920s saw the beginning of modern mass culture, characterized by film, radio, books, and magazines. Some messages advocated self-improvement for the sake of the individual, others for humanity. Still others praised self-fulfillment through pleasure or love in contrast to those that criticized any ideas not leading to a renewed spiritual commitment to emperor and nation.

Pundits at the time and historians since have seen a gap opening between town and country in terms of prospects for a decent livelihood as well as in values. While urban folk were too busy exploring the wonderful variety of activities and ideas newly available to them to pay much attention to the farms, the reverse was not true. Contempt for the city had less to do with status and security than with a deep fear of spiritual complacency, of merely material well-being. Although Matsuura Isami wanted all his children to succeed, he doubted the value of that success as long as it was coupled with the urban lifestyle (Chapter 8).

During the 1930s, Japanese life became increasingly harder. Although Emperor Shōwa took the throne in 1926, the first two decades of his reign are usually associated with the looming shadow and substance of war. The worldwide depression led many countries, including the United States, to erect high tariff barriers in an effort to protect domestic industries. Although Japan's industrial base grew and expanded into more technologically complex manufacturing processes, the benefits did not necessarily trickle down to the worker. Crops failed in northeastern Japan in 1933, leaving many tenant farmers on the verge of starvation. Following the takeover of Manchuria, the military had party rule replaced by transcendental cabinets that were supposed to put national goals ahead of politicking. It became increasingly dangerous to be associated with any ideas that did not tout Japan's unique national essence. Deviant thought or behavior was not to be tolerated. Yoshiya Nobuko and Takahashi Masao faced increased pressure to conform, yet they managed to survive with spirit intact to deal with the new world wrought by Japan's defeat.

CHAPTER 8

Matsuura Isami

A Modern Patriarch in Rural Japan

GAIL LEE BERNSTEIN*

For people who could afford it, education became the great leveler of twentieth-century Japan. Those fortunate enough to take full advantage of its benefits were given the opportunity to succeed in business, administration, and politics. Although people continued to take pride in their ancestry and the new aristocracy centered on the emperor tried hard to preserve the tradition of hereditary privilege, most jobs went to those with the right scholastic credentials, not family background. Nonetheless, access to education remained unequal. Few women went beyond the six years of compulsory education mandated in 1907, partly because of the time and money required, partly because many parents believed that educating women was counterproductive. Women who wanted to go to college were shut out of the elite national and private universities open to men only. Their only access to the prestige accruing to graduation from the top-ranked universities was through marriage. For the vast majority of men as well, a college education required too great a financial commitment to be practical. That a rural landlord such as Matsuura Isami (1880–1962) managed to send all fourteen of his children to college was an extraordinary achievement.

Education was but one of the forces that transformed the Matsuura family. All of its members experienced the effects of urbanization, imperialism, and war that had concrete consequences for the nation as well as for the patterns of everyday life followed by increasing numbers of Japanese. Isami's personal philosophy well illustrates the attraction to and revulsion

*I am grateful to the Northeast Asia Council of the Association for Asian Studies for a research grant in 1993 and the American Philosophical Society for travel funds for two research trips to Japan in 1993 and 1995. Valuable research and writing time was made possible by the Dean of the Social and Behavioral Sciences College of the University of Arizona, who awarded me both a one-semester sabbatical leave and a one-semester, funded-research leave in 1995 and granted me a one-course "buyout" in the fall semester of 2000. Insightful comments by Julia Clancy-Smith and Moniqua Lane helped shape the final version of this chapter.

from city life, although most of his children sought urban middle-class respectability. A number traveled to or lived in Japan's colonies. None was left unchanged by World War II.

Professor of history at the University of Arizona, Gail Lee Bernstein is the author of Japanese Marxist, A Portrait of Kawakami Hajime *(1976, translated into Japanese in 1991); and* Haruko's World: A Japanese Farm Woman and Her Community *(1983; updated in 1996). Her edited or coedited books include* Japan and the World: Essays in Japanese History and Politics in Honour of Ishida Takeshi *(1988), and* Recreating Japanese Women, 1600–1945 *(1991).*

Father is a . . . remote, august, figure. He is not called upon as a last reserve of sternness and punitive power. If bodily chastisement is resorted to, it is usually administered by the mother. . . . It is outside the gate that the dominion of the male begins and ends. To his children he is in some degree god-like; strong, helpful, loving, and removed from petty affairs.[1]

There are four things to be feared: earthquake, fire, thunder, and father.—*Japanese saying*

In a rice-farming village deep in the cold, mountainous region of Japan's northeast, around the turn of the twentieth century, a slender, handsome young man of twenty-one, well educated for his day, married his fourteen-year-old cousin in a match arranged by his father, the village head. The groom, named Isami (1880–1962), was the family's oldest son and heir; the bride, Kou, was his aunt's granddaughter. Although younger than the average bride of her day, according to the Japanese way of counting, Kou was fifteen—three years above the legal age of marriage. The couple's first child was born fifteen months later, in March 1903. Sustaining a harmonious marriage that spanned a half-century, Isami and Kou produced and reared a total of eight girls and seven boys.[2] Remarkably, all but one of their offspring survived childhood and led long lives.

What role did Isami play in the lives of his many children? What was the nature of his relationship to them as a father, and did this relationship differ according to their age and sex? Was he indeed viewed as a remote, authoritarian figure "removed from petty affairs"? Was he feared? Or did he follow the advice in popular magazines in the 1920s, which urged fathers to be "lovable" and "playful" while leaving the main work of discipline and education to their wives?[3]

We have only sparse information on men as fathers in modern Japan. However, we do know that Isami's social background—the scion of a large, wealthy family prominent in local government—surely cannot be considered typical. Nor was it typical to have fifteen children by the same woman (though Isami's parents had had eleven children, four of whom died before adulthood). Indeed, Isami's daughters called him "an original." According to his oldest daughter, he "never imitated anybody."

Yet, Isami's active involvement in child-rearing may not have been exceptional. In rural families, men tended to participate in household labor, including the physical care and education of their children.[4] Japanese historians of fatherhood have argued that before the modern period, fathers, including "members of the elite samurai class," were closely involved in child care.[5] In this sense, Isami was no exception.

The roots of Isami's family reached back eleven generations to the late seventeenth century, when the original ancestor first assumed the role of village head. By Isami's time, the family was among the wealthiest in their prefecture, with landholdings of more than four hundred acres. For at least the first three decades of his marriage, income from tenants renting family land and from soy sauce-manufacturing enterprises comfortably supported Isami and his offspring. Nevertheless, Japan's forced opening to trade with the Western world only twenty years before Isami's birth had ushered in a new society that threatened to leave rural areas behind.

Isami wholeheartedly embraced Japan's late-nineteenth-century reform goals of rapid industrialization and military strengthening. He echoed the sentiments of many of his countrymen for whom education, and especially Western education, provided the route to Japan's rise as a world power and to their own upward social mobility. Though formally educated through the age of nineteen, Isami had had only a limited introduction to the new foreign learning, but it was sufficient for him to glean the trend of the times. The future lay neither in farming nor in old-style Chinese books; modern education, and especially mathematics, science, and foreign languages, provided the ticket to success. Familiarity with Western customs, etiquette, and fashions was also necessary to function in a world dominated by European and American diplomacy and trade. As the family heir and successor to the village headship, Isami was expected to remain in the countryside. However, for his children—girls as well as boys—he had other plans, which, in only one generation, promised to catapult them, like so many other Japanese persons of this era, from peasants, albeit wealthy ones, into the new urban middle class.

Unlike the image of contemporary Japanese fathers as removed from domestic life—strangers in their own homes—and of their wives as the primary caregivers and "education mothers" (*kyoiku mama*), Isami was a hands-on parent, not only by choice but of necessity. The family's country house swarmed with children—Isami's own and his siblings'. Kou was frequently pregnant or recovering from childbirth, with her youngest infant carried Japanese style on her back. Even with the female servants and nursemaids to assist her in feeding her large brood, sewing and laundering their clothes, and supervising them, Kou needed her husband's help.

Isami's fathering represented more than "masculine domesticity"—a term used to describe child care that socializes boys especially into male activities, such as hunting.[6] His active involvement in domestic work extended equally to all his children, and not merely to his firstborn son and heir. According to his daughters' recollections, Isami performed tasks which, by the early twentieth century, within the middle class, were increasingly viewed as the natural responsibility of mothers. He cut the children's hair, bathed the babies, washed cuts or wounds with an antiseptic that resembled vinegar, ministered to upset stomachs and colds with a tiny pill that was probably a Chinese herbal remedy, and baked oatmeal cookies in a large stone oven for the children's snacks. He also played with his children, but the play had an edifying purpose: development of their physical strength. After their bath, the young ones would do exercises, such as hanging by their arms from Isami's shoulders as he spun them around.

A well-defined philosophy of child-rearing guided Isami and his young wife in their challenging job of nurturing over a dozen children in an isolated farm community and preparing them for a new society. Late into the 1920s the nearest train station and doctor were two-and-one-half miles away. A rickshaw pulled by a servant was the sole means of local transportation. Family members usually traveled on foot to the train. Yet this remote rural setting, precisely because it demanded hardiness, had its pedagogical advantages.

Isami believed that the three secrets of successful parenting were a good "blood line," fidelity to one's spouse in a monogamous marriage, and a healthy natural environment, with clean air, sunshine, and ample outdoor play space.[7] He assumed that he and his wife had inherited the first trait, he faithfully practiced the second, and the countryside where the children grew up provided the third.

The children were encouraged to engage in strenuous physical activity in close contact with nature. They hiked in the nearby mountains and swam in the river that ran along the edge of the village. In autumn they jumped from the roof of the house onto beds of fallen leaves. They played indoors during the winter, entertaining themselves by wrestling, singing, or juggling bags filled with sand or buckwheat.

The couple's views on child-rearing echo similar teachings of Fukuzawa Yukichi, the nineteenth-century popularizer of Western learning who was held in great esteem by Isami. Fukuzawa, too, had preached the value of physical exercise and even "rough sports" for both girls and boys, and he had advertised the benefits of country living for children. Fukuzawa considered many children of wealthy families to be "both mentally and physically feeble," because it was the "tradition of their houses to overprotect and overfeed and overdress the children, and to have too easy a life, leading to a lack of activity."[8]

Despite their goal of preparing their children for modern, urban life, Isami and Kou criticized city mothers for pampering and spoiling their children. Such women, they charged, by worrying excessively about their children's health and hygiene, turned them into delicate hothouse flowers. Neither Kou nor Isami believed in coddling the young. Every child, even if suffering from a cold or already fallen asleep, had to follow the Japanese custom of the nightly hot bath. "Throw away the thermometers and the *haramaki* (stomach warmers)," Isami advised.[9]

The couple also criticized mothers who instilled in their offspring the twin vices of consumerism and materialism. They attributed these traits in particular to the "class of educated women" who tried to exert too much control over their children. In their excessive attention to their young charges, they "put nice clothes on them, fuss over them, teach them things they don't need to know, and destroy their innocence. They are proud of their creations, but the children are sacrificed."[10]

Isami and Kou frowned on store-bought toys, which had become available in the cities. Expensive and dangerous (many were made of glass) manufactured toys, in the couple's view, discouraged creativity.[11] Their own children played with whatever they found in the fields around them and used their imagination to improvise. Sticks became swords, a piece of bamboo turned into a horse, leaves served as bowls, and pebbles were candies.

Although Isami's children enjoyed exceptional freedom during playtime, he and Kou were adamant about instilling good manners in their offspring. Ordinarily the children ate together at a separate table from Kou and Isami, and a maid served their food. Nursemaids and older siblings helped the younger ones and kept them in line, sometimes with a rap on their heads. When guests visited, the children were sent out of the room. The couple also enforced strict rules against fighting or dishonesty. They mediated arguments and intervened in fights. Children as young as three who behaved dishonestly or selfishly were lectured by their parents. After three episodes of misbehavior, they were punished with a spanking. Such incidents were evidently rare. "We never had any problems due to fighting among the children," Kou once told a journalist who visited their home in the late 1920s for a story on "the good family." She added, "The younger ones learn from the older ones, and the older ones take care of the younger ones."[12] The reporter noted the seeming paradox of a family that maintained "a traditional life-style in old Japan," but reared children to become "successful in Tokyo—the heart of modern Japan."[13]

What is striking about these idealized views on child-rearing, clearly articulated in the interview with the visiting journalist, is the sense they convey of two parents operating as a team. Early-twentieth-century urban discourse on parenting in how-to books variously advised fathers to assert "strictness" and mothers to exercise "love," or fathers to be "playmates" and mothers, "teachers."[14] However, Kou and Isami did not observe such a gendered division of labor in the shaping of their children's character.

Both parents displayed a combination of affection and strictness. Described by her youngest daughter as "very gentle" and by the journalist who met her as "cheerful," Kou also showed a tough side. "Mother spoke her mind directly," recalled one of her daughters. Children home from school in the summer were expected to do household tasks after only one day's vacation. At the same time, one way that Kou showed her love for her children was by making new summer clothes for them. Her "mother's intuition," as another daughter put it, enabled Kou to sew clothes in the right size, even for children who had been studying away from home, by guessing correctly how much they had grown over the year.

Isami's daughters spoke of him with respect, viewing him as authoritative but not oppressive.[15] It is true that at times he was *kowai*, fearsome. He observed the customary disciplinary practice of putting a misbehaving child outside the house even at night—the Japanese equivalent of sending a child to his room. His second daughter vividly remembered this punishment: she was only five when it was imposed on her. He occasionally made decisions that disappointed the children, and they could not easily disobey or challenge his will. "Father made decisions without wavering," said his youngest daughter. "Once he decided on a course of action, he did not like to change plans."

Nevertheless, Isami's children recognized that he looked out for their well-being, at least as he interpreted it. In talking about their lives, the daughters mentioned instances in which he seems to have tried to follow their wishes as long as he felt that, in so doing, they would not be harmed and he would not damage the family's reputation. Because one daughter expressed an interest in studying music, for example, he personally inspected the facilities of a music school in Tokyo. Not liking the behavior of the boys there, he sent her to a private women's college instead. He discouraged his fourth son from trying to become a professional singer, arguing that singers had a bad reputation: they were associated with theater people, popular amusements, and prostitution. The boy would endanger his siblings' marriage prospects if he entered the entertainment world. Isami persuaded him to study medicine instead.

Both parents displayed emotional attachment to their children. Into old age, daughters cherished memories of physical intimacy with both their mother and their father. One recalled how Kou carried the infants directly against her naked back and how Isami observed the Japanese custom of sleeping on tatami mats alongside the older children. When his eleven-year-old daughter died of peritonitis, to honor her memory the distraught father built a pool by damming a nearby stream and composed a haiku, linking her to the reflection of flowers in the water.

The parents' sense of joint responsibility for their children's upbringing extended to their education as well, although here Isami played a dominant role. Married young, Kou probably had no more than four years of compulsory education. The couple's oldest daughter remarked that her mother "could not keep up with" her father. Kou frequently asked Isami to explain terms unfamiliar to her, such as the new Western political institutions introduced into Japan. One day she asked, "Dear, what kind of a system is a jury system?"[16] Isami's worldly knowledge left other family members behind as well. When he heard news of the death of a leading novelist and called out, "Natsume Sōseki has died!" the oldest daughter, then thirteen, remembered thinking "it was a relative of ours."

The children began their formal education in the local public school, a simple wood structure that their family helped to build and maintain. In their first five years of schooling, they received instruction in arithmetic and the phonetic Japanese writing system, and they also began to acquire the discipline needed to memorize the Chinese characters that form the basis of Japanese writing. Before leaving the classroom, children were required to look up unfamiliar ideographs from the day's lesson. The family's large living room functioned as a study hall. Like schoolteachers, Kou and Isami set up desks for themselves in one corner of the room and doled out assignments. The older children might read from the writings of agrarian reformer Ninomiya Sontoku, known as the "Peasant Sage." Younger children might be asked to practice drawing an apple.

In his emphasis on the children's formal schooling, Isami's behavior came closer to the stereotypical image of the stern Meiji-era, authoritarian father. He closely guided arithmetic homework, for example, and made the children practice their sums before going out to play, occasionally hitting them if they made mistakes. "Father did not like stupid children," one daughter recalled.

Isami's position as father was bolstered by the Civil Code of 1898, which gave legal recognition to the househead, who was usually male. He controlled his children's marriages and had legal superiority over his wife in matters of divorce, business transactions, and inheritance. As the heir of a wealthy landowner and village leader, Isami also enjoyed economic power; villagers were beholden financially to the Matsuura family. These legal and economic privileges were tempered, however, by Isami's paternalistic sense of responsibility. The village head, explained the local priest, was the "father" of the village.

A towering figure of strength and rectitude, Isami provided, as needed, advice, money, encouragement, and a firm moral compass for the many people who came in contact with him—not only his children, but relatives, servants, and villagers. His second son recounted, in his seventies, how, on the eve of his departure from home for the first time to attend middle school, he received from his father a "long letter whose contents I do not recall but that sounded like moral instructions."[17] "When I was in college," his youngest daughter remembered, "students were asked to choose a motto for themselves. I asked my father what I should select. I think he realized I always felt trapped between my older sisters and my younger brothers—who tended to act like older brothers with me. So, he recommended as my motto, 'Be harmonious but do not be affected by others.' "

Isami's advice usually counseled a focused resoluteness in the face of difficulties. To a son-in-law in medical school who was neither studying hard nor supporting his wife and daughter, he sent a certified letter saying, in essence, "Until you finish medical school, you can't see your family," and he had his daughter and grandchild move back into his household. To the teenaged son of the village priest who, after the deaths of his parents, started doing poorly in school and associating with an unruly group of boys, Isami preached tough love. He "took him in hand," as one family member described it, and urged him to be more "stouthearted," but he also arranged for the boy to receive instruction at a Buddhist temple in Yokohama. The grateful young man eventually assumed his father's position as priest of the village temple. At Isami's funeral many years later, he broke down and wept.

One of Isami's goals as father was to preserve family continuity and harmony. He kept careful records of key events, and in his later years he wrote a family history. In her seventies, one of Isami's daughters-in-law gently urged his cantankerous eldest grandson to be more polite to his aunts (Isami's daughters) by murmuring, "Father would like it." By that time, Isami had been dead for thirty years.

The patriarch's domestic work also extended to preservation of kinship ties with relatives on both his and his wife's side. He paid calls on kin related by blood or marriage, attended weddings and funerals, helped arrange marriages for extended family members, and oversaw the maintenance of the ancestral graveyard. Such work, performed by housewives in urban areas, was men's work in the rural Japan of Isami's time. His nurturing of family ties left a lasting impression on his daughters, who followed his example in their married lives and conscientiously sustained a social network among their siblings.[18]

Above all, however, Isami was remembered by his children for his commitment to lifelong learning. Well rounded in his interests and talents, he read avidly (including foreign works in translation), wrote poetry, painted, and dabbled in inventions, such as a mechanical rice-husker and a washing machine. He even devised a way to draw electricity from the nearby river in order to provide lighting for the family's residence beginning in 1914.

Isami as father was thus a model of creative and intellectual endeavors as well as an exemplar of moral values, a visible presence in daily interaction with offspring of both sexes, a protector, teacher, and guide. He was conscious of his role as parent and clear about his methods and goals. But he did not give his children a notion of work— paid labor—in the outside world, nor did he himself work the family's agricultural land. He was supported by the family's income from land rents.

Beginning around 1920, however, Isami became increasingly more involved in his own entrepreneurial activities. He attempted unsuccessfully to patent and manufacture the rice-husker and washing machine that he had designed. He had more success with an oatmeal factory, which he established in the 1920s in Tokyo and turned over to his oldest son to manage. He also explored investment opportunities in hydroelectric plants, but again with only limited success. Although these business ventures, and his assistance to his father, occasioned trips to Tokyo or to other prefectures, he never followed a fixed, daily work routine.

The work ethic, if not the actual skills, that the children would need in their adult lives came from school and from observing their grandfather, Yūya, the village head between 1901 and 1937. Although his office was on the grounds of the family's property, across the garden from the main house, every morning he carefully dressed for work in a samurai-style pleated skirt (*hakama*). He returned to the main house for lunch and went back to the office again in the afternoon.

Grandfather Yūya was paterfamilias of four or five generations of kin living in the same household:

Abbreviated Genealogy of the Matsuura Family

7th generation	Isami's great-great-grandmother Chise (d. 1887)
8th generation	Isami's great-grandfather Daisuke (d. 1890)
	m. second wife Moto
9th generation	Isami's grandfather Jinsuke (d. 1917)
10th generation	Isami's father Yūya (d. 1937) m. Miyo (d. 1934)
11th generation	Isami (d. 1962) m. Kou (d. 1955)
12th generation	Children of Isami and Kou

Yūya's great-grandmother—the widow of the seventh-generation household—lived until 1887, his grandfather until 1890, and his mother until the middle of the 1890s. Yūya's father—Isami's grandfather—suffered from weak eyesight and retired relatively early but took a second wife and lived until 1917.

As village head for over thirty years, Yūya was the equivalent of father for two hundred households. For his work as a village functionary, Yūya received no salary. Nonetheless, he threw himself into community projects, budgets, and tax collection. He supervised the school, built a farmers' cooperative, and devised a new tax payment plan that became a model for other villages while also overseeing, with the help of three paid clerks, the family's agricultural lands and businesses. (They gave up their sake business in 1913.) "He was so busy," Isami recalled, "he did not have time to change his clothes."[19]

Yūya taught by his example the virtues of diligence and frugality. Even though he was wealthy and contributed generously to the village's Buddhist temple and school, he was known as a tightwad among family members. His grandchildren remembered that he used the same tea leaves all day and recycled envelopes. He also taught them, however, not to envy others. If somebody expressed envy at another's good luck, wealth, or talent, he would ask, "Has he died?" One did not know what fate held in store for a person.

Children of the household thus learned many lessons merely by observing the adults in their midst—male as well as female, servants as well as siblings, cousins, and grandparents. The presence of multiple caregivers of both sexes was not uncommon in Japan.[20] Children were influenced by a number of people of different ages and in a number of ways. They learned domestic skills by overhearing their mother teach servants how to wash kimonos or cook miso, and charity by seeing her give old clothes to a beggar who came to the house. They saw their father tinkering with inventions. "I learned to work from grandmother," said Isami's youngest daughter. "I weeded the garden with her early in the morning before going to grade school." In fact, the grandmother (Isami's mother Miyo) suffered a paralyzing stroke while weeding in the garden— against his advice—on a hot summer day.

Grandparents were an especially important part of children's lives. In fact, it is misleading to speak of either mothers, fathers, or both, as being primarily responsible for their children's care. Kou was too busy to give each child very much individual attention. Younger children had nursemaids, and older children slept with their grandparents in the separate retirement cottage in the family compound.

Isami himself was reared in his early years by his great-grandparents. As the oldest son and heir of his generation, the boy was taken under the wing of his scholarly, older kinsman, who had retired from his duties as village head twelve years before Isami was born. Beginning at the age of five, Isami lived in the retirement cottage and received instruction in reading from the eighth-generation patriarch, a learned man in his sixties whom Isami adored. From his great-grandfather, Isami gained his love of learning, which he sought to pass on to his children. From Daisuke's second wife, Moto, who was eight years older than her husband, literate, and a devotee of the theater, Isami may have acquired his commitment to women's education and to a loving relationship with his own wife. Moto had helped raise her stepdaughters after their mother died. She had traveled with her husband to Tokyo—then called Edo—in the 1860s and gone on pilgrimages with him. "She had a good head and fine character," Isami wrote in his family history. "They were an excellent couple."[21]

Shortly before his death in 1890, his great-grandfather took Isami, then ten years old, on his first trip to Tokyo, approximately 125 miles away by train. To commemorate this visit to the nation's capital and the center of foreign learning in Japan, he commissioned a painting of the two of them that still hangs in the retirement cottage. Plans for Isami's Tokyo education were squelched, however, when a local luminary consulted by the family reasoned that the boy would never agree to return home once he received a modern education in the big city. Isami completed his schooling in his home prefecture, but he determined to give his children the Tokyo education he had been denied.

All the children of Isami and Kou, daughters as well as sons, were educated in Tokyo from around the age of ten, with the exception of the three youngest sons, whose schooling was temporarily interrupted by World War II, and the daughter who died before reaching adolescence. All fourteen children graduated from college. While in Tokyo the children lived in the house that Isami built for this purpose on the northeastern edge of the city, next to his brother's house. Two live-in servants cared for them. Once a month, Isami made the six-hour train ride to

Tokyo to check on the children's progress. He interviewed the heads of various private women's schools before determining which one was appropriate for each daughter and spoke with their teachers. He also showed up unexpectedly in their classrooms or at school concerts. In the words of his oldest daughter, "He was an education papa."

Higher education for women was rare in Japan in the 1920s and 1930s, and one might wonder why the Matsuura girls were favored by their already overburdened father with such an expensive investment in their schooling. In addition to the inspiration provided by Isami's literate and wise step-great-grandmother, he was probably also following the precedent, already established by the early nineteenth century, of wealthy peasant families furthering their daughters' schooling in order to enhance the family's reputation and to increase the young women's value in the marriage market.[22] Moreover, like many other men of his time, including government officials and the famous educator Fukuzawa Yukichi, Isami believed well-educated women would benefit the country by raising intelligent and healthy children. Mothers were assigned an important nationalist role in reaching Japan's goal of "civilization." They were enjoined to be "good wives and wise mothers."[23] Isami's daughter explained that her father thought it would not help the country to educate men alone; "women too needed to be *erai* [important or great]."

Encouragement of the children's education reaped rewards, at least at first. The sons gained entry into the nation's most competitive public and private institutions of higher learning—Tokyo Imperial University and Keio University. The daughters studied at private women's colleges, rubbing elbows with the daughters of wealthy industrialists or members of the court aristocracy. After they graduated, their father arranged marriages for them to men destined to be financially secure and socially respected—doctors or white-collar employees of large corporations. The eldest daughter's husband, a member of a prominent family with samurai lineage, bluntly told her he would not have consented to marriage with a country girl if she had not graduated from a prestigious Tokyo women's college. Elated by the match, Isami presented her with a diamond ring.

In matters of marriage, a more conservative side of Isami emerged. Although his daughters viewed him as "progressive" in his support of their higher education, he chose to follow custom when arranging matches for his children. He squelched his daughters' desires to work before marriage and tried to interfere with a younger son's romantic attachment. In these ways he countered the growing influence of Western values, and especially of individualism and greater freedom for women outside the home. Worried about appearances, he persuaded a younger daughter's suitor to marry her older sister instead. Otherwise, he said, people would wonder what was wrong with her, and then all the younger ones would have trouble finding suitors. Fortunately for the older girl, she wanted to marry the man. According to her account, her father knew as much and also knew that even he could never persuade her to marry a man she did not like.

Isami departed from custom, however, in seeking spouses for his children who were not, like his own wife, rural dwellers and relatives. Determined to push all his children into the more respectable and secure urban middle class, he needed to cast a broader net. For his sons' wives he sought women who, like his daughters, were graduates of women's colleges, not local farmers' daughters, for they, too, would be living in the cities. Curiously, even for the firstborn son, whose assigned role was to assume the family headship and return to the village, a city girl unfamiliar with farm life was chosen, a decision Isami would later regret.

On the surface, Isami's strategy worked. His children metamorphosed in one decade or two from hayseeds to sophisticated urban consumers with cosmopolitan tastes. One daughter could dance the tango and sew Western clothes, another majored in English literature, and a son worked overseas in Australia. Two daughters married physicians. Two other daughters accompanied their husbands, one a geologist and the other an engineer, on overseas assignments to Manchuria, one of Japan's colonial outposts in the 1930s. The children's life trajectories epitomized the breathless changes transforming Japanese society as a whole from a largely rural, isolated island country to a major industrialized nation and imperialist power.

Isami tried to transform himself as well. On frequent trips to Tokyo over the years he persisted in promoting his inventions. These efforts, like his several business investments, rarely succeeded. In the meanwhile, the expense of educating and marrying off fourteen children in prewar Japan took its toll. As befitted the upper-class aspirations of the family, each daughter was given an expensive trousseau and items of furniture. A bride gave gifts to all members of her husband's family together with the servants. Weddings were held at a famous catering establishment in Tokyo. By the time Isami became village head in 1937, he had sold off much of the family's agricultural land to cover costs; and when the last of the brood was married, in the late 1940s, he was financially strapped. U.S. Occupation land reforms after World War II took most of his remaining holdings. "Father did not mind," remarked one of his daughters. "He said that although you can lose your wealth, you can never lose your learning."

His children's graduation from college and their marriages did not end the patriarch's commitment to their well-being. During and immediately after the war, those who were not overseas returned to their parents' large country home, with their own children, to escape American bombing raids over Tokyo and then the food shortages. Some brought their in-laws with them. Isami and Kou fed and sheltered a household of more than thirty members. For the first time, their daughters and daughters-in-law learned how to tend crops.

Wartime disrupted the lives of all the children, but Isami's sons fared less well than his daughters. The second, third, and fourth sons were drafted into military service, while the education of the three youngest ones was interrupted. The fifth son in his teenage years exhibited symptoms of a nervous breakdown and was called back to the village from his middle school in Tokyo. The sixth son, at the age of seventeen and after only one year of naval preparatory school, became the pilot of one of Japan's famed Zero bombers. Miraculously, all the sons and sons-in-laws survived the war, though the fourth son, caught in the brutal Battle of Guadalcanal, came home seriously ill from malaria, and the brilliant second son, who was the apple of Isami's eye, stayed in Indonesia to serve as an interpreter for the Dutch military war crimes tribunal.

After the war, unlike their well-credentialed brothers-in-law, the sons had trouble finding employment. Isami tried various stratagems to help them. He used his contacts to get them jobs, lent them money to launch their own enterprises, and employed them in his own newly formed and ill-fated company, selling stone used for making macadam. These efforts failed, and the boys floundered. One of their sisters sympathetically described them as "victims of the war."

Wartime dislocations were not the sole cause of the sons' difficulties. Isami's strong personality, in many ways an asset, seems to have intimidated his male children. In his family history, he attributed one or another of his sons' problems to certain weak traits of character—one did not work hard enough, another "lacked a strong will," a third got cocky or self-confident too soon.[24] His youngest daughter added that most of her brothers "lacked direction."

Isami blamed himself in some cases for his sons' disappointing performances. He thought perhaps he and Kou had been too easy on their first son, who "married early and afterward enjoyed a lazy life, pursuing pleasure."[25] He also regretted the hours he had spent away from home during the childhood of the youngest children, between 1925 and 1935, when he had been busy lobbying for a railroad station for the local community. The children had grown and "advanced in their desired directions," but he had been too preoccupied with political activity to enjoy them. "Without realizing it," he wrote in a poem, "ten years passed and I did not notice the flowers and the autumn leaves."[26]

The strain of living up to their father's expectations in wartime and occupied Japan proved too much for the sons. The heir—who had nothing left to inherit—became an alcoholic. The second son stayed in Indonesia for almost twenty years after the war's end, establishing a new life for himself and ignoring his father's pleas to return, although he did send money to his family. By the time he went back to his embittered wife in Japan, he was a stranger to his own children and a foreigner in his own country.[27] The third son, who before the war had been a journalist, after a failed campaign for political office became a local high-school teacher and lived in a family-owned house. The fifth son dropped out altogether. Like his father, he showed a flair for inventing and even had one of his inventions patented, but he ran up debts trying to manufacture the others. His wife and their children eventually left him because he could not support them. "He could never work for others in an office," his sister explained. He married again, to a woman he met on a train, and became a taxi driver, estranged from his siblings. The sixth son married against his father's wishes and quit veterinary school. Unemployed, he tried working in his father's struggling business but, assigned to solve a thorny problem involving moving stone over an unpaved road, he came close to a nervous breakdown.[28]

Only the fourth son, pushed to become a doctor when he had hoped to become a singer, approximated the standard set by his father. Although unable to finance a medical practice in Tokyo where his well-bred wife had grown up, with family funds he managed to open a clinic in the same nearby town as the third son. In place of the ne'er-do-well heir and his wife, the third and fourth sons and their wives helped care for Isami and Kou in their old age and until they died, Kou in 1955 of tuberculosis contracted during the war, and Isami in 1962 of a stroke.

Isami and Kou's daughters, on the other hand, were more firmly grounded in the urban middle class and, for the most part, financially better off than their brothers, due to their spouses. Their rural childhood, nevertheless, had hardly prepared them for the kinds of relationships they would have with their husbands or for their own roles as parents. First, "city men" were absent from the day-to-day care of their children. Absorbed in their professions as busy doctors or as white-collar employees of large corporations, Isami's sons-in-law worked away from home and were preoccupied with the demands of job and nation. Their wives became the main child-rearers and household managers, a circumstance that would have puzzled their own father. Second, the families of Isami's children were smaller. With a few exceptions they lived without servants and without multiple generations under one roof. In contrast to their mother's extraordinary fecundity, only two of the six daughters were able to have more than one child. Two daughters who were infertile each adopted a girl. One of the sons was childless, also.

Also foreign to Isami was the emotional gap between his married daughters and their husbands. His own faithful and companionable marriage to Kou contrasted with the separate spheres, emotionally and sometimes physically, in which husband and wife operated in postwar urban Japan. The men had left their family homes for long terms, as they were drafted into the army during the war and sent to different cities or overseas by their companies after the war. On their return, they relied on their wives for almost all the domestic work and saw much less of them and their children than Isami had. Even when living in the same city, husbands were still "not there," as they worked long hours and arrived home late, often after the children's bedtime. At least one of the marriages was strained almost to the breaking point for many years by the presence of another woman in the husband's life.

In the transition to the new urban middle class, husbands became more like providers than companions to their wives and fathers to their children. The generation of Isami's grandchildren, at least according to the standards of parenting he had set, was fatherless.[29]

NOTES

1. Kurt Singer, *Mirror, Sword, and Jewel* (New York: George Braziller, 1973), 36. Singer observed Japan in the 1930s.

2. Information on the Matsuura family comes from interviews with members of the twelfth generation, whose cooperation I gratefully acknowledge, and from Matsuura Isami, *Yamashiraishi o ko* [To tell about Yamashiraishi], the family history that Isami published in 1961 (hereafter referred to as Isami).

3. Harald Fuess, "Playful Patriarchs: New Middle Class Fatherhood in Taisho Japan," paper delivered at Symposium in Honor of Professor Albert M. Craig, Harvard University, Cambridge, Massachusetts, May 1999, 8–9.

4. Kathleen S. Uno, "Women and Changes in the Household Division of Labor," in *Recreating Japanese Women, 1600–1945*, ed. Gail Lee Bernstein (Berkeley: University of California Press, 1991), 17–41.

5. Harald Fuess, "A Golden Age of Fatherhood? Parent–Child Relations in Japanese Historiography," *Monumenta Nipponica* 52, no. 3 (Autumn 1997): 381–97. Such generalizations are based on a small number of cases, however.

6. Ibid., quoting Ralph LaRossa, *The Modernization of Fatherhood: A Social and Political History* (Chicago: University of Chicago Press, 1997), 31–34.

7. Uezawa Kenji, "Yon fūfu jūyonji ikka hanjōki Fukushima ken no yamaoku ni Toyo Taikō jidai kara renmen to shite sakaeru Matsuura shi o otonaou," *Fujin no tomo* 23, no. 1 (1929): 64.

8. "Early Marriage or Late Marriage," in *Fukuzawa Yukichi on Japanese Women*, trans. and ed. Eiichi Kiyooka (Tokyo: University of Tokyo Press, 1988), 133–34.

9. Uezawa, "Yon fūfu," 64.

10. Ibid., 65.

11. Ibid., 65–66.

12. Ibid., 65.

13. Ibid., 60–61.

14. Fuess,"Playful Patriarchs," 4–13.

15. The distinction is made by Joelle Bahloul, in *The Architecture of Memory: A Jewish-Muslim Household in Colonial Algeria, 1937–62* (Cambridge: Cambridge University Press, 1966), 57, regarding Jewish fathers in Algeria, who were both.

16. Uezawa, "Yon fūfu," 63.

17. Matsuura Kojirō, *Indoneshia sanjūnen* [Thirty years in Indonesia] (Tokyo: Jigyō no Nihonsha, 1977), 5.

18. Gail Lee Bernstein, "Social Networks among the Daughters of a Japanese Family," paper delivered at Symposium in Honor of Professor Albert M. Craig, Harvard University.

19. Isami, 30.

20. Kathleen S. Uno, *Passages to Modernity, Motherhood, Childhood, and Social Reform in Early Twentieth Century Japan* (Honolulu: University of Hawai'i Press), 1999.

21. Isami, 24.

22. Anne Walthall, "The Life Cycle of Farm Women," in *Recreating Japanese Women*, 49.

23. Sharon H. Nolte and Sally Ann Hastings, "The Meiji State's Policy toward Women, 1890–1910," in ibid., 151–74.

24. Isami, 57, 60, 70.

25. Ibid., 71.

26. Ibid., 42.

27. Matsuura Kojirō, *Indoneshia sanjūnen*, 71–73.

28. Isami, 59.

29. On contemporary families, see Hiroshi Wagatsuma, "Some Aspects of the Contemporary Japanese Family: Once Confucian, Now Fatherless?" *Daedalus: Journal of the American Academy of Arts and Sciences* 106, no. 2 (Spring 1977): 181–210.

CHAPTER 9

Yoshiya Nobuko

Out and Outspoken in Practice and Prose

JENNIFER ROBERTSON

By the early twentieth century, Japanese society was well on its way to modernity. Vastly more people were literate than ever before. Industrialization created many new types of jobs, and the people who filled them had disposable income to spend on entertainment. The appearance of mass culture made it possible for authors to earn more substantial incomes through the sale of their work than had ever been possible before. Magazines targeting specific audiences developed an insatiable appetite for serialized novels and short stories. Publishing houses churned out best-selling editions of popular writers' work. Nevertheless, government censorship meant that authors were never entirely free to write as they liked lest they offend public decency. During Japan's long war with China and later the United States, between 1931 and 1945, only writers whose work could be read as supporting the military machine could find their way into print. As we will see in Chapter 10, writers deemed dangerous to the state were imprisoned; others fell silent or joined the appropriate patriotic organizations. Although unknown in English-language translations, Yoshiya Nobuko was one writer who established her reputation before the war and continues to be read today.

Yoshiya's importance goes far beyond her significance as a writer. In her life as well as in her work, she exhibited a thoroughly modern sensibility. She took full advantage of the new public space for relations between women. As a writer, she communicated directly with women readers. As a woman who lived with another woman, she challenged the conventions of family life. It was no accident that Yoshiya's open avowal of her sexuality appeared just when the intensification and specialization of modern medical research into human behavior led a new breed of professional, the sexologist, to coin a new term for same-sex relations (dōseiai). Both practice and theory point to ways of conceptualizing human relations that would have made little or no sense fifty years earlier.

Jennifer Robertson is professor of anthropology at the University of Michigan. She is the author of Native and Newcomer: Making and Remaking a Japanese City *(1991) and* Takarazuka: Sexual Politics and Popular Culture in Modern Japan *(1998).*

"𝓜any women have never heard of the Women's Patriotic Association (Aikokufujinkai), but there isn't a woman alive who hasn't heard of Yoshiya Nobuko."[1] Ikeda Hiroshi, a literary critic, made this declaration in the popular magazine *Hanashi* (Talk) in 1935, by which time Yoshiya (1896–1973) had emerged as one of the most prolific and well-known writers in Japan. She was also the best-paid writer. She earned three times more than the prime minister, although she still resented paying taxes, "especially since women do not have the right to vote."[2] The overwhelmingly favorable public reception of her novel, *Onna no yūjō* (Women's friendship), serialized in the monthly *Fujin Kurabu* (Women's Club) between 1933 and 1935, had secured her celebrity status, on which her publisher capitalized by printing a twelve-volume anthology of her fiction shortly thereafter. Yoshiya's star never dimmed during her lifetime, and her numerous publications, which include "girls' fiction," historical novels, social commentary, and autobiographical essays, continue to be reissued. Although women in general are absent from the Japanese literary canon, it is hard to fathom why Yoshiya is also absent from (especially Anglophone) anthologies of Japanese women writers published to incorporate women into the otherwise androcentric canon of "pure literature."[3]

Born the year after Japan's victory in the Sino-Japanese War (1894–95), Yoshiya grew up in a social environment shaped by a succession of wars marking the transformation of Japan from an isolated and feudal country to an aggressive imperial power. She was raised as a privileged and affluent member of the small but growing urban middle class, yet her life choices clashed with "traditional" norms—especially with respect to sex and gender roles—underlying even the political and literary avant-garde. Neither an activist nor apolitical, Yoshiya, the writer, was more of a maker of future worlds than a fixer of the real world. Doubtless, her careful negotiations of the social and political instability and confusion that characterized early-twentieth-century Japanese society enabled her both to choose her own future and, most *atypically*, to secure financial independence outside of marriage, which she eschewed.

COMING OUT

Yoshiya Nobuko was born on January 12, 1896, in Niigata city, the youngest child and only girl among her four siblings. Both of her parents claimed prestigious samurai genealogies, and the affluent Yoshiya household retained the atmosphere of an earlier, feudal time. Capitalizing on Nobuko's precocious reading abilities, Yoshiya Masa kept her daughter hostage to moral and instructional texts for girls and women and taught her how to sew and cook, two skills at the core of the dominant "good wife, wise mother" gender role. Her father, Yoshiya Yūichi, was the Niigata police chief, and one might speculate that his job to enforce law and order influenced the conservative politics and disciplinary rigor of the Yoshiya household. The adult Nobuko herself was a paragon of self-discipline. She reserved mornings for writing and wasted no time—she was reputedly a "fast writer."

Yoshiya Nobuko's precocious literary talent was apparent to her teachers by her third year in elementary school (in Ibaraki prefecture, where her father had been transferred), when she wrote an essay on "Mizu" (Water). Her mother, however, was unimpressed by her daughter's skill, and their relationship grew increasingly strained. Nevertheless, Nobuko continued to write. By 1908, when she was twelve years old, her short stories were published in *Shōjokai* (Girls' Circle), *Shōjo Sekai* (Girls' World), and *Shōjo no Tomo* (Girls' Friend). Five years later, readers encountered her prose in such prestigious literary magazines as *Bunshō Sekai* (Literary World) and *Shinchō* (New Tide). She also won first place in a girls' fiction contest sponsored by *Girls' World* for her submission, "Narazu no taiko" (Soundless drum).

The trajectory of Nobuko's life began to diverge from that of her parents in 1915, when her father was transferred to Utsunomiya, where he assumed the directorship of the Red Cross, and she moved to Tokyo to live with her youngest brother, Tadaaki, who was a student of agricultural science at Tokyo Imperial University. Nobuko's eldest brother Sadakazu had opted to pursue an unillustrious career as a fine arts painter, and her middle brother, Michiaki, had also disappointed their father by displaying no aptitude for higher education. Tadaaki had always been supportive of his sister's literary aspirations. Not only did he keep Nobuko supplied with the latest publications, he often argued on her behalf when their parents sought to terminate her education, fearing that too much erudition would spoil her chances of an upwardly mobile marriage.

What actually spurred Nobuko's move to Tokyo was a letter from the celebrity artist, Takehisa Yumeji, a good friend of Sadakazu. Yumeji's hugely popular pictures of willowy, wide-eyed young women complemented Nobuko's fictional characters in ambience and affect. Recognizing their shared feminine aesthetic, Yumeji wrote to Nobuko suggesting that they meet in Tokyo and discuss ideas for collaborative projects. Despite her low opinion of his decadent and philandering behavior, Nobuko agreed to have Yumeji illustrate some of her work. During her first year in Tokyo, she also embarked on an eight-year project that propelled her into the literary limelight. This was the series of short stories, *Hanamonogatari* (Flower tales), serialized for eight years (1916–1924) in the popular magazine, *Shōjo Gahō* (Girls Illustrated).[4] Today, many female authors claim that *Flower Tales* inspired them to pursue a literary career.

The celebrity of both Yumeji and Nobuko was contingent in large part upon the turn-of-the-century emergence of a new target audience and category of consumer: the *shōjo*, or girl, but literally, a "not-quite-female female." A "really real" female was a married woman with children. The so-called *shōjo* period defined the emergent space between puberty and marriage that began to grow into a life-cycle phase, unregulated by convention, as more and more young women found employment in the service sector of the new urban industrializing economy. Included in the *shōjo* category were the "new working woman" and her jaunty counterpart, the flapperlike "modern girl," or *moga* (*modan gāru*), who was cast in the popular media as the antithesis of the "good wife, wise mother." Obviously, the spectacle of women working and cruising was not a brand-new phenomenon; rather, the prefix "new" denoted middle-class forms of urban employment for girls and women, who served as clerks in department stores, ticket sellers for trains, schoolteachers, telephone operators, typists, nurses, writers and journalists, actors, and café hostesses. These women were among Yoshiya's loyal readers and fans.

Few urban employment opportunities were available for women over the age of thirty; male employers preferred young women up to twenty-four, at which age they should be getting married. Women who, like Yoshiya, could support themselves, were treated as social anomalies, irrespective of their sexual practices. Similarly, "modern" signified a Westernized woman, not in the sense of a woman fluent in a European language but one who eschewed wifehood and motherhood and acted like a man, particularly like a flaneur. Such a woman was often referred to in the critical media as a garçon (*garuson*), one of the many labels pinned on Yoshiya by her detractors.[5] As early as 1890, social critics had claimed that women were becoming more mannish as a result of Japan's Westernization. In sum, when applied pejoratively to girls and women, "new," "modern," and "Western" were euphemisms for "unfeminine," "un-Japanese," "disorderly," and "dangerous."

The treatment of the *shōjo* and the *shōjo* period by the popular media in turn-of-the-century Japan reveals a Janus-faced object and subject of scrutiny. The latter was perceived by some as a downright dangerous phase of unstructured social interaction and unconventional behavior. Since *shōjo* "girlhood" was not determined by chronological age, unmarried adult women in general were regarded as morally depraved and biologically immature. The *shōjo* was reified by critics as a barometer of decadent and unwholesome social transformations. The ambiguous figure as the "not-quite-female female" inspired countless articles on "normal" and "deviant" sexual desires, for *shōjo* was a label that, among other things, implied heterosexual inexperience and homosexual experience. In fact, the term *dōseiai* (same-sex love) was coined at this time to refer specifically to a passionate but supposedly platonic friendship between girls or women, although sexologists found it difficult to distinguish friendship from homosexuality: Where did one end and the other begin? [6] Such friendships were regarded as typical among girls and women from all walks of life, but especially among girls'-school students and graduates, educators, civil servants, and thespians. The *ai* alludes to the term's original definition. Often translated as "agape," *ai* is contrasted with *koi*, or "eros." Because female (homo)sexuality was understood as spiritual and male (homo)sexuality as carnal, the neologism *dōseiai* was preferred by some sexologists to underscore the spiritual aspect of same-sex love between women. [7]

Controlling the *shōjo* was desirable because she was fascinating, attractive, and weak, and it was necessary because she was powerful, threatening, and different. According to some pundits, *shōjo* were "no longer discreet, obedient, or domestically inclined" due to the influence of the masculinizing tendencies attributed to various modern practices and Western popular culture. [8] Statements such as these were anachronistic and misleading, since the category of *shōjo* was a newly discovered social phenomenon. Yoshiya herself and other women who did not fit the label of "good wife, wise mother" were classified as *shōjo*. However, by eschewing a conventional female and feminine life-path, Yoshiya and others effectively expanded the dimensions of the *shōjo* period so that it defined not a phase of life, but an actual lifestyle and subculture as well.

Tamura Toshiko was one of Yoshiya's friends who also spent part of her adult life with another woman. She created a sensation with her short story, "Akirame" (Resignation, 1910), an exploration of "the sensuous nature of a young woman's attraction to another woman." [9] There were also many "ordinary" females in early-twentieth-century Japan who either lived together or who wanted to live together. Not a few of them attempted suicide, often together, out of desperate frustration at rigid social protocols that denied legitimacy to their relationship. [10] In fact, by the 1930s, the preponderance of lesbian suicide attempts reported in the press led one prominent sexologist to wonder, "Why are there so many lesbian double suicides reported in the society column of the daily newspapers? One can only infer that females these days are monopolizing homosexuality." [11]

Yoshiya is credited with playing a key role in developing and defining the genre of *shōjo* fiction aimed at this entirely new female audience cum subculture of reader-consumers. Her *Flower Tales* epitomizes the nascent genre. Each of the fifty-two chapters is named after a flower.

The stories are set in girls' schools—often mission schools—in Japan, and the sometimes lonely, self-sufficient maverick heroines who populate the stories are foils for coquettish girls and unhappily married women who acquiesce to convention. The boys and men who do appear in the stories tend to be distrustful or inconsequential and remain relatively undeveloped as characters.

Ideas for the various scenarios in *Flower Tales* grew out of Nobuko's own experience. A year after her move to Tokyo, Tadaaki left for North China as part of his new job to survey forests, and Nobuko found lodging in a women's dormitory in the Yotsuya district managed by American Baptist missionaries. She also began to study English at that time. However, the dorm's early curfew interfered with her penchant for spending evenings and nights at the movies in Asakusa, the lively theater district. Within a year she had moved to the more liberally managed YWCA in Kanda, a district known for its universities and used book stores. Nobuko's roommate there was Kikuchi Yukie (of Tsuda Women's College), who became the model for Akitsu, one of the two protagonists in her *Yaneura no nishojo* (Two virgins in an attic), penned in 1919. This book is recognized as her earliest effort to write explicitly about lesbianism. Akitsu is a self-sufficient and determined young woman living in a women's dormitory who guides her roommate Akiko through the process of self-discovery and a concomitant rejection of patriarchy. The story ends with the two women deciding to leave the dorm and set out together on a lifelong journey.

Whereas Akitsu is modeled after Kikuchi, Akiko's transformation into a resolutely woman-identified character charts the progress of Yoshiya's own evolution under the tutelage of her YWCA roommate. The YWCA bore the reputation of being a refuge for women eager to escape an arranged marriage or married life itself. It was also a proving ground for lesbian relationships, including the one between Kikuchi and Yoshiya. Their archived correspondence and passages in Yoshiya's diary suggest that Kikuchi was an aggressive and jealous partner. Kikuchi clearly flouted the prevailing stereotype of women, for it was taken as common sense, or the ruling definition of the "natural," that only courtesans, prostitutes, and widows experienced sexual desire.[12] Yoshiya herself wrote in her diary (on January 25, 1920) that "SEX [*sic*] is a most natural human desire. But the irritating thing about Yukie [i.e., Kikuchi] is the way she equates sex with possession and ownership, the way men do. The physical act is just a cover for a coarseness of spirit."[13]

Yoshiya wrote the "Suiren" (Water lily) chapter of *Flower Tales* around the same time as this diary entry. It is about a young woman, much like herself, trying to stand on her own two feet. Not surprisingly, Yoshiya applauded her contemporaries who publicly declared their rejection of the self-sacrificing role of "good wife, wise mother." For example, she was deeply impressed by a "divorce petition" published in a leading daily newspaper by a popular poet, Byakuren (Itō [née Yanagihara] Akiko), seeking to sever ties with her philandering husband of ten years. Byakuren's petition for a divorce in the form of a "tearful confession" of her unhappy marriage to the wealthy Itō Den'emon, a coal-mining tycoon twenty-five years her senior, was printed verbatim in the evening edition of the *Tōkyō Asahi Shinbun* on October 23, 1921. Yoshiya was so moved by the petition, excerpted below, that she copied and underlined parts of it in her diary and included a fictionalized reference to it in her short story, "Moyuru hana" (Burning flower), which was being serialized in the same newspaper.[14]

> All that comforted me during my ill-fated marriage to you was my poetry. The hurt from the pathos of a loveless marriage was so deep that at times I would resign myself to the curse of a pointless life that would end behind a dark curtain. Fortunately, however, I have fallen in love with someone [the anarchist lawyer Miyazaki Ryūsuke] whose love will help me to rejuvenate my life and turn it around. Following my conscience, I have decided that it is time for me to fundamentally restructure the unnatural daily life of my past. That is, I must now leave behind the fictions and falsehoods and adhere to the truth. You respect only the power of money and have an utter disregard for women. Therefore, with this letter I hereby announce our separation.[15]

Byakuren's courageous choice of love and politics over financial security deeply impressed Yoshiya, who, a year earlier, in 1920, had decided to end her own relationship with the possessive and petulant Kikuchi. Yoshiya became briefly involved on the rebound with an older woman she met at the YWCA. That relationship, too, deepened her disillusionment about love—until January 1923, when she was introduced to Monma Chiyo, the woman who became her life partner.

TRUE LOVE

Three years younger than Yoshiya, the twenty-four-year-old Monma was a mathematics teacher at a higher girls' school in Tokyo's wealthy Kōjimachi district. Her first, and not so subtle, impression of the popular writer was of a "cute Ainu woman" on account of Yoshiya's unusual haircut.[16] Two years earlier, in 1921, Yoshiya had decided to cut her hair short and hence was one of the first Japanese women to do so despite the (rarely enacted) law against short hair on females. Whereas short hair on males signified the rationalization of everyday life, on females it was the mark of a maverick, construed as a sign of social disorder and sex-and-gender confusion. Moreover, the short, or "masculine," haircut was interpreted by conservatives writing in the early twentieth century as a symbol of lesbian sexuality to which young women were all too susceptible. Yoshiya's *kappa* (water imp) haircut was unique and wholly unlike the trendy Eton-crop and pageboy styles sported by the sexually ambiguous "modern girl." Her hairstyle, in short, was not at all fashionable; rather, as she claimed, it embodied a manifesto of liberation from state-sanctioned womanhood. Significantly enough, Yoshiya never changed her trademark coiffure.

Yoshiya and Monma were virtually inseparable from the day they met. Until they began living together under one roof as a couple in 1926, they wrote each other letters on a regular, sometimes daily, basis. In 1924, when they were separated for ten months while Monma was teaching at a girls' high school in Shimonoseki, 1,000 kilometers west of Tokyo, the two women exchanged over 150 letters, most of which averaged between five and ten pages in length. The passionate and erotic nature of their relationship was evident not just in the sheer number of letters exchanged but also in their steamy content. These and hundreds of other pieces of Yoshiya's correspondence formed the basis of a biography—the first of only several on Yoshiya—by the feminist historian Yoshitake Teruko.

As an aside, although the loanword "love letter" was introduced to the Japanese public in the early twentieth century, letters of love (*koibumi*) have a centuries-old history in Japan. Letters incorporating poems were a staple form of communication in the gender- and ritual-bound Heian Court (795–1193), where it was considered a gross breach of etiquette for a man to neglect to send his lover a morning-after letter and poem as soon as he returned to his quarters. It is significant that during their "courtship period," Yoshiya never failed to write a letter to Monma after returning home from an outing with her.

Unlike her fiction, Yoshiya's letters were not flowery but rather crisply, if passionately, penned, as in the following poemlike example:

> Beloved Chiyo
> I will love you no matter what
> I do not wish to make you lonely
> Nor do I want to be lonely
> I want you to be the source of my strength
> And, if you will let me, I would like to be the source of your strength
>> May 23 [1923], 8:30 P.M.
>> Arriving home soaking wet from the rain
>> Nobuko[17]

Monma's letters were almost loquaciously melodramatic in comparison:

> Beloved elder sister. I am unspeakably lonely when you leave. My heart becomes hollow, and all I am able to do is to sit in a chair and stare blankly

at the wall. It's now nighttime, isn't it? As I wrap my unlined black kimono around my bare skin and adjust the hem, my body is aroused by feelings of longing [for you]; instead, what stretches confusingly before my eyes is dusty reality. Ah, this evening. My heart finds no consolation in this evening dream of mine or in reality. My heart sinks from a heavy sadness. If only on this night we were together in our own little house, lying quietly under the light of a lantern, then my heart would gradually warm and neither would you be so sad. I am so sad that I won't be able see you either tomorrow or the day after. Let us please meet again on Tuesday. Farewell for now; I am forever yours. Why have I written such things, I wonder? Please don't worry too much about me. Goodbye, and please take care of yourself.

    May 11, [1923] midnight
    Thinking of my elder sister.
    Chiyoko[18]

Other letters express their passionate love somewhat more graphically. In one of her longer letters to Monma (in 1924), Yoshiya writes, "I crave your lips. Do you know how much I crave them? When I get into bed alone at night I begin to burn deeply for you. . . . I am staking my entire life on you, on a woman—every prayer, every desire, every happiness, even my art [I am staking on you]. I need you and you alone; I have no life without you."[19] Kisses, caresses, and warm embraces were mentioned regularly in their letters along with subjects more overtly political and polemical than Yoshiya's published pieces. Monma's tenure in Shimonoseki inspired especially ardent missives between the two women, who also used the opportunity to polish their antipatriarchal rhetoric and to strategize against the state's paternalistic family system. Monma, for example, in a letter to Yoshiya in February 1925, vented her feelings about society's double standard:

> I can only think of how soon we can arrange to live together. There's nothing I need more than your warm embrace. It is unfortunate that we are not a male and female couple, for if you were a male, our union would be quickly arranged. But a female couple is not allowed. Why is it that [in our society] love is acknowledged only by its outward form and not by its depth of quality—especially since there are so many foul and undesirable aspects to heterosexual relationships?[20]

Yoshiya's response was an audacious manipulation of historically traditional practices in the direction of radical change:

> Chiyo-chan. After reading your letter I resolved to build a small house for the two of us. . . . Once it is constructed, I will declare it to be a branch household (*bunke*), initiate a household register [listing, by law, all family members], and become a totally independent househead. I will then adopt you so that you can become a legal member of my household (adoption being a formality since the law will not recognize you as a wife. In the meantime, I aim to get the law reformed). We will have our own house and our own household register. That's what I've decided. . . . We'll celebrate

your adoption with a party just like a typical marriage reception—it will be
our wedding ceremony. I want it to be really grand. We will ask Miyake
Yasuko-san and Shigeri-san [the couple who had introduced them] to be
our go-betweens [a formal role at weddings]. I wonder what kind of wedding kimono would look best on you? . . . In order for us to realize this
event, I would like you to retire from your teaching position. . . . I just can't
wait any longer.[21]

Yoshiya kept her promise and built a new house in Shimoochiai, a suburb of Tokyo, to mark their partnership. She did not formally adopt
Monma until February 1957 for two reasons. First, Monma's parents
initially objected to their daughter's adoption; and second, and most important, Yoshiya was keen on having their relationship legally recognized as a bona fide marriage, not as a "mother-daughter" pairing. Only
when it became clear to her that the postwar constitution would retain
the patriarchal ideology of its predecessor did she adopt her partner,
thereby ensuring that Monma would be recognized legally as her successor. From that point onward, Monma was known legally as Yoshiya
Chiyo.[22] As the option of forming a branch household was noted by
another famous lesbian couple in 1935, it is probably the case that this
was a primary strategy for "nontraditional" couples to achieve a modi-
cum of legitimacy as a corporate unit.[23]

Monma agreed to quit her teaching position and became Yoshiya's
fulltime secretary in 1931. Their Shimoochiai house was a landmark
modernist building infused with sunlight pouring through numerous sliding glass doors. Yoshiya had a passion for architecture and often claimed
that had she been born a male, she would have become an architect.
Sharing this extravagant home were two maids and a German shepherd.
Yoshiya built eight houses in all; moreover, she was one of the first Japanese to have a car of her own, and at one time she owned six race horses!
She was generous with her wealth and offered support and mentoring at
her home to many women who aspired to a literary career. [24]

SEXUAL POLITICS

The families and childhood experiences of Yoshiya and Monma were
very different in every respect. Yoshiya was the youngest and only daughter
of five children; Monma was the eldest of seven children (three sons and
four daughters). Yoshiya's father was a government official and bureaucrat; Monma's was a scholar of Japanese literature.[25] And, although both
of their mothers could be characterized as "good wives and wise mothers," Yoshiya's was wholly unsupportive of her daughter's professional
aspirations, while Monma's encouraged her daughter to pursue a profes-

sional career. Biographer Yoshitake Teruko avers that the "goodness" of her mother imparted in Monma an affirmation of "same-sex longing," whereas Yoshiya's mother was adamantly opposed to her daughter's literary ambitions, deeming them to be patently unfeminine. Unlike Monma, Yoshiya did not grow up with a favorable image of women. Rather, as Yoshiya commented in her diary, her mother embodied the plight of Everywoman forced into a loveless arranged marriage and relegated to a demoralizing life devoid of any semblance of agency and self-determination.[26]

Although I find it problematic to make causal links between daughters' gender identity and sexuality with the attitudes and circumstances of their mothers, I do not doubt at all that Yoshiya and Monma's mothers—and fathers—played a role in fostering a domestic environment that either supported their daughters or created challenges for them to overcome. In fact, the notion that Monma's "same-sex longing" was nurtured by the positive influence of her mother is a relatively recent departure from the enduring notion introduced in the late-nineteenth century that lesbian sexuality was caused by mean mothers and abusive stepmothers, among other negative familial and environmental factors.[27] Like Yoshiya's mother, some conservative pundits perceived higher education as one of those negative environmental factors and were especially hostile to early-twentieth-century attempts to popularize sex education and sexual hygiene.[28] Similarly, politics was deemed an unsuitable interest or profession for women. The Peace Preservation Law enacted in March 1900 forbade political activity, broadly defined, by women (along with soldiers, police, priests, and minors). The establishment in 1911, of Seitōsha, or Bluestocking Society, a literary, urban, middle-class women's organization, signaled the public presence of self-conscious women whose political ideas and behavior far exceeded the narrow cognitive range of the "good wife, wise mother" role. The society was forced to disband in 1916.

Yoshiya Nobuko herself was deeply influenced by the Bluestocking Society. She was especially inspired by the founder, Hiratsuka Raichō, who had introduced the reading public to the concept of the "new woman" (*atarashii onna*) in 1913. Like Hiratsuka, ten years her senior, Yoshiya was a strong supporter of the American Margaret Sanger's campaign to introduce birth control both as a "positive" eugenics policy and as a fundamental right of women. She also lambasted women—including her own mother—who became pregnant without any forethought.[29] Perhaps the literary efforts of the Bluestockings inspired Yoshiya to found *Kurosōbi* (Black Rose) in 1925. This was a monthly literary magazine that she intended as a forum for exploring the more unconventional dimensions of her own fiction without worrying about censors and salability.

However, it proved to be too great an effort even for her workaholic self and was discontinued after the eighth issue.[30]

Although I cannot elaborate here, I suspect that Yoshiya's diary entries and letters to Monma were proving grounds for the gender-bending ideas that, rendered in tamer rhetoric, infuse her novels and commentaries alike. Similarly, what some critics dismissed as "children's stories," namely, *shōjo* fiction, constituted for Yoshiya and her readers an interstitial space where new or unconventional configurations of everyday life might achieve materiality and practical importance and where they might question received convention. In contrast to her private correspondence, Yoshiya was artfully indirect about sex in her published work. An article titled "Dannasama muyō" (A husband is unnecessary), published in the left-of-center intellectual journal *Kaizō* (Reconstruction) in January 1931, is telling. Yoshiya defends, with exasperation, her unconventional life through subtle satire and humor, as revealed in the following excerpts:

> "Why don't you marry?" everyone asks politely. Is it that I'm the epitome of a wife? People greet me with that question instead of, say, a "Good morning," or a "Good evening.". . . They might as well ask me if I'm simply indulging in a reckless adventure fueled by a pathetic determination to be a barren woman.
>
> "You must be lonely?" everyone asks politely. . . . Rest assured; I am not at all lonely! The outdated notion that an unmarried woman is lonely, bitter and angry is completely foreign to me. I write novels, which for me, is the great work of my life.
>
> For 365 days of the year I work from morning to night, from deadline to deadline, . . . and in the process, I completely forget about the great defect in my life: the absence of a husband. If I hadn't been blessed with a talent for writing, I'd probably have ended up unusually lonely, barely able to endure each minute of the day as I sobbed and wailed. . . . I offer my thanks to the *kami* (gods); for some reason, the omniscient *kami* made me a novelist instead of a wife. Now if the *kami* had first asked me to choose between having a husband and becoming a novelist, I . . . most certainly would have asked to become a novelist, not because a woman like me couldn't attract a good husband, but because with some practice, I could become a good novelist.
>
> "Don't you like men?" Many people ask me this. Please, everyone! For crying out loud, don't make such ridiculous assumptions! . . . Why would I dislike men? . . . Please, everybody, just think for a minute. There are two types of humans, males and females. Just two types. To dislike one of them is truly too sad for words.[31]

Although Yoshiya herself was quite extraordinary, she wrote from the perspective of a young woman of the urban middle class who sensed that something was missing from her life but could not quite put a finger on just what it was. Her emphasis on heroines and same-sex friendship and love was pathbreaking. Despite her polite, ornate prose, she managed to convey rather radical ideas to her middle-class readers, female and male, married and unmarried alike, who collectively outnumbered her strictly *shōjo* fans. She stretched the parameters of the status quo and, at the same time, broadened the minds of her readers. It was for her readers, in fact, that Yoshiya consciously and constantly crafted the politics of her narrative. Thus, for example, after returning in 1929 from a year of traveling with Monma throughout Europe and the United States, which was de rigueur for Japanese women writers at the time, Yoshiya, who was "impressed by the liberated women of America," vowed "never again to write about female characters who cried a lot and simply endured their miserable lot in life."[32] Yoshiya's account of her worldwide travels, titled *Bōfū no bara* (Stormy rose), was serialized in 1930 in the women's magazine, *Shufu no Tomo* (Housewife's Friend).

During their yearlong trip, Yoshiya and Monma rendezvoused in Moscow with two writers, both women, who, unlike Yoshiya, would become part of the Japanese "feminist" literary canon: Miyamoto Yuriko[33] and Yuasa Yoshiko. In September 1928 they traveled to Paris via Moscow by train from Manchuria because, as Yoshiya explained, she "wanted to set foot in the Soviet Union, where a revolution had succeeded."[34] She and Monma made the most of a twenty-four-hour layover in Moscow where, guided by an elderly Korean man who spoke fluent Japanese, they toured the Kremlin and other sites. They then continued on to Paris for an extended stay, and in the summer of 1929 met up again with Miyamoto and Yuasa before heading for the United States. Their writer friends returned to the Soviet Union.

Miyamoto had been living in Moscow since October 1927 with Yuasa, a journalist and scholar of Russian literature. There, Yoshiya first met Yuasa; the two women later became fairly close friends, meeting at coffee shops and going to movies together back in Tokyo. The once-divorced Miyamoto and Yuasa, an "out" lesbian, lived together at that time as a couple and often visited Yoshiya's Shimoochiai home until Miyamoto decided to marry again. Yoshiya kept sympathetic tabs on her activist colleague through the mass media, for the frequent arrests of Yuasa and the eventual life sentence meted out to her husband for their activities on behalf of the Japan Communist Party made splashy headlines.[35] Yoshiya's own politics were far tamer.

CANONS AND CANNONS

Komashaku Kimi, a feminist writer and activist, subtitled her critical biography of Yoshiya, "hidden feminist." "Hidden," not because Yoshiya was silent about feminist issues—she was not—but because her feminism was expressed neither in the context of the Japanese feminist movement nor in a politicized vocabulary. Nevertheless, her ideas about female citizenship, marriage, household succession, and so forth were patently feminist and wholly radical. Yoshiya was and remains "hidden" in another sense as well. She was snubbed by her male contemporaries, particularly those who, claiming membership in the canon of "pure literature," defined themselves against "popular literature," the category in which they lumped Yoshiya's corpus. Kobayashi Hideo, eulogized today in academe as a doyen of pure literature, was among her harshest and most misogynist critics. Parroting the dominant sex-gender ideology of the time, he dismissed Yoshiya as a "child" and her work as "childish" in a 1936 review of *Women's Friendship*, of which he could "bear to read only a few pages."[36] Yoshiya had long since honed her ability to respond acerbically to such sexist condescension, and Kobayashi was not spared. Shortly after his review was published in *Bungakkai* (Literary World), she cornered him at a well-attended party hosted by the newspaper, *Tōkyō Nichinichi*, and fired a salvo of her own:

> You refer to my work as rubbish, but would major newspapers [and magazines] serialize rubbish? You assert that I write like a child, but how old must a woman be before you cease calling her a child? *Women's Friendship* was first serialized in *Fujin kurabu* (Women's Club) [a journal for adult women]. Do you regard women as children by definition? Moreover, you have no business criticizing what you do not read from beginning to end. You cannot claim to be a literary critic if all you do is pick out short segments of my work on the basis of which you then denounce it in its entirety. That is hardly proper behavior for one who claims to be a discerning and knowledgeable man![37]

According to another of her biographers, Yoshiya's awesome popularity and lesbian sexuality provoked petty jealousies and base prejudices on the part of Kobayashi and other contemporaries. It would seem that similar attitudes today continue to impede recognition of her considerable and varied literary achievements. [38] Collectively, Yoshiya's feminist (and only) biographers have sought to dismantle the defective lens through which the image of the versatile writer has been warped and to (re)position her as an outspoken critic of the patriarchal status quo whose choice of career and life-partner alike were radical acts.

Yoshiya's sexual politics impinged upon but were not contained by political theories of either the left or the right. Because she perceived all women to constitute a discrete social class on account of their oppression by men, she not only felt alienated from her socialist contemporaries who identified with the proletariat but was equally perturbed by the overt militarization of the country in the wake of the 1923 earthquake that leveled Tokyo.[39] The brutal murders by the police of the anarchist couple Ōsugi Sakae and Itō Noe shortly after the earthquake shocked Yoshiya, who had known Ōsugi since childhood and Itō through the Bluestocking Society. Nevertheless, about fifteen years later, she joined—or rather, was impelled to join—the Pen Corps (Pen butai), the popular name for the cultural propaganda unit organized in 1938 by the powerful Cabinet Information Bureau following Nazi precedent.[40] I should note in this connection that Yoshiya was not alone in playing some type of supporting role in the military regime. Most feminists at the time were heartened by the state's emphasis on maternal health as an adjunct to a "positive" eugenics policy aimed at improving the conditions of reproduction in order to increase the size and stature of the Japanese population.[41] Likewise, twenty-two of the most renowned writers of the time, with few exceptions—Miyamoto Yuriko was one—were organized by the bureau as literary war correspondents charged with supplying the Japanese public with riveting accounts of key battles and ethnographic stories about the diverse cultures contained within the growing empire. Yoshiya was assigned to the navy's branch of the Pen Corps, headed by the writer Kikuchi Kan; the army's branch was headed by litterateur Kumei Tadao and included novelist Hayashi Fumiko, all good friends of Yoshiya. The two women were the only females included in the "official" Pen Corps—other women writers traveled there under different auspices. In stark contrast to Yoshiya's avowed timidity in the face of war, Hayashi proved to be an intrepid and indefatigable correspondent, risking her life to visit battlefronts in central China.[42]

Yoshiya was perceived ambivalently by the wartime military regime. On the one hand, some of her fiction was deemed unfit for girls and women to read due to its affirmation of free will and liberalism. This was the reason given for the withdrawal from the *Ōsaka Mainichi Shinbun* of her serialized short story, "Atarashiki hi" (A new day), in 1942, although it was snapped up by the jointly published newspapers, *Tōkyō Nichinichi* and *Ōsaka Asahi Shinbun*, which had republished her perennially popular *Flower Tales* in serial form two years earlier. On the other hand, the state sought to harness her enormous popularity and celebrity for the purposes of raising the morale of weary citizens. As a member of the Naval Pen Corps and a special correspondent for *Housewife's Friend*, Yoshiya toured and sent regular dispatches from central and north China, Manchuria, Indonesia (Java), Thailand, Vietnam (Indochina), and other areas under Japanese domination. She also wrote a play, *Mura to heitai* (Village and soldiers), staged in 1939, and published in such wartime magazines as *Sensha* (Tank) and *Sukōru* (Squall).[43]

Yoshiya's months-long tour of Indonesia at the end of 1940 followed the "diplomatic" mission headed by Kobayashi Ichizō, then minister of commerce and industry, to secure petroleum and other resources from the Dutch colonial administrators. The mission ended in failure, and the Japanese successfully invaded the Dutch East Indies at the beginning of 1942, securing imperial hegemony over Southeast Asia and the South Pacific. Kobayashi was the founder of the famous all-female Takarazuka Revue and, like Yoshiya, built a dream world around passionate romance, although he colored it heterosexual. Not surprisingly, the revue staged parts of Yoshiya's *Flower Tales* in 1926, from which time onward she maintained a close relationship with Kobayashi until his death in 1957 and remained a loyal "Takarazuka" fan.[44]

When not reporting from colonial outposts overseas, Yoshiya focused on her new passion for haiku, studying with Takahama Kyoshi, a renowned poet and novelist. She also oversaw the construction of a new modernist home for herself and Monma in Kamakura (now a private museum devoted to her work). Apart from her penchant for architecture, perhaps she realized that the seaside resort south of Tokyo was much safer than the metropolis, which by 1944 was undergoing heavy bombing by the Allies—and, in fact, her Tokyo home was destroyed in an air raid.

EPILOGUE: LAST BLOOM

For reasons related to the "wartime amnesia" precluding (until very recently) any critical national reflection on Japanese militarism and imperialist aggression, Yoshiya's published reports and travelogues from her tours of duty with the Pen Corps have been omitted from anthologies of her work. Relatively little is known of her wartime activities or those of her contemporaries.

After the war, Yoshiya continued to publish fiction and nonfiction prolifically. She won prestigious prizes for her writing, which defied the strict division between pure and popular literature. She was awarded the Women's Literature Prize (Joryūbungakusho) in 1951 for her short story, "Onibi" (Will-o'-the-wisp), serialized in *Fujin Kōron* (Women's Review), and the Kikuchi Kan Prize for her ambitious historical novel, *Tokugawa no fujintachi* (Tokugawa women, 1966) in November 1967. Her earlier works were republished one by one—with the exception of her wartime essays, scripts, and reports. Her novel, *Ataka-ke no hitobito* (The people of the Ataka household), serialized in the *Mainichi Shinbun* from August 1951 to February 1952, was translated into six languages.

Yoshiya began to write historical novels in the late 1960s, in part to redress the inadequate and stereotyped representation of female characters in the historical novels written by her male contemporaries, and in part to restore the images and voices of girls and women to Japanese cultural history itself. One representative example of her historical work is *Toki no koe* (The voice of the times), a "docu-novel" serialized in the *Yomiuri Shinbun* between 1964 and 1965 on the antiprostitution movement in Japan orchestrated by the Salvation Army.[45] *Tokugawa Women* and *Nyonin heike* (Heike women, 1971) are her other two major historical works. Both were serialized, and the latter was also made into a television series.

Yoshiya and Monma had moved back to Tokyo in 1950 into a newly constructed house located in Kōjimachi. Noise and pollution that accompanied the rapid and unregulated postwar growth of the city forced them back to Kamakura twelve years later in 1962, when preparations for the 1964 Olympics exacerbated the problem. Yoshiya's health took a turn for the worse a few years after the move. She had been plagued all of her life with gastrointestinal problems and in the early 1940s had suffered from gallstones. Eventually, in May 1972, she was diagnosed with metastatic colon cancer. Monma withheld the diagnosis from Yoshiya, the first time that she had ever kept anything from her partner, but the fact that Yoshiya both agreed to be hospitalized and wrote out her will suggests that she suspected the worst. The energetic maverick was finally slowed by disease. She died at home on July 11, 1973, at the age of seventy-seven, holding Monma's hand.

Only recently have several Japanese feminists resurrected Yoshiya as a prototype of the self-sufficient female ideal for late-twentieth-century Japan, and it is from their biographical studies and other primary sources that I have culled information for this essay. That a writer of Yoshiya's celebrity and prolificacy could be ignored by scholars underscores how narrowly constructed is our knowledge and understanding of Japanese cultural history, the place of girls and women in it, and their gendered and sexual practices. Yoshiya sought to write women into her nation's cultural history and to develop a new vocabulary of female agency in her fiction. It is our responsibility to write Yoshiya back into Japanese literary history and to complicate the discourse of sex, gender, and sexuality in Japan (and Japanese Studies) by rescuing her voice from the "well of loneliness."

NOTES

1. Ikeda Hiroshi, "Yoshiya Nobuko-san no seikatsu o nozoku" [Looking in on Yoshiya Nobuko's daily life], *Hanashi* 8 (1935): 212.

2. Quoted in Yoshitake Teruko, *Nyonin Yoshiya Nobuko* [The woman Yoshiya Nobuko] (Tokyo: Bungei Shunjū, 1986), 215. The postwar (1946) constitution included universal female suffrage.

3. See, for example, Yukiko Tanaka and Elizabeth Hanson, eds., *This Kind of Woman: Ten Stories by Japanese Women Writers, 1960–1976* (New York: Perigee Books, 1984); Yukiko Tanaka, ed., *To Live and To Write: Selections by Japanese Women Writers, 1913–1938* (Seattle: The Seal Press, 1987).

4. Ōtsuka Toyoko, ed., "Yoshiya Nobuko nenpu" [Yoshiya Nobuko chronology], in *Taishū bungaku taikei* [An outline of popular literature], vol. 20 (Tokyo: Kōdansha, 1972), 384–85; Yoshitake, *Nyonin Yoshiya Nobuko*, 40–81.

5. " 'Watashi' wa 'boku' e" [From (feminine) "I" to (masculine) "I"], *Ōsaka Mainichi Shinbun*, February 10, 1932.

6. Yasuda Tokutarō, "Dōseiai no rekishikan" [History of homosexuality], *Chūō Kōron* 3 (1935): 151.

7. Makoto Furukawa, "The Changing Nature of Sexuality: The Three Codes Framing Homosexuality in Modern Japan," trans. Alice Lockyer, *U.S.–Japan Women's Journal* (English Supplement) 7 (1994): 115–16.

8. Sugita Naoki, "Shōjo kageki netsu no shindan" [An analysis of the feverish interest in *shōjo* revues], *Fujin Kōron* 4 (1935): 274.

9. Tanaka, ed., *To Live and To Write*, 60.

10. For details, see Jennifer Robertson, "Dying to Tell: Sexuality and Suicide in Imperial Japan," *Signs: Journal of Women in Culture and Society* 25, no. 1 (1999): 1–36.

11. Yasuda, "Dōseiai no rekishikan," 150.

12. Yoshitake, *Nyonin Yoshiya Nobuko*, 87.

13. Ibid., 122.

14. Ōzawa Hisako,"Yoshiya Nobuko no genten to natta shōjo shosetsu" [Yoshiya Nobuko's first work of girls' fiction], *Shōjoza* 1 (1985): 25; Yoshitake, *Nyonin Yoshiya Nobuko*, 19.

15. "Den'emon e Akiko saigo no tegami" [Akiko's last letter to Den'emon], *Tōkyō Asahi Shinbun*, October 23, 1912, evening edition.

16. Yoshitake, *Nyonin Yoshiya Nobuko*, 130. The Ainu are an indigenous minority people who reside primarily in the northernmost regions of Japan. The Ainu were subjected to forced assimilation (Japanization) by the imperial state from roughly the midnineteenth century onward. Only in 1997 were they given legal recognition as a "Japanese minority" group.

17. Quoted in Yoshitake, *Nyonin Yoshiya Nobuko*, 138–39.

18. Ibid., 139–40. Monma referred to Yoshiya as *onēsama* or "older sister," a popular euphemism then and now for one half of a lesbian couple. Yoshiya called Monma by her first name, which she feminized and rendered diminutive by adding either a *ko* or *chan*, a sign of affection in this context.

19. Ibid., 189.

20. Ibid., 193.

21. Ibid., 194.

22. Ibid., 286–87. Initially, Yoshiya had adopted her brother Tadaaki's second son and his wife to serve as her successors. However, that arrangement was annulled a year later, when Yoshiya realized that the only way legally to ensure that Monma would inherit her estate was to adopt her formally.

23. See Robertson, "Dying to Tell," 19, 30.

24. Ikeda, "Yoshiya Nobuko-san no seikatsu," 214; Yoshitake, *Nyonin Yoshiya Nobuko*, 239, 220.

25. Yoshitake, *Nyonin Yoshiya Nobuko*, 40, 132.

26. Ibid., 54, 64, 132–33.

27. Hirozawa Yumi, "Iseiai chōsei to iu fuashizumu" [The fascism of compulsory heterosexuality], *Shinchihei* 6, no. 150 (1987): 67–73; Jennifer Robertson, *Takarazuka: Sexual Politics and Popular Culture in Modern Japan* (Berkeley: University of California Press, 1998), 70.

28. See Sabine Frühstück, "Managing the Truth of Sex in Imperial Japan," *Journal of Asian Studies* 59, no. 2 (2000): 332–58.

29. Ikeda, "Yoshiya Nobuko-san no seikatsu," 217; Komashaku Kimi, *Yoshiya Nobuko—kakure fueminisuto* [Yoshiya Nobuko—hidden feminist] (Tokyo: Riburopōto, 1994), 119–26; Yoshitake, *Nyonin Yoshiya Nobuko*, 54, 63, 109. "Positive eugenics" refers to the improvement of the conditions of reproduction, including maternal health, as a way of creating a "superior" population.

30. Yoshitake, *Nyonin Yoshiya Nobuko*, 183.

31. Yoshiya Nobuko, "Dannasama muyō" [A husband is unnecessary], *Kaizō* 1 (1931): 128–29.

32. Quoted in Yoshitake, *Nyonin Yoshiya Nobuko*, 203–4.

33. At that time she was known by her family name, Chūjō; she married Miyamoto Kenji in 1932.

34. Yoshiya Nobuko, *Jidenteki joryū bundanshi* [An autobiographical history of women writers] (Tokyo: Chūō Kōronsha, 1977), 75. The constituent chapters were originally serialized in a variety of journals from 1962 to 1966.

35. Hirozawa, "Iseiai chōsei," 69.

36. Quoted in Yoshitake, *Nyonin Yoshiya Nobuko*, 252.

37. Ibid.

38. Tanabe Seiko, "Kaisetsu" [Commentary], in Yoshitake, *Nyonin Yoshiya Nobuko*, 321.

39. After the devastating Tokyo earthquake of 1923, Yoshiya and Monma decided to spend a year in Nagasaki, where they befriended an English nun from whom they took English lessons. Yoshiya also continued to attend church on Sundays, a ritual since her days at the YWCA.

40. Komashaku, *Yoshiya Nobuko—kakure fueminisuto*, 272; Sakuramoto Tomio, *Bunkajintachi no daitōa sensō—PK butai ga yuku* [The intelligentsia's Greater East Asia War—the PK Corps advances] (Tokyo: Aoki Shoten, 1993), 11–16, 33, 40.

41. See Sumiko Ostubo, "Feminist Maternal Eugenics in Wartime Japan," *U.S.–Japan Women's Journal* (English Supplement) 17 (1999): 39–76; Jennifer Robertson, "Japan's First Cyborg? Miss Nippon, Eugenics, and Wartime Technologies of Beauty, Body, and Blood," *Body & Society* 7, no. 1 (2001).

42. Yoshiya, *Jidenteki joryū bundanshi*, 55–61; Sakuramoto, *Bunkajintachi*, 21.

43. Komashaku, *Yoshiya Nobuko—kakure fueminisuto*, 272–73; Yoshitake, *Nyonin Yoshiya Nobuko*, 255; Ōtsuka, "Yoshiya Nobuko nenpu," 836–37; Ōzasa Yoshio, *Nihon gendai engekishi, Shōwa senchūhen* [History of modern Japanese theater, Shōwa wartime], vol. 2 (Tokyo: Hakusuisha, 1994), 586–87. These works include "Utsukushii nekutai" [Beautiful necktie, August 1940] and "Genchihōkoku: ran'in" [Frontline report: Dutch Indonesia, May 1941], respectively.

44. Yoshiya Nobuko, *Watashi no mita hito* [People I have observed] (Tokyo: Asahi Shinbunsha, 1963), 27–30; see Robertson, *Takarazuka*, for a history and analysis of

the "Takarazuka Revue." Revue fans were also readers of *shōjo* fiction. There was and is much overlap between the two media.

45. Yoshitake, *Nyonin Yoshiya Nobuko*, 293–94, 288; Komashaku, *Yoshiya Nobuko— kakure fueminisuto*, 242.

CHAPTER 10

Takahashi Masao

Flexible Marxist

LAURA HEIN

Even before the death of Emperor Meiji in 1912, the introduction of radical and universal doctrines that seemed to threaten the vaunted particularity of the Japanese state had upped the ante on political discourse. We have seen how Ishizaka Shōkō and Jahana Noboru tried to put the ideals of the People's Rights movement into practice. By the early twentieth century, anarchism, nihilism, socialism, and communism had been defined as dangerous thought and censored under the Peace Preservation Law. During the short reign of Emperor Taishō (1912–1926), parliamentary democracy gained a brief upper hand in government, starting in 1918 when the party politician Hara Takashi became prime minister. Hara and his successors can be considered liberals only in contrast to the few remaining genrō, *the elder statesmen whose achievements in building modern institutions led them to take a proprietary attitude toward the government. No prime minister saw any reason to deplore anarchist Ōsugi Sakae's murder by the police following the great Kanto earthquake of 1923 or that of his six-year-old nephew.*

Despite government repression and police brutality, the so-called dangerous thoughts attracted bright young men and women who saw in them solutions for the social ills plain to them. Takahashi Masao's intellectual biography dramatizes the appeal of socialist thought for a highly educated economist whose research and experience led him to perceive all too many weaknesses in capitalism and the state systems that supported it.

Laura Hein is associate professor of Japanese history at Northwestern University. She is the author of Fueling Growth: The Energy Revolution and Economic Policy in Postwar Japan *(1990) and coeditor of* Living with the Bomb: American and Japanese Cultural Conflicts in the Nuclear Age *(1997) and* Censoring History: Citizenship and Memory in Japan, Germany, and the United States *(2000).*

Takahashi's Masao's early life exemplifies the opportunities for a small number of very bright poor boys to rise within the meritocratic educational system, with the benevolence of an early patron. He was born in 1901 in the provincial capital of Sendai, the youngest of six children. His

175

father was a mail carrier whose greatest pleasure was watching his children eat; the older man knew that providing the basic necessities for his children was both precious and uncertain. Young Takahashi was at the top of his class, but his family could not afford to educate him beyond elementary school. At that time, about 15 percent of boys his age attended middle school, the gateway to all white-collar jobs. Takahashi was only able to continue his education because a wealthy neighbor offered to pay for his middle school. The neighbor also encouraged him to think big; when Takahashi wanted to go to a vocational school, he urged him to try an academic one, since he could always move down to vocational or military officer training if the academic track proved too difficult.

This was his great opportunity. Takahashi went to a local missionary-run middle school where he learned mathematics and English. In 1919 that school awarded him a scholarship to the Number 2 National Higher School, also in Sendai, where he majored in economics so that he would soon be able to send money home to his family. He continued in English and also studied German, French, mathematics, and political science. He entered the Economics Department of Tokyo Imperial University in 1922. At that time, less than 1 percent of Japanese boys (and only a handful of girls) went to higher school, let alone college. Takahashi also worked part-time from the age of ten, first selling caramels in a movie theater (and carrying clandestine letters from male to female high-school students) and then delivering daily newspapers at 4 A.M. In later years, those quiet morning hours became his writing time.

Takahashi also developed an early interest in politics. In 1920 or 1921 he went to hear the famous anarchist, Ōsugi Sakae, who never showed up. He had been arrested at the train station, but the audience of two hundred was kept by the police, who took their names before they could leave the room. Takahashi and his fellow student Okuda Shinzō (who remained a lifelong friend) knew that if their presence were made public, they would be expelled from higher school. Desperate, they went that night to the house of the provincial police chief to beg him not to tell their school. He agreed, warning them not to go to such meetings again but to study hard, and recounted terrifying tales of dangerous leftists. The police chief, who of course had just had Ōsugi arrested simply to prevent him from giving a speech, took a far more paternalistic attitude with the two young men from his own town. That incident captures not only the political repression of the supposedly liberal Taishō era but also how vital personal relations were in prewar Japan; the two students had approached the police chief in his home at night and made a personal appeal—which worked. When the Tokyo police murdered Ōsugi three years later, Takahashi undoubtedly thought about that incident again, with a renewed sense of both outrage and relief at his own good luck.

In college, Takahashi studied French economics and also statistics, because he planned to work in an insurance company or a bank. As he approached graduation, however, he decided to go to graduate school instead. He seems to have been motivated by a combination of intellectual and political curiosity. I suspect that the insurance company seemed deadly dull and that Takahashi wanted the opportunity to think more carefully about the political and economic ideas that had begun to excite him. This was the second decision that changed his life, allowing him both an academic and a political career rather than the life of a middle-class, white-collar "salary man." Graduate school was also where he discovered Marxism.

Why did Takahashi find Marxism so attractive? First, he was originally drawn to Marxism not for the theory but because he wanted his work to directly benefit poor people like his own family. He looked for intellectually coherent and immediately practical answers to the social problems he saw in front of him. As a young man, Takahashi thought the government was shockingly inadequate because it did little to alleviate grinding poverty in the poorer parts of Japan, including his native Tōhoku. When he was a middle-school student, Takahashi had seen soldiers fire on people protesting the sudden increase in the price of rice. (He ran away so fast that he lost one of his wooden sandals.) Surely, it was wrong for the government to allow its people to starve and then respond to their desperate pleas with bullets. Takahashi saw political activism as one way to change the world for the better, and scholarship as another, related one. He felt a strong sense of social responsibility, in part because of his own access to rare higher education. He wanted to improve life for his fellow citizens and make a difference in the world rather than simply build security for himself.

Second, he was part of a substantial group of idealistic and socially concerned young men and (fewer) women, both in the university and outside it. These were his friends. They drank coffee and argued about the world together, went to movies and concerts, and dropped by one another's homes. The elite contacts he made in middle school, higher school, and college remained crucial throughout his life, helping him find jobs and gain influence at an extraordinary variety of levels. The graduate student network was also the main route by which he discovered illegal Marxist writings. There was enormous interest in revolutionary social theory in all the elite educational institutions in Japan in the years after World War I. As one of Takahashi's closest friends, Arisawa Hiromi, put it, "At the very least there was a feeling that the old ways of doing things would not suffice for the future and that economics had to change too to be useful in that new society. Marxism was very popular. . . . I think we were moved by the feeling that we as scholars had to get to the bottom of analyzing what capitalist economics is in order to explain the conditions of society."[1] Political commitment was the thread binding Takahashi's social set together. They discussed the nature of Japanese capitalism almost every day.

Third, this was an international phenomenon. All over the world in the 1920s and 1930s, young people seriously studied and engaged Marxism. Takahashi and his friends knew that—they read socialist works in English, French, and German, and a few even learned Russian—and thought of themselves as part of a global intellectual community. They prized their membership in that community highly and saw modern social science as a tool for all people, not an alien Western concept. Throughout his life, Takahashi remained convinced that the world outside Japan's borders provided valuable lessons—both positive and negative—for the nation's future development. His contribution, as he saw it, always included searching out those lessons and interpreting them for his countrymen.

Moreover, Takahashi and his friends were inspired by the Marxist vision of society itself. They liked Marxism's scientific, modern, and rational qualities because they allowed critical distancing from the reigning concept of Japanese society and state—the concept of an organic, mystical entity captured in the figure of the emperor, who was not only both the supreme religious and political leader but also the embodiment of the state itself and the metaphorical father of all ethnic Japanese. Takahashi thought of "science" as a philosophy of life rather than just a discrete body of knowledge about the physical world. He explained this concept as follows: " 'Scientific' means, indirectly, 'things as they are' (*ari no mama*)." But, he went on, humans try to visualize their ideal of heaven, and scientific research is one kind of effort toward that goal. All attempts to define the limits of human existence, understand the mechanisms governing social change, and extend human thinking are "scientific" in this view.[2]

Takahashi was also moved by the idea that all societies pass through the same stages toward a universal future, precisely the aspect of Marxism that is most criticized today. Unlike many other international academic theories popular at the time, Marxists thought of Japan as fundamentally like European societies rather than intrinsically inferior on the basis of race, climate, history, or some other attribute. In other words, Marxism's international egalitarianism made it valuable to Japanese critics. Takahashi was thrilled by the idea that Japan's working class and its society could "advance along the path of history," like all other societies.[3]

Takahashi and his friends also found attractive Marxism's focus on society as a unit rather than on the individual, the emphasis on combating poverty and social injustice, and, of course, the promise that the future would be fairer. Social problems, particularly those of class-based economic inequality and poverty, seemed to Takahashi the crucial issue around which he should structure his life's work. Class struggle seemed to him a reasonable response to the huge gap between daily life for rich and poor in prewar Japan. Like his friends, he approached this as a moral imperative as much as a technical one and gave commitment and passion to this task for many decades. Marxism appealed to Takahashi and his friends precisely because it allowed them to combine passionate engagement with methodological rules. Rather than openly champion morality, these men sought to introduce technocratic, universalistic, and rationalist qualities to public life in Japan. They thought that establishing that base would lead directly to social and political improvement. In the end, this faith in method was a utopian assumption, but one they shared with technocrats of their generation everywhere around the globe.

Most thoughtful young Japanese of the 1920s and 1930s rejected the egoism and pursuit of individual profit at the heart of capitalism, which seemed to them incapable of leading to the kind of society where the weak were protected by the strong. They took that critique in two very different directions. The majority of the Japanese people, including government leaders, gravitated toward a far more aggressive variety of nationalism over the course of the 1930s and became convinced that solutions to the country's problems lay in resistance to the decadent West, military conquest of China, national spiritual renewal, and tighter ideological control at home.

To Takahashi, that response was both intellectually and emotionally unattractive. His was, however, the minority view. Many nationalists thought that the Marxists were a grave danger to Japan (because they believed that simply by talking about class conflict, the Marxists would create it) and persecuted them. They, too, were part of an international trend; governments across the globe panicked when confronted by domestic socialists in the years after the 1917 Bolshevik Revolution in Russia. That harsh response only strengthened the Marxists' belief that the government was a tool of the capitalists and did not serve the best interests of the people.

Although all of them engaged in illegal acts, neither Takahashi nor any of his closest friends joined the Japan Communist Party (JCP). Takahashi explained why in terms that reflect his social-scientific bent. He was immensely attracted to the ideas and ideals of the JCP but always a bit suspicious of the men in action. His main reservation was based on his sense that they were insufficiently rational. As he put it, "Too much support, trust, hate, revulsion, etc. was expressed—they were too emotional to be neutral."[4] He did join the Rōnō-ha in 1928, a study and policy group that developed and published theories about the nature of Japanese capitalism and advised working-class activists on strategies to gain political and economic power. Direct political activity of that kind was defined as illegal under the 1925 Peace Preservation Law. Some of the founding members of the group had been JCP members previously, but had left the party and its own study/policy group in December 1927.

In fact, it was only barely legal—and increasingly dangerous—to study Marxist theory openly. Takahashi had to work on something else if he hoped to find a job after he graduated. He picked Keynesian economics for that reason, and published a book on John Maynard Keynes's *Treatise on Money* in 1936. "My strategy from then was to pretend (*neko o kaburu*) as much as possible so that I could study overseas. . . . It was very good for me. The big event in non-Marxist economics then was the Keynesian revolution."[5] That plan worked. Normally, a scholar with Takahashi's credentials would have become a professor at Tokyo Imperial University after graduate school, but he was denied a post because of his interest in Marxism. In 1928 he accepted a job at Kyūshū University arranged by Minobe Tatsukichi (himself a famous legal scholar), who was the father of Takahashi's good friend and fellow graduate student, Minobe Ryōkichi. Thus, partly to get and keep a job, Takahashi learned what would soon become the most important scholarship of his era. His need to hide his true research interests ironically helped stretch him intellectually and pushed him to approach Marxism as one of a number of legitimate and useful bodies of work, rather than to accept it uncritically.

Takahashi and his friends became famous for their ability to mix economic approaches eclectically when they pursued both economic theory and economic policy in the post–World War II era. They borrowed from neoclassical, Keynesian, and Marxist traditions throughout their careers. They also moved easily between international theory and local empirical data, convinced that both investigations were necessary. This eclecticism is their proudest legacy. Thus, it is instructive to reflect on the fact that they originally engaged in this dual exploration in order to find work and stay out of prison. Their choices in their course of study were shaped by official anxiety about "dangerous thought" as much as by their own intellectual concerns. After the war, they were able to put together ideas and policies from a number of intellectual traditions, creating what we think of today as the Japanese economic system. They retained much of the Marxist framework although, eventually, the doctrinaire quality of Marxist political movements and the inability of Marxist theory to directly explain individual economic behavior became more disturbing to them.

The opportunity to go overseas was highly prized by these men and was the source of much of their social and intellectual prestige as well as of their professional ideas. Travel abroad was a rare privilege because it was terribly expensive, although most of the top students at elite schools won government scholarships. Often, they went abroad as graduate students or, more commonly, early on as professors. They usually went for two years, studied at a European or American university, bought trunkloads of books, improved their language skills, and learned first-hand about the world beyond Japan's shores, particularly the new developments in their chosen discipline. These scholars used the knowledge and materials gathered on their trips for decades to come, both for their own work and for training students. Most of them traveled extensively during their years abroad, often putting in at several Asian ports along the route west and then returning from Europe via the United States. Once ensconced in Europe, they also went to plays, museums, and concerts, hiked in the Alps, and enjoyed the cafés and beer halls, too. The friendships and intellectual connections they made in places such as Berlin and London often endured for decades. The travelers also attended the sort of political events that were banned or dangerous in Japan: congresses of communists, socialists, and anarchists, labor union meetings, May Day parades and demonstrations, and speeches by recent visitors to the young Soviet Union, for example. Even more than most people, these student-scholars associated travel with intellectual stimulation and forbidden ideas. Indeed, the men who went to Europe between the end of World War I and 1932 found the freer political atmosphere there tremendously exciting. The degree of tolerance in Weimar Germany, the main destination of Japanese scholars in the 1920s, far outpaced Japan even in the heyday of "Taisho democracy."

Takahashi won a government scholarship to study in Europe in 1936, a testimony to his great skill at keeping his illegal activities hidden from the authorities. He was deeply affected by his trip, but not in the ways he had anticipated. By the time he arrived, repression against leftists and Jews was well under way—and not just in Germany. Wherever he went—and Takahashi managed to see an extraordinarily large portion of Europe—his expectations that European society was far more hospitable, democratic, and protosocialist than his own were dashed. Moreover, to his astonishment, the problems of poverty and oppressive class relations were just as evident in Europe as in Japan. Far from serving as the model-ideal as it had for earlier visitors, Europe now seemed a dark warning of the dangers of fascism.

Takahashi made Paris his base of operations. He had one good friend there, Etienne Dennery, a demographer who had visited Tokyo Imperial University in 1925 or 1926 while Takahashi was a graduate student. The two men had traveled around Japan together, walking through little villages, trading stories, and becoming friends. In 1936, Dennery, who was Jewish, housed Takahashi in the apartment of another academic who had already emigrated. He told Takahashi, "Masao, I am letting you stay here because you are not an anti-Semite." The open anti-Semitism throughout France shocked Takahashi. Dennery also urged Takahashi to think seriously about the possibility that he might be arrested himself when he returned to Japan. And, of course, the socialists and labor leaders Takahashi traveled to see increasingly reported on episodes of intimidation, violence, and arrest.

Unlike a decade earlier, when Germany had seemed the best model for leftist Japanese, Takahashi found 1937 Germany creepy. He visited a left-wing bookstore in Berlin where his friends had gone previously, but he found the shop much changed. Its window sported a huge sign identifying it as a Jewish business, and the contents were only the kinds of books that could be sold in Tokyo. Shortly thereafter it closed. As Takahashi described Germany, "The provincial cities were full of Hitler posters—as though they'd been blown in by a rainstorm. 'Heil Hitler' had replaced 'guten-morgen,' 'guten tag,' and 'auf wiedersehen.' College professors began and ended their lectures with 'Heil Hitler.' " Many of the Germans he spoke to defended Hitler and argued that democratic rules were unnecessary, making Takahashi very uneasy. Even worse, many of the Japanese he met in Germany agreed. Takahashi attended a public lecture on racial science where the professor explained to his audience that the Aryans were the purest of races and the Jews the most debased. Takahashi thought it was pretty far-fetched, but a Japanese colleague explained to him that not only Germans were Aryans but that Japanese enjoyed that status, too. Takahashi wrote: "At that moment I knew that the definition of race was political rather than scientific."[6] Small wonder that he associated perversion of knowledge with right-wing thought.

Europe forced Takahashi to rethink his assumptions in other ways as well. He spent several days with a friend at his ancestral home in the French countryside where the local farmers behaved with traditional deference, something he had thought was peculiar to "semifeudal" Japan. He was also deeply shocked by the poverty he saw in Glasgow, "the nerve center of the great British Empire." To his horror, people really were living on porridge. Then, in Ireland, he met people who were even poorer than the Japanese emigrants to Manchuria, his previously unchallenged standard of abject poverty.[7]

After the Great Depression spread around the globe in the early 1930s, Takahashi became convinced not only that capitalism was a central part of the problem but also that it was in decline. In this he was not alone. When he went overseas, he still thought in terms of Japanese deviance from the European norm of economic and political development. His observations, however, left him far less convinced that Europe was a better model. In other words, while the experience confirmed both Takahashi's underlying moral vision and his belief that societies should be based on fair, rational, and scientific principles, it also provided a platform from which he could critique the West as well as Japan.

This trip also marked Takahashi's first starting to think of the USSR as anything other than a workers' paradise. Although he had long thought the Soviets were wrong about Japan and had made a serious error in their instructions to Japanese communists, it had never occurred to him that there were problems within the socialist country itself. While traveling in Europe he heard disturbing stories about the Soviet Union and then he read Leon Trotsky's *Revolution Betrayed*, a critique of the Soviet Union and Lenin from within a Marxist framework. As he put it, "If it hadn't been for encountering Trotsky, today I might be like [doctrinaire Japanese Marxist] Sakisaka—the Sakisaka who still maintains that the USSR leads the world in both standards of living and democracy. As always, fortune has smiled on me."[8]

In short, Takahashi's experience overseas was a two-year exercise in instilling skepticism. He saw the clay feet of both the great giants of capitalism and socialism. Of course, the next few years would raise doubts in all quarters that Europe in general or either Germany or the Soviet Union in particular was a great model to emulate. But Takahashi and the other Japanese political scholars who traveled to Europe in the mid-1930s learned this lesson earlier and more intimately than most.

At the same time, opportunities for political expression were shrinking in Japan, just as in Europe. Most of Takahashi's close friends had been arrested while he was overseas and charged with advocating the overthrow of the state (*kokutai*) and the system of private property and conspiring "to advise the proletarian movement, enlarge the Rōnō-ha, and activate communism." Takahashi himself was arrested on the dock when he arrived at Yokohama, although the police allowed him to eat lunch with his waiting mother before they locked him up.[9]

At his pretrial hearing, Takahashi argued that the state could not charge him with being anticapitalist, given that it had itself just passed the National Mobilization Law, making all private property rights subordinate to the state. That was socialism, was it not? Takahashi's argument shows the common logical thread between prewar orthodoxy and Marxism. The judge was not impressed by his cleverness, however, and Takahashi went to jail for his ideas.

He spent two years in prison, at first in preventive detention while under investigation for contravening the Peace Preservation Law. Takahashi's treatment during his arrest and incarceration was deeply inconsistent. He was alternately treated with enormous deference and obvious contempt, and occasionally with surreal contradictions. The police wanted a confession from him. First, they allowed him neither soap nor a razor, and he gradually "began to look more and more like a criminal." Then they pressured him to write about illegal acts committed by others. At other times, the police allowed him up to the second floor office, fed him tasty meals, let him see his family, and work. He ghost-wrote reports for them. But relations with the police gradually worsened as Takahashi failed to confess.

Then, "One day, what I had been waiting for finally came." The police beat him up and warned him that the beatings would get worse until he confessed. They also told him (probably falsely) that all the other Rōnō-ha people had implicated him already. He asked to see those confessions "because it might help me remember" and was horrified to find out how much was recorded there—what he had written, which pen name he had used, where they had met, what post offices they usually used, everything. In the end, he admitted to writing the article he thought was least incriminating. It argued that the Manchurian conquest was harmful both to the national economy and the domestic standard of living. That was what the police wanted. They could call it a confession, clear their books, charge him, and send him off to Sugamo prison.[10]

Before he left for Sugamo, the police at his first jail, including the Special Higher Police, threw a party for him, partly to apologize for "that time" they beat him up and partly to thank him for writing their reports to headquarters, which had won them a commendation. Then, in 1940, Takahashi was found guilty and given a two-year suspended sentence in addition to time already served. He was the only Rōnō-ha member to get a suspended sentence. Takahashi knew he was lucky; at least two of his friends died after rough treatment at the hands of the law.

After he was released from prison, the National Police Agency briefly considered hiring him—the new bureaucratization meant they needed an economist. In the end, they decided it would be inappropriate to hire a Peace Preservation Law violator. Takahashi was relieved as he also had begun to think it would be inappropriate for him to take such work. Instead, his friend Arisawa Hiromi (himself out on bail at the time) turned down an offer in Shanghai and recommended Takahashi, who took the job as reporter with the *Tairiku Shinpōsha*, a newspaper affiliated with the army. Takahashi thought of those years as his second opportunity to study abroad. His job was not very taxing, and he spent most of his time studying Chinese and traveling around the country observing. He reports that he was "bothered by the fact that I could not say I was not an imperialist," but his only attempt at protest was an article for his newspaper suggesting that taking food from peasants rather than buying it was not the way to win Chinese hearts. That small gesture earned him a threatening visit from a military police officer. Takahashi also spent time with a number of his Chinese former students from Kyūshū University, who urged him to return to Japan when "the scent of defeat grew stronger." He did so in January 1945.

Then the war ended, and suddenly Takahashi's fortunes changed for the better. His antimilitary reputation, strong foreign language skills, and, above all, his economics training gave him great credibility with the Occupation Government (known as SCAP). Takahashi and his friends were the future of the country as far as the Occupation economists and technocrats were concerned. At the same time, SCAP monitored their political activities, for example, investigating Takahashi's connections to the Communist Party in August 1947. Like many other Japanese who had been persecuted for their ideas, Takahashi passionately supported the new protections on speech, publication, and assembly that were part of the postwar constitution as well as the new legal protection against torture and inhumane prison conditions.

His main efforts as an economist went toward building an effective statistics infrastructure for Japan, a task that he saw as leading to the same goal as his political efforts. He put his greatest faith in institutionalizing rational thought and reliable data, which elements had been completely lacking in national policy during the war. Takahashi was appalled by the wartime regime's reliance on "the Japanese spirit" and "the national essence" to overcome all obstacles.

Takahashi turned down the opportunity to work for the government in the new economic planning bureau, however. Together with his closest friends, he simply could not bring himself to trust the political and bureaucratic leaders, much to the frustration of his allies within the government. One bureaucrat who had been arrested during the war and was active in economic reconstruction afterward, Wada Hirō, was extremely harsh in his assessment of Takahashi, attributing his refusal to cowardice and terming it "the betrayal of the citizens at large."[11] Although Takahashi never admitted it publicly, I think he regretted that hesitation in later years. Certainly, he never again had the opportunity to participate in government at so high a level. Instead, he went back to the University of Kyūshū to resume his teaching career and specialized in the "mixed" capitalist and socialist economy of Yugoslavia. His politics mirrored his economic interests. He was a consistent advocate for strategies that bridged the Cold War divide and charted territory independent of both Cold War superpowers.

In the immediate postwar years, Takahashi had assumed that socialism was not only desirable but also inevitable in Japan. Many Europeans also thought at this juncture that a transition to socialism was the dominant trend of the times. Takahashi was an active member of the newly legal Japan Socialist Party and closely followed European developments, such as the economic policies of the British Labour Party. More generally, the two systems of capitalism and socialism seemed to be converging everywhere after the war. For example, all the major capitalist countries expanded their social welfare programs at the insistence of their citizens, who had given so much to the war effort.

Takahashi described his life just after the war as extremely busy, in a time when "the 'postwar democracy' boom flowered together with postwar inflation. Labor unions and democracy circles sprouted like bamboo shoots after the rain. I went everywhere I was asked." He gave a series of public lectures on politics and economics for workers, which was then published as *Talks on Socialism* (*Shakaishugi no hanashi*) in June 1946 and sold unexpectedly well. Ironically, the royalties from that critique of capitalism enabled him to buy land, build a house, and become a property owner for the first time in his life. Takahashi at last felt physically and financially secure enough to marry Nishimura Yoshiko in 1947. Their only child, Masako, was born in 1950, when Takahashi was forty-nine years old.

In his 1946 book, Takahashi explained that socialism was not yet fully distinguishable from capitalism in terms of its capacity to provide a livelihood for all citizens. Here he saw the transition as likely to be peaceful. He explained that some capitalist trends were positive harbingers of socialism—such as the development of science and technology—although he believed that these areas would expand far faster when freed from the "stingy limits" imposed by the desire of capitalists to profit from their scientific and technological inventions. He simply referred to the negative aspects without describing them and commented that these would gradually disappear. Interestingly for us now, Takahashi saw the dynamics of capitalist competition itself as a positive force, driving the economy toward socialism. As he explained it in a later essay, "Free capitalism pushes capitalists to make products better and cheaper and leads to technological improvement and the development of productive power." So, although he rejected the idea of unregulated capitalism, he recognized and accepted the idea that the market could serve as an important mechanism for economic development and technological innovation. He also saw that as an appropriate strategy to pursue.[12]

The logic of that argument would mean a tolerant attitude toward capitalists, who, through no desire of their own, were hastening the arrival of socialism with every new efficiency they introduced. Yet, the Afterword to *Talks on Socialism* began with a stern warning that people who stood in the way of this trend had to be stopped—jailed and, if necessary, executed. Although the entire essay was couched in the language of reason and pedagogy, in this section, Takahashi explicitly rejected these strategies as useless with these "saboteurs of socialism, who cannot forget the [capitalist] past." It is a disturbingly bloodthirsty moment, and one rarely repeated in his later writings.

Takahashi's 1947 book, *Politics and Economics at a Turning Point* (*Tenkeiki no seiji to keizai*), was a call to political engagement as well. After defining state authority, he argued that political power is often naturalized, obscuring the methods by which some people gain and retain it. Then, "The dominant class is happy when people say 'politics is bad, or boring, or dirty,' or that honorable people don't get involved in it." Rather, Takahashi argued, if serious people want to change society, they must get involved in politics. He minimized the difference between democracy and socialism. For him, democrats emphasized the crucial argument that there should be no discrimination based on differences between the sexes, or religion, or language, nor should there be political or legal discrimination. Ending economic injustice was, he argued, but a small step from there. Socialism was for him "democracy in action."[13]

By 1949, Takahashi had worked out a calmer position on violence and class struggle. Typically, he presented this as an historical choice, drawing on Europe for both his exemplary and his cautionary tales. He argued that the more fully developed the most admirable political values of capitalism, then the more peaceful would be the inevitable transition to socialism. He presented Great Britain as the best example of a peaceful transition, noting that the Labour Party had won power through the democratic process and then had "decided on their own to quit capitalism and adopt socialism. . . . There, the class that loses political power in an election, abides by the election results." Thus, the fact that there were no arrests or imprisonment of opponents reflected the high development of capitalism. By contrast, Lenin's fledgling government in 1917 feared its internal and external opponents and sacrificed "bourgeois freedoms" in the name of security, thus revealing the weakness of the new government's position. "In Britain, the ruling class's power and self-confidence is great so they don't feel the need to step outside the framework of democracy—[the British Labour leaders] are strong in a way that Russia's rulers are not."

Takahashi thought the dynamic power of capitalism itself could be the mechanism for the shift to socialism because the "better" capitalists would gradually overpower the inferior ones, then develop monopolies and cartels. Gradually, there would be fewer and fewer people committed to capitalism as a system, as all the ruined entrepreneurs took jobs as wageworkers in the sprawling conglomerates of the successful capitalists. If society is sufficiently democratic, when the workers begin to desire socialism, they can use the parliamentary process to achieve it.[14]

The true subject of this passage, of course, was the choice facing the Japanese: a peaceful or a violent transition to socialism. Takahashi argued here and consistently thereafter that the exercise of democratic freedoms and civil rights was the most important way to achieve peaceful change. He appealed to Japanese vanity about its level of civilization. Only the most modern and highly developed nations, he claimed, are able to pull off both peace and socialism. He also reminded them of the absence of political freedom in Japan before defeat. By making socialist thought illegal and jailing laborers who sought improved working conditions, the presurrender state guaranteed that determined critics would attempt to disrupt the social order by force, thus creating the violent opposition they most feared.

Takahashi assumed that socialism, that is, state control of basic industries, would powerfully transform the economy. Essentially, it would remove most barriers to human and economic potential, "leaving only the limits of technology and science." By liberating industrial operations from the need to generate capitalist profits, those state enterprises would regenerate the whole economy in ways that liberated the technological potential of things and the creative potential of humans. He assumed that the inefficiencies of capitalist industrial production and the likely efficiencies of state-led production were so great that replacing one with the other would transform the economic structure and, eventually, social, political, and cultural life as well. This was a fantasy of the power of rationality imagined as the rationalization of production, the reordering of distribution networks, the liberation of human minds, and the humanizing of society, because "the state takes on responsibility for supporting jobs and livelihoods for all individuals. So both materially and spiritually, life under socialism is very different from life under capitalism."[15] Reading this fifty years later, I am most struck by the scale of the transformation he imagined. He thought that selfish profit-taking, corruption, and mismanagement were so great that eliminating them would transform the economy. He also saw them as distorting the natural workings of a system that, when allowed to revert to its own logic, would be efficient and rational. He was wrong, but he shared this view with many others around the world in the years immediately after World War II.

This argument was also directed at the Japan Socialist Party, which by that time was already mired in the fierce factional fighting that would hobble it for the next half-century. As he explained, "If the Socialist Party is to play a leadership role in bringing about socialism, then there must be freedom for criticism and debate within the party." Without that freedom, several key developments could not take place: democratic traditions, a democratic relationship between the party and the working class, and democratic practices within working-class organizations. "That is, if there is insufficient belief in the value of the individual, then the dictatorship of the proletariat, which is necessary for the development of the realization of socialism, will be stuck at the level of the dictatorship of the party or of splits and factions within the party." In his view, these were fearsome developments that would lead to "bureaucratism, the principle of control by insiders, privileges according to one's position, opportunism, power by seniority, selfishness, essentialism, or a feudalistic socialism—something even worse than a feudalistic capitalism."[16] Takahashi remained close to the Japan Socialist Party but was disillusioned by the factional infighting, embarrassing scandals, and political maneuvering of the party activists.

At the same time, Takahashi saw himself as a scholar and teacher first and a political activist second. He clearly believed that the main contribution he could make to the socialist revolution was in training the intellect of as many Japanese citizens as possible. He saw his role as fundamentally that of an educator, and he assumed that if only enough people had a firm grounding in rational thought and could "make the connections between work and ideas and politics, we can make democracy and socialism in Japan." He argued in another essay that education should teach people to question their society in fundamental ways. Presurrender education in Japan, by contrast, operated to stop knowledge in the sense of questioning the status quo; and that, Takahashi argued, explained why so many student groups were seen as a "thought problem." Again and again, throughout his life, he defined critical thinking as his contribution to political life in postwar Japan.

In the 1947 book, Takahashi had extended his ideas about socialism as a political stance. He presented himself as a public intellectual, striving for a more open debate—offering his ideas in a quest to extend knowledge and pursue study for its own sake as well as exercising the new freedom of inquiry in order to keep alive the right to do so. This stance became an enduring feature of his work, and nearly all of his postwar books begin with the comment that his intended audience is young people, both students and workers, and his goal is to stimulate debate and encourage people to think for themselves as much as it is to persuade them. Putting the same idea another way, he defined his goal as helping to make clear not only the meaning of "socialism" but also that of "democracy" for Japan. He firmly believed that the great majority of the Japanese people had been irresponsible in letting fascists take over in the 1930s. Only by actively striving for economic and political participation could they prevent disaster from striking twice.

His goal was to raise the cultural and intellectual level of the working masses up to that of his own, which he saw as the prerequisite to socialism. This is a patronizing stance, which comes through very clearly in the early postwar essays, but it also describes his own successful trajectory from poor Tōhoku boy to esteemed professor at a national university. Academic learning and cultural literacy had changed his life; it is reasonable that he believed they would change power relations at larger social levels as well. He wrote approvingly of smart workers and farmers who at the same time continued their studies and engaged in political work, giving the example of one young "Red" who organized both an agricultural cooperative and a farmers' union.[17] In his vision of socialism, human productive potential—like that of the economy—would be liberated by freedom from money worries. Education was the route by which people could express that potential: "In society today, the human capital of bright but poor youths is wasted. Under socialism it will be completely different. The level of natural resources—that is, talent—will be decisive."[18]

Over the next forty years, Takahashi wrote twenty-five more books on economics and left-wing politics and countless articles. In 1962, after one of the biggest factional fights that split the JSP into two wings, he started his own journal, called *Peace Economics* (*Heiwa Keizai*), which specialized in analyzing government economic policies and offering socialist alternatives. He edited it until he was in his nineties. He retired from Kyūshū University in 1965, and in 1967 his graduate school classmate, Minobe Ryōkichi, became governor of Tokyo. Takahashi helped develop his economic policies and also acted as a liaison between Minobe's office and both the Socialist and Communist Parties for the next twelve years.

As time went on, Takahashi's politics gradually grew less revolutionary and more reformist, or, as he himself put it, by the 1970s, "We settle for 'reasonable equality' and semi-democracy and a planned system called market mechanisms of capitalism tinged with socialism. My socialism now is not of the rice riots but of human self-development."[19] His new perspective reflected several changes. First, in Takahashi's view, postwar Japan was a far more democratic and equable society than was presurrender Japan. Second, it had been very difficult to think about the limitations of socialist economics until after the war, since it was impossible to try out ideas or even read much about socialism in practice elsewhere in the world. Third, by the 1970s, Takahashi recognized that socialism was not politically achievable in Japan (at least in the near future), nor did he think violent revolution was desirable. His willingness to rethink his goals earned Takahashi the nickname "flexible Marxist" in an economics journal in 1989. That intellectual flexibility was in short supply among leftist thinkers in both pre- and postsurrender Japan.

Takahashi had articulated a dissenting tradition for twentieth-century Japan, one that remains relevant today. He died in 1995, active as a scholar and writer to the end of his life.

NOTES

1. Arisawa Hiromi, *Gakumon to shisō to ningen to: Arisawa Hiromi no Shōwa shi* (Tokyo: Tokyo Daigaku Shuppankai, 1989), 54.
2. Takahashi Masao, *Kagakuteki shakaishugi no tachiba kara* (Tokyo: Itagaki Shobō, 1948), 29–30.
3. Ibid., 20–21.
4. Takahashi Masao, *Happō yabure—Watakushi no shakaishugi* (Tokyo: TBS-Buritanika, 1980), 99–102.
5. Takahashi, *Kagakuteki shakaishugi no tachiba kara*, 12–13.
6. Takahashi Masao, *Nijū seiki no gunzō: Takahashi Masao no shōgen* (Tokyo: Daiichi Shōrin, 1989), 49.
7. Takahashi, *Happō yabure*, 167–68, 171, 182.
8. Ibid., 165–66.
9. "20-nen mae" interview with Ōuchi Hyōe, Arisawa Hiromi, Wakimura Yoshitarō, Minobe Ryōkichi, and Takahashi Masao, *Sekai* (April 1958): 117–25.
10. Takahashi, *Happō yabure*, 191–92.
11. Ōtake Keisuke, *Maboroshii no hana—Wada Hirō no seijun* (Tokyo: Rakuyū Shobō, 1981). Quotation is from Wada's diary, 402–3.
12. Takahashi, *Kagakuteki shakaishugi no tachiba kara*, 53–61.
13. Takahashi Masao, *Tenkeiki no seiji to keizai* (Tokyo: Ōdosha, 1947), 6, 44.
14. Takahashi Masao, *Shakaishugi shoron* (Tokyo: Junshindō, 1949), 23–30, 77–80.
15. Ibid., 11–12, 67–77, 95–97.
16. Ibid., 109–10.
17. Takahashi, *Tenkeiki no seiji to keizai*, 33.
18. Takahashi, *Shakaishugi shoron*, 94–96.
19. Takahashi, *Happō yabure*, 1.

SUGGESTED READINGS

Takahashi's major publications include: *Keinzu no kaseiron no kenkyū* (Research on Keynes's theory of money, 1936); *Shakaishugi no hanashi* (Talks on socialism, 1946); *Tenkeiki no seiji to keizai* (Politics and economics at a turning point, 1947); *Kagakuteki shakaishugi no tachiba kara* (From the perspective of scientific socialism, 1948); *Shakaishugi shoron* (Short text on socialism, 1949); *Marukusu to keinzu no taiwa—gendai no sekai to Nihon* (Conversations between Marx and Keynes—Contemporary Japan and the world, 1963); *Nihon keizai o dō suru ka* (What should be done about the Japanese economy? 1966); *Shakaishugi o kangaeru* (Thoughts on socialism, 1970). Details of his life come from two autobiographies: *Happō yabure—Watakushi no shakaishugi* (Wandering along—my socialism, 1980); and *Nijū seiki no gunzō: Takahashi Masao no shōgen* (The twentieth-century group: Takahashi Masao's account, 1989). Also see Arisawa Hiromi, *Gakumon to shisō to ningen to: Arisawa Hiromi no Shōwa shi* (Scholarship, ideas, and people: Arisawa Hiromi's Shōwa history, 1989); and "20-nen mae" interview with Ōuchi Hyōe, Arisawa Hiromi, Wakimura Yoshitarō, Minobe Ryōkichi, and Takahashi Masao, *Sekai* (April 1958).

For prewar education, see Byron Marshall, *Learning to Be Modern: Japanese Political Discourse on Education* (1994). For Ōsugi Sakae, see *The Autobiography of Ōsugi Sakae*, most recently translated by Byron K. Marshall (1992). Prewar Marxism is discussed in Germaine Hoston, "*Ikkoku Shakai-shugi*: Sano Manabu and the Limits of Marxism as Cultural Criticism," in J. Thomas Rimer, ed., *Culture and Identity: Japanese Intellectuals during the Interwar Years* (1990); and Andrew Barshay, " 'Doubly Cruel': Marxism and the Presence of the Past in Japanese Capitalism," in Stephen Vlastos, ed., *Mirror of Modernity: Invented Traditions of Modern Japan* (1998). The Rice Riots of 1918 are examined in Michael Lewis, *Rioters and Citizens: Mass Protest in Imperial Japan* (1990). Tetsuo Najita and H. D. Harootunian, "Japanese Revolt against the West: Political and Cultural Criticism in the Twentieth Century," in *The Cambridge History of Japan*, vol. 6 (1988), explains prewar nationalist thought; see pp. 711–74. For the constant and byzantine bickering within the postwar Socialist Party, see Masumi Junnosuke, *Postwar Politics in Japan, 1945–1955*, translated by Lonny E. Carlile (1990). Wada Hirō's biography is by Ōtake Keisuke, *Maboroshii no hana—Wada Hirō no seijun* (1981). For the Occupation period generally, see John W. Dower, *Embracing Defeat: Japan in the Wake of World War II* (1999).

PART V

World War II and the Postwar World

It could have been predicted that Japan's entry into World War II would prove devastating to its people. The long China war had sapped men and matériel, but while laborers conscripted from Korea replaced workers at home to some extent, Japan's military and factories required resources far beyond those provided by the mines of Manchuria. In the drive to build heavy industry, for example, Japan's planners had decided to design steel mills that required scrap iron as raw material. In 1941 most of this scrap was imported from the United States. Modern armies ran on oil; the nearest source for Japan at that time was in the Dutch East Indies in what is now Indonesia. The threat by the United States and its allies to embargo oil unless Japan pulled out of China led Tokyo to view war as inescapable. Although Japan's army and navy managed to capture the oil fields by 1942, the unrestricted use of submarine warfare by the United States meant that most of the oil ended up polluting the ocean.

Japan had mobilized its forces to fight in a huge theater. Even though it had signed a neutrality pact with the Soviet Union, it still kept an army in Manchuria. It had troops strung out across China, occupying cities, guarding railways, fighting up the Yangtze River against the Nationalists, and trying to dig the Communists out of the hills in Yenan. The soldiers who captured Hong Kong in December 1941 then had to roust the French from Vietnam and the British from Malaya and Singapore (February 1942) while attacking Indonesia. With the Americans driven from the Philippines in May 1942, Japan's hegemony over the western Pacific was complete, yet its bastions consisted in large part of fortified atolls and garrisoned islands. Easily cut off from supplies and communications, the soldiers stationed on these outposts suffered unbelievable hardships, as we learn in Chapter 11. The effect on indigenous civilian populations was devastating.

Conditions on the home front were better, at least until the last months of the war. Even though strictly rationed, food was available, and anyone with access to even a bit of a garden could hope to grow a little extra. People had to be careful of what they said; complaining about hardships was unpatriotic and might bring down a visit from the *kenpeitai*, or thought police. The government tried to protect the best and brightest young men as long as possible. Only at the end of 1943 did it start drafting college students. In the next year, women were encouraged to leave their homes and take over the jobs of hauling steel and driving trucks heretofore monopolized by men. Life got dramatically worse after the fall of Saipan in November 1944, when the Japanese islands came within reach of American bombers. The firestorms that they brought to Japan's cities destroyed houses and killed or maimed hundreds of thousands of men, women, and children. By the time Tokyo surrendered, ninety cities had been at least partially destroyed, and almost three million people had died.

Under the surrender terms signed by the government on September 2, 1945, Japan was occupied by foreign troops under General Douglas MacArthur, the Supreme Commander of the Allied Powers (SCAP). MacArthur's goals were to demilitarize and democratize Japan; to this end, he and his staff carried out sweeping reforms designed to erase the last vestige of militarism and all that supported it. They revised the constitution of 1889 to wrest sovereignty from the emperor and invest it in the people; they instituted universal suffrage; they purged bureaucrats associated with the military regime and Japan's colonial empire; and they initiated land reform (see Chapter 8). They tried to make the educational system more democratic by giving more authority to local school boards, encouraging more open classrooms through parental involvement, and vastly expanding the opportunities for higher education. (The only reform not undone after the Occupation was the last.) SCAP censored songs, movies, and books deemed supportive of the war effort, and American products seemingly threatened to overwhelm all that was distinctively Japanese. A bulwark against this flood of American culture was the singer Misora Hibari (Chapter 12).

The road to economic recovery and then status as an economic superpower was long and difficult. Small start-up companies such as Sony and Honda had trouble getting the licenses and capital needed to manufacture their products; government ministries preferred to help the enterprises its bureaucrats knew before the war. The remedy for inflation was so draconian that the economy would have ground to a halt had it not been for the fortuitous outbreak of the Korean War, which pumped procurement orders and capital into Japanese industry. Following the end of the Occupation in 1952, government and business leaders embarked zealously on promoting an economic expansion that promised benefits for all. Agricultural productivity soared with mechanization and the use of powerful chemical fertilizers and pesticides; consumers discovered a wealth of new products designed to make life easier and more comfortable; and Japan's first postwar generation worked long hours for the sake of company and country.

Japan's defeat and occupation transformed the country just as the Meiji Restoration had not quite eighty years earlier. It would never do to underestimate the continuities with the previous period—among many, the erosion of the old landlord system, the introduction of a parliamentary system even if not necessarily a democratic one, and the creation through education and training of human capital without which high-speed economic growth would have been impossible. Despite such continuities with the past, however, ordinary people found that their lives changed in ways they had little imagined and over which they had little control.

Yokoi Shōichi

When a Soldier Finally Returns Home

YOSHIKUNI IGARASHI

Japan captured the South Pacific islands of Wake and Guam just days after its attack on Pearl Harbor. Slightly smaller than Molokai with a land area of 203 square miles, Guam witnessed a fierce battle before being reconquered by American marines in August 1944. Even after the war ended a year later, small units of Japanese soldiers continued to hold out, not fighting but not surrendering until decades later.

Like Rip Van Winkle, one of these soldiers eventually found himself caught in a time warp. Yokoi Shōichi never experienced the nadir of Japan's devastation at the end of the war and the postwar period of recovery and reconstruction. By the time he returned home in 1972, the country had far surpassed its prewar peak of economic growth and was enjoying an unprecedented prosperity. For a man fresh out of the jungle, it must have been a shock.

Yokoi was one of a number of soldiers who reappeared years after Japan's surrender. Those confined to Siberian prisoner-of-war camps had not stayed away voluntarily, of course, and some soldiers remained on the Pacific islands evading enemy detection. Yokoi and the others who returned from the Pacific force us to examine issues of how they managed to survive, why they remained out so long, how they were received upon their return, and how their stories were inserted into the master narrative of war memories.

Associate professor of Japanese history at Vanderbilt University, Yoshikuni Igarashi is the author of Bodies of Memory: Narratives of War in Postwar Japanese Culture *(2000).*

When I first learned that Mr. Yokoi was discovered in a cave in the jungle, I was excited to hear that my "war buddy" had returned alive and simultaneously caught aback as if somebody had called to me from the dark. What indeed is this fearful thing? I cannot easily answer that question.

—Yasuoka Shōtarō[1]

197

CAPTURE OF A STRAGGLER

On January 24, 1972, two local hunters on Guam captured a Japanese soldier who had been hiding in the jungle for twenty-seven years since the Japanese defense forces collapsed in August 1944. The man identified himself as Yokoi Shōichi from Aichi prefecture in central Japan. The Japanese news media immediately published the report, initially with skepticism, and then with intensity once the prefectural relief bureau confirmed his identity. On this small South Pacific island, as many as 120 Japanese news reporters competed to cover every aspect of Yokoi Shōichi's experiences. (Witnessing their aggressive approach to Yokoi and information gathering, Guam residents likened them to kamikaze pilots.) For the next several weeks, the story of the soldier who continued his lone battle in the Pacific and his return home fascinated millions in Japan and other countries, and the name of Yokoi Shōichi became one of the most prominent markers of Japan's postwar period.

Yokoi's reemergence from the Guam jungle brought back memories of the war to postwar Japan, invoking various reactions. Many former soldiers saw themselves in the emaciated figure of Shōichi, who was merely an ordinary man from a rural community. Some bereaved relatives of fallen soldiers superimposed the images of their beloved sons or brothers over his. The younger generations who had no personal experiences of the Asia Pacific War cast a curious gaze on the man who had been imprisoned by the wartime social mores. To many of them, Yokoi's behavior was simply incomprehensible.

The return of a "fallen" soldier shook postwar Japan society and reopened the psychological wounds of war. Commenting on Yokoi's return, for example, one writer claimed, "I feel we owe something to the dead soldiers, and we have to return what we owe to them. I feel we need to respond to their deaths."[2] Another writer, Yasuoka Shōtarō, who had also served in the wartime military, admitted his surprise when realizing that Yokoi's reappearance had brought back long-repressed memories of war. At least for these writers, Yokoi Shōichi had come back from the nether world to settle the account with the war dead.

However, 1972 Japanese society failed to comprehend the nature of the challenge that Yokoi's return posed. Like his emaciated body, the disturbing image of the former imperial soldier was readily rehabilitated into that of a more likable character in the affluent society, where war experiences had already been transformed into a nostalgic commodity. Yokoi himself readily accepted his newly assigned role in postwar Japan as a vital tool for his postwar survival.

YOKOI SHŌICHI'S WAR

The first half of Yokoi Shōichi's life was as unremarkable as the lives of millions of Japanese men who were mobilized in Tokyo's war efforts in the 1930s and 1940s. He was born in 1915 in a rural community in Aichi prefecture as the only son of Yamada Shōhichi and Tsuru. His parents separated when he was three months old, and young Shōichi stayed with Tsuru, who eventually married Yokoi Eijirō in 1926. At the age of sixteen, Yokoi chose to be apprenticed to a tailor in Toyohashi City, about forty miles away from home. He experienced a typical apprenticeship, he recalled in his 1974 memoirs, waking up at six and working all day until his eleven-thirty bedtime. Aware of his lowly status as an apprentice, he tried not to eat too much, so despite being a growing teenager, he never got to eat enough of even a frugal meal. It was not an easy life, but the skills that he acquired at the tailor shop later turned out to be indispensable for his survival in the Guam jungle. After five years of apprenticeship and one extra year of work at the shop, Yokoi finally returned to his parents' house to open his own tailoring business. He kept his business running for two years until he was called up to serve as a soldier in an army supply unit in 1938.

Like many young men before him, Yokoi began building a life for himself on the basis of the skills he had acquired through hard work. And, like most in his generation, he had to interrupt his career trajectory in his prime to serve as a soldier in Japan's colonial aggression. The country was deep into a war against China long before it declared war against the United States and the other Allied Powers in 1941. In September 1938, Yokoi was mobilized to be part of a unit stationed in southeast China. The unit was sent back to Japan in February of the following year, and he was discharged from service shortly thereafter. Yokoi worked hard to rebuild his business only to find his life disrupted again, this time for much longer than anybody anticipated. In August 1941 he was called up to serve with the Twenty-Ninth Infantry Division in Manchuria. There he spent two and one-half uneventful years on what was then a colony on Japan's northern frontier. The army remained in firm control of the region during his tour of duty; he saw no heavy fighting. Yet he did not return to his hometown until 1972.

In February 1944 his unit was transferred to the South Pacific to support the effort to halt the advance of U.S. forces. The Japanese navy was steadily losing control of the region, and many transport ships had already been lost to enemy submarine attacks. Although the ship that carried Yokoi's unit was damaged by a torpedo, it managed to reach its final destination, Guam, in March. By the end of April, a total of 19,000 soldiers had arrived on the island. Yokoi's unit was immediately engaged in the construction of a defensive line along the island's southwestern coast. Yet, facing the far better prepared U.S. invasion forces of 50,000, the defenses that the Japanese had constructed proved to be utterly ineffectual. Bombardment by U.S. warships prior to the invasion neutralized much of what little firepower the Japanese soldiers had left, and the actual U.S. landing took only a single day.

On July 21, U.S. forces came ashore on the western coast of the island. The Japanese units were incapable of maintaining their defensive positions and retreated inland in chaos. Out of desperation, their commander, General Obata, ordered all soldiers still alive to launch an all-out attack four days later to press U.S. forces back to the landing points. Lacking a means to counter enemy firepower and air attacks, the Japanese failed to organize an effective offensive and lost more than 80 percent of their men. After this debacle, the commander chose to fight a defensive battle in the jungle and gathered the remaining 3,000 soldiers in the northern part of the island. These forces were annihilated, however, in an early August attack on U.S. tank units. General Obata committed suicide on August 11. The Japanese forces' organized effort to defend the island had come to an end.

Despite the annihilation of the Japanese defense forces and the collapse of General Obata's headquarters, there were still a few thousand Japanese soldiers scattered in the Guam jungle. Communications among the defense units had been disrupted in their retreat, and some units were omitted from the command network. Without a central command system, the surviving soldiers were left to their own devices. Yokoi's platoon, in the southern part of the island, were unaware either of the all-out attack on July 25 or of General Obata's death. The platoon commander opted for survival rather than a desperate suicidal attack on the American stronghold, eventually ordering his thirty-some men to form smaller groups to avoid enemy detection. The platoon was thus divided into three groups in early September. Yokoi, whose prolonged combat experience by then had earned him the rank of corporal, led one of them into a battle of attrition. The focus of their fight shifted from the exchange of fire to sheer survival in the jungle while waiting for the arrival of friendly forces.

Yokoi and four other soldiers moved inland toward the upper reaches of the Talofofo River, seeking a safer location in which to hide from the intensifying American clean-up operations. Two other soldiers soon joined the group, and together they built a hut as a base for their operations. It was by chance that they were in the southern part of the island where food was more abundant, yet much of their energy was still expended in searching for it, and relations among them became strained over its distribution. These Japanese Imperial Army soldiers were reduced to leading a life of hunting and gathering, experimenting with local foods, and constructing crude huts with local plants. Indeed, in the second half of Yokoi's memoirs, the part that covers his life in the Guam jungle, he reports mostly on the food that he and other stragglers ate and the dwellings that they built.

In the early years of their struggle for survival, Yokoi and others gradually acquired valuable knowledge about local foods and sustained themselves with what the jungle offered them—breadfruits, coconuts, federico nuts, papayas, potatoes, lizards, snails, toads, rats, cats, wild pigs, and deer. (Some of these, such as federico nuts and toads, were poisonous, and they had to learn how to process them properly.) Later, when Yokoi lived in a smaller group, they added prawns and eels from the Talofofo River to their diet. As they spent more time in the jungle and hiding became their raison d'être, Yokoi and his fellow stragglers completely stopped appropriating food from local residents' cultivated land in order to leave no traces of their presence.

Clothing and footwear were also a central concern for the surviving soldiers who had no prospect of receiving future supplies. At first they were able to find man-made materials by digging through war wreckage left in the jungle. Yet, once they had depleted these limited resources, they had to find alternative ways to repair their clothing. Before long they were wearing sandals made out of palm fiber and patching their uniforms with dried toad skins. They later produced needles from scrap metal. One of the stragglers, Shichi Mikio, who survived until 1964, put to use his knowledge of the basics of blacksmithing. Yokoi eventually devised a method to produce fabric out of wild hibiscus trees and tailored his own "suits." When he was discovered in 1972, he was wearing a handmade shirt and shorts that he had put together literally from scratch. Many in Japan were amazed by his ingenuity. Combining their job skills and the skills they had learned growing up in the rural communities of prewar Japan, the stragglers managed to wage their battle against the elements.

Although Yokoi's group gained valuable experiences essential for survival at its first location of semisettlement, its members eventually decided to move farther into the jungle to hide from American soldiers. With the addition of several other stragglers, the group grew to include as many as ten men by June 1945. (Yokoi kept a rough calendar by observing the moon.) However, three of them were shot and killed by patrolling American soldiers in July. Two left of their own volition in September because of conflict within the group.

Further discord divided the group into smaller units: Yokoi, Shichi Mikio, and Nakahata Satoru left the other two in 1946. Two years later, Shichi and Nakahata left Yokoi alone in the jungle. However, the three of them resumed living together the following year, frequently changing their location until, in 1950, they decided to dig an underground cave to live in.

Without proper tools, digging a suitable cave was no easy task. Yokoi, Shichi, and Nakahata spent a month working on their first cave only to abandon it after a month of living in it. The cave was simply not suitable for human habitation. Several months later they began digging a second cave at another location. They completed it despite rising groundwater in the rainy season, but left it after six months. They had to abandon three more caves before completion because of the groundwater problem. Finally, the three stragglers returned to living aboveground. After experiencing another breakup (during which Yokoi lost almost all his possessions in a fire), the three reunited and managed to finish a satisfactory cave in 1959. Yet they ceased to live together in 1960—this time for good. Disagreement over food—how to consume and conserve it—led to Yokoi's decision to leave the other two. Yokoi spent more than three months digging his own cave about 500 meters away from the one he had left behind. It was barely large enough for one person, but Yokoi built an inside toilet and lined the walls, ceiling, and floor with bamboo. This cave turned out to be his permanent dwelling for the rest of his time on Guam.

After separating, Yokoi and his companions maintained amicable relations until Shichi and Nakahata died in 1964. The cause of their deaths was not clear to Yokoi or the Guam medical examiners who later viewed their remains. Yokoi simply suggests in his memoirs that the living conditions in the Guam jungle gradually took a toll on their bodies. When visiting Shichi and Nakahata in January 1964, Yokoi had noticed that their health was visibly declining. Ten days later he discovered their corpses, already reduced to skeletons, in their cave. Yokoi then lived in the jungle in silence, with no human contact, for the next eight years, refraining even from talking to himself for fear of being discovered by local residents. He later claimed that he never slept deeply— even the sound of cockroaches mating woke him up. When he could not bear his complete solitude in the middle of the night, he would cry and shout, banging his head against the walls of his cave.[3] In those eight years, his body and mind reached the limits of their endurance. His encounter with the local hunters was perhaps a desperate, albeit subconsciously motivated, attempt finally to free himself from his self-imprisonment.

YOKOI'S CHOICE

The Asia Pacific War ended in Japan's defeat in August 1945, and Yokoi learned about the surrender and the Potsdam Declaration within a year through a Japanese newspaper he picked up in the jungle. So he claimed, at least right after he was discovered on Guam.[4] He told a different story later, however, in his memoirs. There he carefully avoided discussing when he learned about Japan's defeat, while insisting that he had remained unaware of it in the early years of his concealment. Instead, he argued that his fellow soldiers deemed information about defeat to be an American deception, designed to trick them into surrender. In his case, only long after Japan's loss did he finally suspect that the war was over, although he did not want to accept it. Even without information from outside, it would not have been difficult to reach the conclusion that the war had ended in the Americans' favor when the only planes visible in the Guam sky belonged to the U.S. military.

Yokoi's selective retelling of his experiences on Guam appears to be a maneuver intended to deflect criticism of his behavior. Once he had returned to his hometown, he received numerous letters from all over Japan, many of which were encouraging. Some of them, however, accused him of having abandoned his duties as an imperial soldier out of fear. If he was aware of Japan's defeat, it was not a larger nationalist cause but cowardice and his egoistic desire for self-preservation that prevented him from coming out of the jungle. It was difficult to rationalize his survival if he could not claim that he chose life over death in order to continue his war efforts in the jungle. For this reason, Yokoi emphasized the ferocious U.S. clean-up operations in his account and his deep-seated suspicion of Americans. If he could convey to his readers his conviction that the war was still going on, then his behavior in the jungle could be justified—he continued to fight the war while awaiting the arrival of friendly forces.

Other reasons may be added for why he stayed in the jungle for so long. Some media reporters found their own reasons and attributed his behavior directly to the *Senjinkun* (Instructions for the battlefield), the document that Tōjō Hideki, then army minister, issued to the imperial soldiers in January 1941. It specifically prohibited soldiers from becoming prisoners of war: "One should not accept the disgraceful fate of POW as long as one is alive." The passage seemed linked to the conduct of the Japanese soldiers who had refused to surrender, and so shortly after his exodus, Yokoi himself began blaming it for his own behavior. However, it was more likely that fear, not an abstract army instruction, kept Yokoi in the jungle. (Moreover, Yokoi's basic army training was over long before the *Senjinkun* was issued.) Many soldiers who fought and eventually hid in the jungle resisted surrender at least in part because they had no assurance of their subsequent safety at the hands of the enemy forces. On Guam, which had been under the U.S. Navy's control since 1917, Japanese soldiers had assumed that the inhabitants harbored pro-American feelings. For that reason, Yokoi and his fellow stragglers were fearful of the local residents as well as of the Americans. Yet their biggest fear was the reaction that their surrender would trigger in their own military. Many believed that once they became POWs and were sent back home, they would be court-martialed, and maybe even executed, as defectors by the Japanese military authorities. Such a fate would only bring disgrace to their family members and hometowns. For these reasons, surrender was simply not an option.[5]

Yokoi also refused to take his own life on Guam. His antiheroic action of hiding in the jungle was a de facto objection to Tōjō's order as well as to a wartime Japanese society that devalued human lives. Thus, the complete isolation that Yokoi had to suffer in the jungle was the result of a choice that he was forced to make between disgrace and death. He could find no honorable way out. Only by wandering as one of the living dead could he escape the stigma of surviving the lost battle. Postwar Japanese society, however, which had managed to repress the trauma of defeat by the early 1970s, failed to understand the nature of his struggle and did not hesitate to transform him into a heroic figure. By accepting his newly found identity, Yokoi quickly found honor in his twenty-seven years of isolation.

YOKOI AND POSTWAR JAPAN

Out of the 19,000 soldiers sent to defend Guam, Yokoi Shōichi was the 1,305th to return alive to Japan. Those who chose to surrender to or were captured by the U.S. forces were eventually repatriated in the postwar period. A number of them had managed to hide in the jungle for many years. Minagawa Bunzō, for example, who spent several months together with Yokoi's group in 1945, and Itō Masahi were both captured by local residents and sent back to Japan as late as 1960. However, the return of these soldiers barely attracted the general public's attention, unlike Yokoi's discovery twelve years later. Even Minagawa's and Itō's sixteen years of hiding failed to trigger any substantial media response in postwar society, where the repatriation of Japanese POWs from the Soviet Union and China had continued well into the 1950s.

Furthermore, when Minagawa and Itō left Guam, Japan was fighting another "war"—the popular struggle over the issue of the U.S.–

Japan Security Treaty revision. In the weeks before the final ratification of the revised treaty on June 19, 1960, literally millions of Japanese rallied to express their opposition to it. Most participants in the demonstrations objected less to the specific articles of the new treaty than to the strong-arm tactics that Prime Minister Kishi Nobusuke adopted for its ratification. To them, Kishi embodied the authoritarian pre-1945 regime. He had served as executive secretary in the puppet state of Manchukuo and then as minister of commerce in the Tōjō Hideki administration when Japan declared war against the Allied Powers. Following the nation's defeat, he was incarcerated as a Class-A prisoner, waiting for his day in the Tokyo War Crimes Trials. Yet his case never came to court. Reflecting the conservative turn in postwar American Occupation policies—prosecution of war crimes became secondary to fear of Communist insurgencies in East Asia—the trials did not extend past the first round, in which twenty-eight defendants at the Class-A rank were judged. Kishi soon returned to politics and subsequently became prime minister in 1957. The opposition to the treaty revision served as a displaced political struggle through which to pass a belated critical judgement on wartime authoritarianism—the authoritarianism that Kishi reenacted in his efforts to ratify the new treaty. Once it was ratified, Kishi resigned from office, taking responsibility for the political turmoil. The opposition movement immediately quieted down. In the 1960s, Japanese society instead fully embraced the conservative Liberal Democratic Party's economy-first policy and enjoyed unprecedented economic growth and prosperity.

By the time Yokoi Shōichi reemerged from the Guam jungle, Japanese society had been transformed, at least in regard to its war memories. The postwar period had begun in a demeaning fashion for Japan, with the nation actively accepting the former enemy's hegemony in East Asia and transforming itself into a client state of the United States (the U.S.–Japan Security Treaty reaffirmed its dependence on the U.S. military). However, economic success rehabilitated the nation's bruised pride enough to conceal the trauma and humiliation of defeat, most of which had been suffered at the hands of the U.S. forces. Economic success also brought material wealth, which rapidly transformed the physical environment of Japan and erased the markers of the past.

On the basis of its newly found economic prosperity, for example, postwar Japanese society celebrated two major international events during the 1960s, and these served to push memories of war farther away. In 1964, the year when Yokoi's two straggler companions perished, Japan proudly demonstrated its reconstruction to the international community by successfully hosting the Tokyo Olympics. A few years later, when Osaka hosted Expo '70, memories of Japan's troubled past were conspicuously absent from the celebration of the country's economic power and prospects for the future. Its past figured merely selectively in the presentations of Japan's (and humanity's) future, witnessed by the 64 million attendees.

While Yokoi was living through his war in the Guam jungle, Japanese society steadily managed to distance itself from its memories of Tokyo's aggression. When he returned home in 1972, the country was optimistic with regard to the future. The people believed that their political environment would remain stable for some time to come. (The Oil Shock of 1973 shattered that illusion.) The image of an emaciated imperial army soldier shocked Japanese society by showing it a glimpse of the war, the images of which had long since been sanitized. Yokoi reappeared as a living fallen hero of the Asia Pacific War to demonstrate that memories of Japan's war could not be so easily repressed. Personally, he felt a great sense of guilt for having survived the battle in which thousands of his fellow soldiers perished. During his hospital stay on Guam, Yokoi was tormented by the sprits of the deceased, who taunted him for abandoning them. Yet as he regained physical strength in Guam and Japanese hospitals, the spirits ceased to torment him, and he was eventually rehabilitated into a participating member of society.

The Japanese mass media mercilessly covered every single word Yokoi uttered and every move he made. According to the accounts printed in the media, he experienced extreme surges of emotion following his capture, swinging between a manic state and depression. The fear of execution by the enemy stayed with him for several weeks. He simply could trust nobody. The newspaper and magazine reporters who swarmed around the hospital where he was recovering and aggressively approached him were none too sympathetic to his plight. Many articles portrayed his bizarre behavior as the result of his psychological difficulty in readjusting to the modern world, without much regard for the larger historical forces at work behind his personal experiences.[6] Yokoi was living through a conflict between two worlds—the pre-1945 Japan he had defended and the postwar society he emerged into. The reporters made little effort, however, to imagine how the world that Corporal Yokoi had preserved on Guam for so long could be as real as the affluent society to which they themselves were accustomed. The majority of the reports were produced from the perspective of that 1972 Japan.

The media were also eager to normalize Yokoi. In describing the human dimension of the man by tracing his family history to his hometown, many reports treated him as the latest hometown hero. Yokoi's own struggle between surrender and death was completely bypassed. His experiences were perhaps too alien for the postwar reporters to compre-

hend. Instead, he was praised for the length of his survival and the ingenuity that had allowed him to achieve it. His rehabilitation into postwar
Japanese society became one of the media's biggest concerns, and this
led them to trivialize his trauma. To complete the process of reentry,
Yokoi had to follow the "normal" life course of marriage and child-
rearing. Thus, his sexual functionality loomed as a significant issue, and
the man who had been tortured by unbearable loneliness was asked by
reporters how he dealt with sexual desire. The interest in Yokoi's sexual
appetite persisted even after his marriage in November 1973, nine months
after his return to Japan.

Yokoi faced a new game of survival once he reemerged from the
Guam jungle, and he learned to play it very well. He, too, began to reha-
bilitate his own image within the perameters of discourse set by the media. In the initial confusion of reentry into postwar Japan, Yokoi claimed
that he fought the war for the sake of the emperor and expressed his
desire to see him in person to return his rifle. However, many commen-
tators claimed that Yokoi's statement was not typical of noncommissioned
officers in the Japanese Imperial Army. A meeting with the Supreme
Commander would have simply been unimaginable for them. Although
Yokoi lamented the state of the imperial family (who now appeared in
mass-produced magazines as popular icons—something that would have
been unthinkable in prewar Japan), he readily exploited the prewar authority of the emperor to rationalize his struggle. Insofar as he could
claim he was fighting a war for a larger pre-1945 cause—for the emperor—he could retroactively find value in his struggle.

When he arrived at Tokyo's Haneda International Airport on February 2, 1972, Yokoi spoke to the thousands of people who welcomed
him there as well as the millions of Japanese who watched him on television. (It was reputed that the airport crowd was far bigger than that which
had welcomed the emperor and empress back from their royal tour of
Europe in 1971.) The first words that he uttered were: "Though embarrassed, I have returned home to tell about the conditions on Guam."
The conditional phrase, "though embarrassed," immediately became a
popular catchphrase. Many Japanese prefaced their statements with it,
while being little concerned as to what the original speaker was embarrassed about. In fact, he was less embarrassed about abandoning the spirits of the war dead on Guam than by the realization that he had been
hiding too long for no good reason. At the point of reentry in 1972, he
was already speaking from the postwar perspective, from which his
twenty-seven years of hiding was simply meaningless because he had
missed the opportunity to enjoy Japan's postwar peace and prosperity.
His embarrassment and regret persisted into his postwar years. When
he returned to his cave in 1973 on his honeymoon, for example, he kept

saying to himself, "I should have come out of a place like this much earlier."[7]

In comparison to Yokoi, Onoda Hiroo, the "last" Japanese imperial soldier who finally emerged from Lubang Island in the Philippines in 1974, had an easier job of justifying his behavior. Onoda had been sent to Lubang Island to serve as an agent to gather information on and subvert the mission of enemy forces. With his fellow soldier Kozuka Kinhichi (who was killed by the Philippine army in 1973), Onoda executed with conviction his duty to assist Japan's war effort in the enemy territory. The two soldiers maintained belligerency with the local people while appropriating their food supplies. Although their family members, with the help of the Ministry of Health, repeatedly visited the island to try to contact and rescue them, Onoda claimed they were convinced that these efforts were enemy plots designed to capture them. Suspicion skewed their judgment, which in turn reconfirmed their suspicion. Even minor typos in the letters the search parties left for them appeared to signal enemy intentions. (Onoda believed that his family members had intentionally made these errors as a warning to him.) In their almost paranoid state of mind, Onoda and Kozuka managed to repress their own conclusions about Japan's defeat.

Onoda managed to live a fiction until the last moment. When communication with him was finally established, he demanded an order signed by his superior officer to relieve him of the assignment. Upon being granted it in person, he finally laid down his rifle and reappeared in society, acting as a soldier who had accomplished a lengthy mission. Despite the fact that the information that he had collected in the past twenty-nine years was completely useless, by receiving recognition that he had been serving on an official mission, Onoda managed to give meaning to his hiding. He fought the war longer than anybody else in Japan and for a higher cause. Because of this conviction, he was not embarrassed to return to his homeland, where he immediately became a nationalist icon.

While becoming a national celebrity, Yokoi Shōichi still had to fight his embarrassment in going back to Japan. When he tried to project a more masculine image of himself several weeks after his return, it backfired. Taunted by letters accusing him of inaction on Guam, Yokoi confessed to reporters that he had killed two local residents several years prior to his capture. After seeing the negative peacetime reaction to this story, however, Yokoi immediately backtracked, blaming the incidents on Shichi and Nakahata. He eventually recanted his story. The Japanese media's investigation on Guam did not produce any concrete evidence that would substantiate his claim. Some reporters were skeptical of his story from the beginning because of inconsistencies in his accounts and because his rifle was not in usable condition when he emerged out of the jungle. In the end, the fiasco over his "murders" only served to dampen the "Yokoi boom" (for example, tourist buses ceased to stop at his home). Through this experience, Yokoi learned to play the roles expected by the media with greater caution.

Financially, Yokoi was well off. It was reported that by May 1972, well-wishers throughout the country had sent at least 31 million yen (about $100,000 at the 1972 exchange rate) to him through the Ministry of Health, media companies, and charity organizations. The gifts included nonmonetary items as well. One ramen producer sent fifteen boxes of ramen noodles to his home immediately after his discovery on Guam. A soy sauce company promised to send him a ten years' supply. Publishers were bidding for his memoirs, ready to offer him a substantial advance. It was also rumored that he would inherit a large plot of land in his hometown, worth tens of millions of yen. Exploiting his celebrity status, Yokoi launched a career as a lecturer on his Guam experience, commanding hefty fees. Although he was planning to reopen his tailor shop in his hometown and put his skills to use, the demands of dealing with the media and his frequent lecture tours left no time for such a mundane business.

With his sound financial prospects and bachelor status, he soon attracted the attention of unmarried women, most of them middle-aged. Many sent letters to him, some literally knocked on his door, offering themselves as his potential brides. Although he initially enjoyed their interest, it did not take long for him to realize that much of it was part of the media hype. Yet, even in his discouraged state of mind, Yokoi managed to meet some serious prospects to whom he was introduced through his acquaintances. He finally decided to marry a forty-four-year-old woman from a well-to-do Kyoto family, Hatashin Mihoko. He was then fifty-seven. The couple married in November 1972, immediately expressing their intention to have a baby, although they failed to conceive one. They canceled their planned honeymoon in light of the news of the death of Kozuka Kinhichi, who had been killed in the Philippines in October. They eventually visited Guam for a honeymoon in March 1973.

Marriage with Mihoko seems to have constructed Yokoi's final bridge to a "normal" life in postwar Japanese society. He acquired the skills to handle the media attention, which eventually dwindled down to a manageable level. His appearances in various venues give the impression that he not only accepted his image as cast by the media but also began to enjoy and take advantage of it. The media expected him to play the role of outsider critic of Japanese society, and he happily obliged. In May 1973 he even appeared in a magazine report on a "Turkish bath," a facility offering sexual services to men.[8] The essay reported that after the services that accompanied a bath (excluding sexual intercourse), Yokoi questioned several women who worked at the establishment. Two months later, another magazine reported that he was appearing as an attraction at a local theme cabaret in Fukuoka, which featured the Japanese imperial military. The female companions available to the cabaret's clients were clad in army nurse uniforms, while the waiters wore army and navy uniforms. Yokoi appeared as army officers of various ranks, including a general. Simply put, he was acting out a self-caricature.

In the early days of Yokoi's discovery, whatever his complaints about Japan—Tokyo's polluted air or congested streets—the media construed his words as profound criticisms of its present conditions and of modern civilization in general. He apparently took the media reactions to heart. In 1974 he even ran for a seat in the House of Councillors, Japan's upper house, counting on popular support. His "platform" was to become a "dog" that would sniff out how the unjust political system actually functions, and he declared that he would spend no money on his campaign.[9] He found another campaign issue in the energy crisis and high inflation that Japan was suffering at the time, which led him to find new meaning in his Guam life—the promotion of self-sufficiency and low consumption. Although he was confident that he would receive at least a million votes, he was disappointed on the day of the election. Of 55 million who actually voted, only some 250,000 cast their ballots for him. While the number was greater than that of those who had bought his memoirs, he fell far short of a seat in the House of Councillors. (He was ranked 73rd among the 112 candidates who ran for 54 seats.) His celebrity status was not enough to sway the voters.

Once the 1974 election was over, the media substantially reduced their coverage of Yokoi Shōichi. His media appearances were limited to occasional social commentaries and discussions of his and his wife's low-budget life. After giving modest attention to his pottery making in the early 1980s, the media treated him as somebody who belonged to the past, featuring him largely in retrospective discussions of the postwar period. In 1991 he briefly met Emperor Akihito, son of Hirohito, at a spring imperial reception. Yet even that meeting came too late (only after Hirohito's death in 1989), and only a few magazines covered it in brief articles.

Yokoi's health steadily declined in the 1990s. He suffered various ailments—a cataract, stomach cancer, a hernia, and backaches stemming from osteoporosis. It got to the point where his body could no longer support his making pottery, the hobby he loved. Several years before his death in 1997 at the age of eighty-two, he discovered that he was also suffering from Parkinson's disease.

On Yokoi's return to Japan, all he had wanted to do was to lead an ordinary life as a tailor. Caught in the media frenzy, however, he was never able to fulfill this wish for his "postwar years." In the end, he lived as a serious yet farcical character—a character behind which he hid much of himself. He left many words behind, but they revealed little of his personal struggle with the trauma of war. When he was captured on Guam, one of the survivors of the Guam battle had lamented: "Mr. Yokoi talks, talks and talks—[look at] that manner [in which he talks]. It is really sad to see him deceiving himself so completely through his own words. We, too [other survivors of the war], continue to lie, while keeping the truth to ourselves and taking it to our graves."[10] In the following years, the situation did not change. Yokoi kept speaking about himself and the war that Japan had fought. Yet what he said was formulaic and revealed remarkably little about the effects of the war and his Guam experiences on his own personal life.

What happened to his cave house in the Guam jungle is perhaps symbolic of Yokoi's whole postwar experience. It was left unattended after his capture and eventually crumbled. The cave now marked on a Guam tourist map was actually dug later by one of his first captors.[11] As of 1999, the original cave was reduced to a foot-deep depression in the ground. Much like the cave reconstructed for tourists, Yokoi's war experiences were painstakingly recreated for the postwar audience. Actual memories of his struggles were buried within the details of everyday life, away from the public's attention. No one could blame the straggler for hiding his painful memories behind the farcical persona that the Japanese media created. Yet, despite his aversion to it, the past kept haunting him. In his "postwar years" and even on his deathbed, Yokoi was kept awake by nightmares of being chased by enemy soldiers. On September 22, 1997, twenty-five years after his dramatic exodus from the Guam jungle, Yokoi Shōichi died in a Nagoya hospital of a heart attack, finally rejoining the fallen heroes he had left in the Pacific.

NOTES

1. Yasuoka Shōtarō, "Yokoi san to Nihonjin" [Mr. Yokoi and the Japanese], *Shūkan yomiuri*, February 18, 1972, 41.

2. Kishida Junpei, "Kigakari na hito tanken: Yokoi Shōichi san to heikasama to soshite . . ." [Exploring the person who is on everybody's mind: Mr. Yokoi Shōichi and Venerable Emperor and . . .], *Josei jishin*, February 26, 1972, 166.

3. He confided to one of the first Japanese news reporters whom he met on Guam his struggle with solitude. In his memoirs, however, he portrays himself as maintaining a cool demeanor no matter how lonely he became. See his "Watashi ga tachiatta, Yokoi, Kotsuka, Onoda san no sei to shi" [Yokoi's, Kozuka's, and Onoda's life and death that I witnessed] in *Sandē mainichi*, March 31, 1974, 28; and Yokoi Shōichi, *Ashita e no michi* [A passage to tomorrow] (Tokyo: Bungei Shunjū, 1974), 226.

4. In the Guam police report, Yokoi claimed that he had learned of the end of the war in 1952. See *http://ns.gov.gu/scrollapplet/sergeant.html* for a summary of the report.

5. Despite strong inhibitions, some Japanese soldiers did intentionally surrender to enemy forces. Yokota Shōhei, who also fought on Guam, surrendered shortly after the U.S. landing. For Yokota's psychological justification for his decision, see his *Watashi wa gyokusai shinakatta* [I did not fight to the last man] (Tokyo: Chūō Kōron, 1999).

6. One weekly magazine article observed that Yokoi was suffering from "Guam autism" [Guam *jiheishō*]. " 'Guam jiheishō' no shakai fukki ni machikamaeru otoshiana" [The traps that await Guam autism's return to society], *Shūkan sankei*, February 18, 1972, 24–27.

7. "Guam tō shinkon ryokō de mita zo Yokoi fūfu no sugoude" [Mr. and Mrs. Yokoi's maneuver on their Guam honeymoon], *Shūkan gunshun*, March 26, 1973, 49.

8. Yokoi Shōichi, "Hazukashi nagara toruko o taiken shimashita" [Though embarrassed, I experienced a Turkish bath], *Gendai*, May 1973, 276–83.

9. "Yokoi san 'yūkoku' rikkōho no ben" [Mr. Yokoi's discussion on his patriotic candidacy], *Shūkan asahi*, June 28, 1974, 151.

10. "Guam tō senyūkai no 'hirō Yokoi' o miru me" [The way the Guam War Association looks at hero Yokoi], *Shūkan bunshū*, February 21, 1972.

11. "Gashi e no omoi atama hararezu" [Thoughts of starvation never left his mind], *Asahi shinbun*, August 15, 1999, Nichiyōban WD, B.

SUGGESTED READINGS

Most of the information in this essay derives from Japanese newspapers and weekly magazine articles. Close to four hundred magazine articles about Yokoi have appeared since 1972. Yokoi Shōichi's *Ashita e no michi* (1974), as well as *Sankei shinbun* and Fuji Television's *The Last Japanese Soldier: Corporal Yokoi's Incredible Years in the Guam Jungle* (1972), provide detailed accounts of his life on Guam, though Yokoi's own account is vague on some key events. Itō Masashi, one of the two stragglers who hid in the Guam jungle until 1960, also published his memoirs, *The Emperor's Last Soldier* (1967). Onoda Hiroo's two books, *No Surrender: My Thirty-Year War* (1999), and *Waga kaisᶿo no Rubangu tō* (1995), demonstrate that his experiences in the Philippines were very different from those of Yokoi's. Yokota Shōhei's *Watashi wa gyokusai shinakatta* (1999) is a valuable account of a soldier who survived the Guam battle by surrendering to the U.S. forces. Yoshikuni Igarashi's *Bodies of Memory: Narratives of War in Postwar Japanese Culture, 1945–1970* (2000) examines the ways in which postwar Japanese society discursively distanced itself from the trauma of war. The Guam government maintains a homepage on Yokoi (http://ns.gov.gu/scrollapplet/sergeant.html), which offers a summary of the police report on Yokoi's capture.

CHAPTER 12

𝓜isora 𝓗ibari

The Postwar Myth of Mournful Tears and Sake

Alan Tansman

Children born during the war grew up to the sounds of martial music: the drumbeat of soldiers marching off to the front and the dirges for the ashes of the war dead on their way to their apotheosis at Yasukuni Shrine. Boys played at being soldier, fighting with swords fashioned from wooden sticks, learning to identify enemy planes, toughening mind and body to withstand the rigors of combat. Girls sewed, rolled bandages, and watched their mothers mourn the return of loved ones in boxes wrapped in white cloth. When hundreds of thousands of civilians died in fire-bombing raids that reduced cities to charred wastelands, many children were evacuated to the countryside. By the end of the war, even young women were trained to fight with bamboo spears against the invasion to come. Japan's surrender left children, like their parents, struggling simply to survive under the U.S. Occupation. They built new lives out of the ruins and ultimately the new Japan, an economic superpower. Misora Hibari was born in 1937, the year the Japanese army invaded north China. Her career as a singer was forged in the crucible of universal hardship. It was a time of unspeakable misery, but for those looking back on it during the prosperity that came later, there is also the taste of a bittersweet triumph of having survived when so many did not.

The story of Hibari, an icon of popular culture, is equally the story of her fans and the medium that made her famous. Even though the ubiquitous television retrospectives of Shōwa music today inevitably include tapes of her performances, her defining moment really came during and right after the Occupation as Japan started pulling itself out of the rubble and reasserting a sense of national identity. Hibari's life refracted through her songs provides one glimpse of what that period means for the Japanese people today.

Associate professor of East Asian languages and cultures at the University of California, Berkeley, Alan Tansman is the author of a study on the postwar woman writer, Koda Aya. He is presently finishing a book on Japanese fascism and culture and is translating and annotating, with Dennis Washburn, Isoda Koichi's "Tokyo as an Idea" and other essays.

When she died in 1989, Misora Hibari's reputation as Japan's greatest postwar singer had ascended to the level of myth. Her voice, wrote one critic and fan in 1990,

> sings of a confession with nobody to confess to. Within her song there is a certain something wrapped in an ancient silence older than even existence: the magnificent speech of flowers in a garden deep in the night that nobody knows the meaning of, the steady gaze of nature. Are not hers the original sounds of all living beings, the songs of ancient birth itself, older than our existence? To whom does her song belong? The singer? Or the listeners nearby? From where does her song emanate? From the singer? Or from the trembling bodies of the listeners?[1]

HIBARI AS SHAMAN

By the end of her life Misora Hibari had acquired a shamanlike aura. To her fans, she was a being grounded in the everyday but touched by a higher power. In her final performance in 1988 she seemed to one fan, "supported on air like a spirit."[2] Yet many Japanese felt about her at her death as they always had: ambivalent. She continues, even now, to be a sort of Japanese Elvis, loved by some and reviled by others. So, too, will Japan continue its uneasy relationship with Hibari, at one extreme seeing in her the atavistic grip of native sensibility, the uneasy reminder of a gloomy past better left behind, and the queasy schmaltz of an outdated culture. At the other extreme, she embodies the essence of the much-vaunted Japanese spirit of forbearance—specifically, of postwar forbearance. Her popularity, and that of the music she sang—*enka*—has never disappeared. It submerges periodically but inevitably reemerges, like a repressed myth.[3]

When she died of pneumonia on May 24, 1989, four months after Emperor Hirohito, the nation mourned. Hibari's final hours were reported with the same religious care and accuracy as the emperor's. News reports and documentaries filled the airwaves, and the newspapers—from the loud pages of the *Nikkan Sports* to the national dailies *Asahi, Yomiuri, Mainichi, Sankei,* and the serious *Nikkei*—ran front-page stories of her death. All spoke of her as having sung with and for the spirit of postwar Japanese. Some lamented the death of that spirit; others editorialized that it, like her, would never die: she was an "immortal bird," still in flight. Her records sold out across the country, thousands stood vigil through the night by her home in Yokohama, and thousands more lined the streets to watch her hearse pass by. Many shed the same tears of awe and gratitude that they had shed for their emperor.

With Hibari's death, a chapter of history seemed to end. In the words of the popular writer Sawaki Hidae, "Hibari expressed the fundamentals of postwar life, and with her death closed the entire Shōwa era, leaving behind the image of Shōwa women, who were allowed such little happiness." The power of her voice, she continues, belongs to "all the nameless fans," and the universal power of her songs derives from the "authority of common feeling possessed by all the nameless."[4]

The romance between the "nameless" and Hibari began in 1949, in the rubble of war-scarred Japan, with her debut as a preternaturally precocious singer, a mere twelve years of age, in the film *Mournful Whistle (Kanashiki kuchibue)*. From the beginning, Hibari was a heroine of, for, and by the people in their resistance to the "democratic" ideal seen to have been imposed by the United States on a defeated Japan. "Her singing voice," wrote one critic, "will undoubtedly be a powerful tool in resisting our artistic colonization." When the Occupation ended in 1952, her rendition of the popular "Apple Ballad" (*Ringo oiwake*) returned to postwar society "that which belongs to the people."[5]

This sad, sweet melody sold 70,000 records, sending Hibari to the peak of fame at age fifteen and to her first important live recital, at Tokyo's Kabukiza Theater. With its melancholy tones and lyrics about the pain of separation felt by a young girl in her country home, the song crystallizes the motifs of *enka*:

> The petals of the apple blossoms
> scattered by the wind
> on a moonlit night, on a moonlit night,
> gently, yes. . . .
> The Tsugaru maiden cried,
> she wept at the painful parting.
> The petals of the apple blossoms
> scattered by the wind, ah. . . .[6]

The mere mention of Tsugaru in northern Japan, like the dust bowl in the Great Depression, raises the specter of provincial poverty and hardship. The biographies, documentaries, fan magazines, and news reports transformed the star Hibari into a provincial maiden (from humble beginnings in a fishmonger's store in Yokohama), weeping at painful partings. Portraits depict her as a four-year-old in the streets of militarized Yokohama, singing with her father's amateur band to those going off to war and to those seeing them off, or at munitions plants to those working for the war. Indeed, she was born amid crisis in 1937, surrounded by economic uncertainty and the sounds of military marches on the radio. Her singing of "The Mother of Kudan" (*Kudan no haha*) at age four when her father departed for the front has the aura of mythic beginnings. She sang of a mother visiting the military cemetery at Yasukuni Shrine in

Tokyo (then and later the object of military affection and right-wing devotion), grieving for her dead son.

A child star who garnered the attention of a generation, Hibari was never a Shirley Temple, bringing to the poor the lost charms of innocent childhood. She has always been the "genius maiden" (*tensai shōjo*)—rebuked by some for her uncannily adult voice—and the very model of a hardworking child (*gambariya*) studying with her home tutor. When the war ended, she sang in the ruins of a destroyed Yokohama, and performed the hits she later made in movies before ramshackle postwar audiences in burned-out cities. She was, like her name, the "skylark of beautiful skies," an innocent bringing new life to a defeated nation, but her voice was also a reminder of the loss of childhood exacted by the war and its aftermath.

Hibari's fans grew up with her, and she remained for them the "genius maiden." Her songs of the late 1940s and early 1950s became an integral part of her concert repertoire in the 1960s, 1970s, and 1980s. For her fans, her songs and the films in which she sang them sustained a feeling of continuity across time, and her admirers continued to call out to her in concerts, as if urging her on. Her performance of "The Homeland Tsugaru" evoked the same passion in 1985 as it did in 1953; she was still referred to in the diminutive of her childhood—"Hibari-*chan*!"— but now by a crowd of old ladies. Even as an adult, Hibari retained the traces of the girl who sang for the trainloads of junior high-school graduates in the early 1950s, arriving at Ueno Station in Tokyo from the hinterlands of Aomori (the modern name for Tsugaru), sacks of apples on their backs, to begin working in small factories and stores. She sang for the anxiety of those youths adrift in Tokyo, parted from their parents and all that was familiar. From the time of her debut, Hibari was—and continued to be—an emotional support for working women. One salesgirl wrote in a fan letter of 1958 that Hibari was her "only joy in life," her "source of inspiration to work hard."[7]

"MOURNFUL SAKE" AND THE PEOPLE'S TEARS

Of Hibari's thousand or more recorded songs, the 1966 "Mournful Sake" (*Kanashii sake*) is the Hibari song par excellence; it is Hibari's signature song, hers and hers alone. That her words were the same and that she cried at the same moment every single time she performed "Mournful Sake" denotes the genius of a performer who makes staged emotion seem real—and indeed, feels it to be real herself. Such blending of artifice and reality reveals Hibari's kitsch genius. Watching her perform, the viewer shuttles constantly back and forth between the extravagant illusion, the spectacle created by sets, lights, costume, makeup, and lyric cliché, and the intensity that makes Hibari appear sincere to her fans—as sincere as Judy Garland, who, after a life of misfortune, cried each time she sang "Over the Rainbow." Hibari trod a fine line between the real and the artificial. Like Judy Garland, she would not merely render a song—she would create it, delivering mawkish lyrics with conviction, revealing sincere emotions beneath a surface of musical and lyrical clichés. When she sang "Mournful Sake," Hibari was not merely the tear-drenched woman staring into an imaginary sake cup at the ghost of the departed. She transformed her sorrows into the beauty of her singing.

Hibari's authenticity could seem both sincere and completely constructed. Perhaps among her fans there were those who recognized this, appreciated her for dissimulation, and valued her not merely for being like them but also above them—for being an artist. Hibari never said why she cried every time she sang "Mournful Sake," and perhaps this silence lent the song its aura.

In her most memorable performance of "Mournful Sake" in 1986, she seems to have perfected a mythic persona that was stripped of all artifice while reveling in sheer staginess. She is draped in blue silk and bathed in white light, standing against a pitch-black background. Clutching her microphone like a talisman, she bites her quivering lips and looks down in intense, sad concentration as if steeling herself against a lifetime of pain. To the lonely plucking of a single guitar, she raises her head defiantly toward a white beam of light and begins to sing in a gently shaking voice,

> Alone at the sake bar,
> the sake I drink
> tastes of the tears of parting.
> I wish to drink and discard
> that image,
> but when I drink,
> it floats up again inside my glass.

"Mournful Sake" shows a Hibari pulled apart yet moving ever forward. She spits out the word "tears," her head shaking with pain, acceptance, and defiance. She caresses every breath, every vowel and consonant, and when she sings "I wish to drink and discard that image, . . ." she gazes fearfully at her hand, as if at her own inner being. She is rebellious as she sings "but when I drink . . . ," then seems to break apart as she lingers, transfixed, on the imaginary "glass" that holds the image of what she has lost. When the image "floats up again," she sinks even deeper into her pain, sustaining the final note with her mouth clenched in an anguished glissando.

Her tears come after the first verse, as she gazes at the glass, when she grasps her arm across her body as if repressing her anguish and speaks, her eyes glistening with tears. By the time she comes to her monologue, she seems spent. With a deep sigh, she begins:

> Ah, the regret that comes after parting!
> Full of lingering desire,
> that person's face.
> So as to forget my loneliness,
> I am drinking, and yet,
> even tonight, the sake makes me sad.
> Oh, sake!
> Why, how should I give up that person?
>
> Oh, sake!
> If you have a heart,
> extinguish the agony in my heart for me!
> When I am drunk from the sake that has made me sad,
> and cry,
> that too is because of love.
>
> Beneath the heart that said,
> "I like being alone!"
> I am crying,
> crying in bitterness for the world
> of the one whom I love but cannot follow.
> The night deepens,
> alone at the sake bar, the sake I drink. . . .[8]

The dam has now broken: as she intones "alone," tears stream down her cheeks, making her nearly choke on her words. But the tears cease as she sings defiantly of "the world . . . I . . . cannot follow." The night darkens as she looks on in "bitterness," a lyric she deepens and extends as if holding on to her last source of strength. Her singing of "night" lasts even longer but sounds gentler and more accepting, as Hibari lifts her head in an elegant gesture. Hibari's interpretations of these phrases are the mark of a master. Her final breath—we feel now that it comes from some bottomless inner chamber—is saved for the night that "deepens." Quivering, she lowers the microphone and, still shaking, bites her lip.

Hibari has a remarkable ability to move rapidly between the sweetest, most fragile high registers, where she seems on the verge of tears, and the darkest, most resilient low registers, where she seems unshakably stoic. She shifts fluidly from her natural voice, in which she speaks to her audience as one of them, breathing from her chest, to her falsetto voice, in which she produces dramatic melismas and throbbing vibratos, drawing breath from much deeper down. With such fluidity, Hibari not only depicts the emotions of which she sings, but she also replicates them in the listener.

Though "Mournful Sake" was composed by Kōga Masao in 1966, it belongs to a genre—*enka*—that Kōga took to its greatest artistic and commercial heights in the 1930s. This was the same period in which the nation's intellectuals were searching for authenticity in Japanese culture. Songs such as Kōga's 1931 "Yearning for Her Trace" (*Kage o shitaite*) and "Sake: Tears or Sighs?" (*Sake wa namida ka tameiki ka*), which sold hundreds of thousands of records at the time, remain among the century's most popular and have attained the status of classics.

Enka is, indeed, tearful music. By the time Kōga's songs popularized the sentimental *enka* melody (though the term was not used at the time) in the late 1920s and early 1930s, with lone guitar, violin, or ukulele accompaniment, its motifs—lament for lost love, homelessness and nostalgia, longing for a lost past and for an unattained future, devotion, a life of wandering and impermanence—had been set in stone, enduring even in postwar song. *Enka* imagery, too—clouds, geese, the moon, train stations, harbors, flowing waters and the foam upon them, shadows, the sound of insects, the world of dreams, to name a few—became clichés that were to last through the postwar period.

The greatest of these clichés, certainly, has been tears, and within the history of *enka*, the most tearful years were those between 1937 and 1940, as Japan rushed into war and hardship.[9] In the 1930s, as mothers grieved for lost sons, wives sent off husbands, and soldiers longed for their homes far away, these tears were colored by the war, the songs often having been solicited by the military. *Enka*, with its themes of devotion and sacrifice, naturally lent itself to such militaristic uses. Indeed, it is still associated with a conservative strain in popular culture. Devotion, however, can cut two ways. In Hibari's *enka*, personal devotion and isolated grieving can overshadow patriotism and communal loss.

The 1930s witnessed a rise in songs depicting boats floating on the water, an image expressing a desire to allow oneself and one's pain to drift off into another world.[10] The tears Hibari shed as she sang Kōga's song in 1966 were such tears of stoicism, yet they were more complex, for they expressed the strength and resistance of her fans—the people—to the social, economic, and intellectual elite of the day, to the erasing of traditions, to artistic colonization.

By the time Misora Hibari first sang "Mournful Sake" in 1966, she and Japan—like Frank Sinatra and the United States in the 1960s—had begun to drift apart. "Even in the 1960s," writes one critic, "she gave off the aroma of the farm, of the trainloads of pupils transported to Tokyo en masse to work."[11] As she sang of enduring the anguish of lost love and of painful partings, in the mournful melodies of the minor pentatonic scale, Hibari's boozy sensibility no longer spoke to many in a nation buoyed by economic success. Though she had suffered with the people in the ruins of postwar Japan, the people had moved on and hence no longer needed her. To many, hers was the music of a dead nation.

But to the generation of Japanese who grew up with her in the post-war rubble, Hibari's music was anything but "the music of a dead nation," and her tears were still real, even in the 1980s. Her music was a dirge for what was threatening to disappear. To them, she cried not only for the death of her own mother, who had devoted her life to her. She cried also for her dead brother, to whom she always remained loyal, though his troubles with *yakuza* gangsters, guns, and drugs sent him to jail and got her blacklisted in the entertainment world (she was temporarily banned from the annual New Year's Eve television songfest, the pop music world's grandest night of promotion). One suspects, with her fans, that she cried, too, for her divorce following a short-lived marriage to a popular film star, and for the painful and protracted bone disease that threatened to end her singing. To the Japanese generation that grew up with Hibari, the extreme highs and lows of "Mournful Sake" spoke the unspoken words of the "nameless" people. They saw that she had made it through and survived—that her life mirrored their lives, that she had persevered without complaint and maintained her dignity in defeat.

With the anguish of a Billie Holiday and the gift to transmute that anguish, Hibari in the final analysis held in thrall an audience more comparable, in size and sociology, to that of Elvis Presley. The passion for Elvis, unabated today, belongs to fans who still respond to him as if he were part of their own lives. Like fans of Elvis, Hibari's fans saw in their star a stoicism and endurance, an honesty and sincerity betraying no ambiguity or irony. This helped them to feel a loyalty to her as a performer and a person. Hibari was not afraid to stand naked, metaphorically speaking, in front of an audience. She had the gift of making her listeners care about her.

One might thus understand Hibari's rise to stardom as due in part to an image that embodied core-but-threatened values, and see her charismatic appeal as especially strong—as was the popularity of *enka*—when the social order seemed uncertain or ambiguous. If, as Whitney Balliett says, jazz is the "sound of surprise," then Hibari's is the sound of familiar, but penetrating, recognition.

Like country and western stars, Hibari created a powerful bond with her audience. It was her ability to "express communal sentiment," in the novelist Inoue Hisashi's words, that made Hibari a genius.[12] "When she sings 'Mournful Sake,' " says Miyako Harumi, Hibari's only rival for genius in the postwar singing world, "there's no 'Mournful Sake' first, and then Misora Hibari later. Misora Hibari and 'Mournful Sake' are one."[13] She was seen to be at her most authentic when she sang for her "nameless, voiceless fans," as they were often called. She knew her audience and could articulate her connection to them. "The people," she said, "are those who don't need to wear sunglasses in front of others. The people are those who can talk looking straight into their companions' eyes."[14]

Hibari's tears reflected the people's experience of Shōwa Japan. In her tears, the people saw their own lives. In her 158 films, she played a cast of characters that cut across history, gender, and mood. She was a poor street kid, boy and girl (her mother, fearing her voice would change in adolescence, got her male roles), a rough young samurai, a samurai's wife, a geisha, a happy teenager, a dancing girl in Kawabata Yasunari's *The Izu Dancer* (*Izu no odoriko*), a maid in Higuchi Ichiyō's *Growing Up* (*Takekurabe*), a *yakuza*.

In song, as on film, Hibari wore many masks. Postwar Japanese song offered its practitioners a profusion of styles, and Hibari sang the entire range. It was a rich mélange—as complex and varied as the literary styles available to writers in late-nineteenth-century Japan—of the most contemporary foreign imports and the oldest Japanese folk melodies. Several could appear within a single composition, sometimes resulting in combinations that were either charmingly creative or absurdly silly, depending on one's taste. For example, in the 1956 *Sword Slashing* (*Chanbara kenpō*), we see Hibari as the brave young samurai, slashing her sword through a group of nasty ruffians to a rockabilly tune. Her renditions of jazz classics put her on a par with her American counterparts, and her version of Edith Piaf's "La Vie en Rose" in English puts her in company with the best chanteuses.

However, her greatest successes, and the songs that most convinced her fans of her authenticity, were the melancholy *enka*. After the Japanese public's drunken craze with American-inspired boogie-woogie in the 1940s, *enka* returned in the late 1940s (with a Kōga Masao revival) and the mid-1950s (when songs of nostalgia peaked) to its lachrymose place in the Japanese popular-culture world. It was perhaps Hibari more than anyone else who restored this melancholy voice to Japan at a time of a generally conservative cultural renaissance—or retrenchment, depending on one's point of view.

ENKA: SONGS OF NOSTALGIA AND RESISTANCE

The pain of the elemental struggle of everyday existence expressed by Hibari through *enka* may not be as raw as the nitty-gritty reality of physical hardship evoked by what Albert Murray calls the blues' "bluesteel and rawhide textures." But *enka* is, like the blues, evocative of the elemental emotion of pain that comes from loss—of the pain belonging to a world distant "from the cloud-like realms of abstraction and fantasy," in Murray's words.[15] Like the blues, *enka* is heard as an authentic expression of emotion; it can be artfully contrived, elegantly playful, and heroic. It has its mythic places—the alleyway, the harbor, the train station, the provincial town—and it has its poetic disposition: to persevere.

Though audiences claim that *enka* sounds and feels authentically Japanese, in reality, like all so-called authentic myths, it is an impure amalgam. *Enka* is marked by a hybrid musical style that can be traced to the importation of Western musical education. In 1872 a repertory of choral "school songs" became a compulsory part of school curricula. Collected and edited by Isawa Shūji (1851–1917), who brought back with him from Lowell, Massachusetts, a teacher of music and a new philosophy of musical education, school songs were short melodies that borrowed from Irish and Scottish folk songs. Like Japanese folk songs, these melodies were in pentatonic scales—accounting for the astounding popularity to this day in Japan of "Auld Lang Syne"—to which were added Japanese lyrics. Often the songs were accompanied by the organ, which had been used in Protestant churches. A compromise was created between Western and Japanese musical scales, the result being a scale without the fourth and seventh notes. Early *enka* synthesized this scale with the popular melodies of a bygone era.

Enka has drawn from a variety of styles. The dramatic vocal flourishes, or melismas, that characterize *enka* were strongly influenced by the sentimental narrative chanting of love and duty born as Osaka popular street entertainment in the eighteenth century, then performed in the late nineteenth in portable huts. The 1920s saw the birth of *ryūkōuta*, the generic term created by Japan's first record companies, Victor and Columbia, to refer to popular music that sounded Western. The success of these songs grew as an accompaniment to silent films—the singer performing at the side of the stage—then appeared on radio (in 1925) and in recordings (in 1928). These songs were the forerunners, both musically and lyrically, of what is now known as *enka*—short songs employing Western instruments and a minor pentatonic scale. *Enka* has drawn as well from Japanese folk songs, chanson, tango, rock, blues, swing, country and western ("Tennessee Waltz," sung in English, was a hit in the 1950s). The minor scale and slow rhythm of songs such as "The Parting Blues" (*Wakare no buruzu*), composed by Hattori Ryōichi and sung by Awaya Noriko in 1937, helped lay the foundation for postwar *enka*.

The dazzling array of prewar musical styles of popular Japanese song was repressed in the musical world from 1940 until the war ended in

1945, to be dominated by the monochromatic songs of war and sacrifice. In this period, "Japanese-sounding songs"—that is, *enka*—became associated with feudalism, nationalism, and, finally, defeat, which were to make them culturally taboo immediately after the war. At that point, the stoic melancholy of Japanese-sounding songs gave way to lighter, Western-sounding melodies of hope. In the first postwar hit, "The Apple Song" (*Ringo no uta*), in 1946, sunny days were here again:

> Putting my lips to the red apple
> I quietly look at the blue sky.
> The apple says nothing, but
> I know how the apple feels.
>
> Shall we sing the apple song?
> If the two of us sing together, it'll be even more fun,
> If we all sing together, we'll be even more happy!
> Shall I tell you of the apple's feelings?
> The apple is so cute, how cute is the apple![16]

The greatest outpouring after the war of joyous—and, some would say, "un-Japanese"—energy came from the frenetic performances by the "queen of boogie," Kasagi Shizuko, singing the boogie-woogie rhythms of Hattori Ryōichi. Kasagi, her skirt hitched up high, could rush through a song with joyous abandon—an almost-American élan—that made the listener forget the day's problems and become lost in a jumble of quick rhythms and ecstatic lyrics. "Tokyo Boogie Woogie" sings of hope for a future in which the universal language of song is all that matters (and Japaneseness is nowhere to be found):

> Tokyo boogie woogie, rhythm uki uki
> heart zuki zuki waku waku
> resounds and echoes in the ocean,
> Tokyo boogie woogie
> the boogie dance is a world dance
> the song, a dream of two.

In "Shopping Boogie," Kasagi transforms the growling of empty stomachs into the joy of words on which the imagination, at least, can feast:

> Carrots, radishes, burdocks, lotus root, Popeye's favorite spinach,
> tomato, cabbage, nappa, cucumbers, lilies, stupid eggplant,
> watermelon, Tokyo leek, leek, boogie woogie button and ribbon,
> shaddock, matches, cider, cigarettes, jintan mints
> yayakoshi (what a bother) yayakoshi yayakoshi yayakoshi
> aah! Yayakoshi. . . .

These were Kasagi's songs, and when Hibari recorded one in 1954, she caused a minor scandal, earning the wrath of the older singer and accusations of being an imitator. Not that Kasagi had much to worry about. When Hibari leaves her métier, the melancholy *enka*, and tries to sing with abandon, as she does in the 1952 "Festival Mambo," her singing seems as stiff as her forced smile or exclamations of "*wasshoi wasshoi*." The festive atmosphere she projects is not infectious. Her greatest successes were always with *enka*, the people's music.

HIBARI AS THE PEOPLE'S SINGER

To her audience, Hibari has always been the "Tokyo Kid," from the 1950 film of the same name: a ragamuffin whose genius made her the object of upper-class curiosity, disgust, and also enchantment, but whose loyalties always remained with the poor and hardworking people. After achieving great fame and financial success, Hibari insisted that she belonged to "the people," not to the entertainment industry. In *Tokyo Kid*, she sings in the most common of postwar locales, an empty lot, as well-dressed bourgeois run to hear her. The soundtrack's lush orchestration virtually drowns out the accompaniment of guitar strings plucked by her longtime costar and friend, Kawade Kiyohisa. But his presence reminds her viewers that she still belongs to the simple world of the street singer and the single string accompaniment—the world of authentic *enka*.

To many fans, Hibari's childish persona not only touched a tender chord, but also gave succor. In the 1951 film, *Dear Dad (Chichi koishi)*, she stands on a bridge leaning against its wall and brings a gentle smile to the man who has asked—indeed, beseeched her—to sing "I Am a Child of the City" (*Watashi wa machi no ko*) to the accompaniment of an accordion. In the 1952 film, *The Maiden of the Apple Farm (Ringo goen no shōjo)*, Hibari mournfully sings what was to become one of the most beloved songs of the entire Shōwa era, "Apple Ballad," for a man at a piano, who looks at her not only mesmerized, but soothed.

But it was the 1949 film, *Mournful Whistle*, featuring Hibari as a ragamuffin turned enchantress of the upper classes, that first turned her into a heroine of the people. The song sold 50,000 records and found a permanent place in many hearts. It was with this song that Hibari's first tears appear. A savior of the poor, she gives an apple to a hungry beggar, returns home, and tells her older sister that she has completed her chores. As she peels onions, she sings the song "Mournful Whistle," and begins to cry.

The film clearly parallels Hibari's life; embodying the hopes of the struggling Japanese, the maiden's star is on the rise. She sings, first and foremost, for them. On a barren plot of land before makeshift hovels, by a dank pond, she sings with joy and abandon. With absolute confidence in her voice and movements, she faces across the pond and toward the camera—at her fans and into a better future. The danger of Hibari's genius, however, was that it could elevate her above her fans, away from the people to the world of cultured elites. When an elegantly attired orchestra strikes up an accompaniment to Hibari's song in *Mournful Whistle*, we fear she has left us. But as if invoking the power of the past, a blind violinist—like the unlettered violinists who first accompanied *enka* singers on the streets—stands up and plays the opening notes of the song, and we are brought back, as we were in *Tokyo Kid*, to the authentic *enka* moment.

In *Mournful Whistle*, Hibari herself reminds her audience, with a wink, that she has never really left them. Elegantly fitted out in tuxedo and top hat, she gracefully swings a black cane and taps, struts, and swings around a spouting fountain, singing to a refined but stiff audience. Suddenly, the twelve-year-old Hibari spots her friends, the people, standing behind a railing, like prisoners behind bars. A fancy gentleman offers her wine, but she playfully refuses (preferring, perhaps, the more authentic sake?) and continues to strut and glide around her aristocratic audience, her lips in a defiant but teasing pout. She seems cocky, as if challenging them. She picks up a flower, brings it to her lips, and then offers it to an elegant lady; but she slyly pulls it away, throwing it into the fountain. The camera lingers on the floating blossom, evoking, in the cliché of Japanese clichés, the poor people behind the railing whose lives, too, are as fleeting as a flower upon the water. As the camera immediately cuts to the assembled ragamuffins, we see they are unkempt and ragged.

When a friend tries to push his way forward from the back, he is stopped by the barrier that separates the haves from the have-nots. But Hibari throws him, and the others with him, a kiss, and one man picks up a harmonica, as if he cannot keep himself from joining her in her sad, but hopeful song. A friend stops him, and Hibari dances on, tapping ostensibly for the aristocrats but actually for the gritty faces behind the railing—and for the working people in the audience. She approaches a couple kissing, but dances away from them disapprovingly, and brings to the dance floor an elegant lady.

The allegory may be unintentional, but in this film it is unmistakable: despite Hibari's claim to be of the people, she dances with the beau monde. The child's appeal to class solidarity in the movie comes from across a divide and is based on her separation from those on the other side. Her popularity depends, ultimately, on her difference from them. She is of the people, but she is also their royalty.

Hibari was loved by the "nameless" common people, to whom she was connected in a song like "Mournful Sake" through emotion and pain, not through knowledge and intellect. But she was scorned by intellectuals. Even in her heyday in the early 1950s, to the educated elite she "smelled old." Her fans were numerous and passionate about her, but as the chroniclers of her life remind us, she also encountered criticism, coldness, and dismissal. In 1957 an overzealous fan threw hydrochloric acid on her. She was popular, they say, but never appreciated. Perhaps, some suggest, her lack of education and her family troubles affected the upper-class view of her. Only poor, hardworking, long-suffering people like her could give her unconditional love.

The obsession among Hibari loyalists with the open contempt shown by intellectuals seems like the obsession of those who feel slighted by arbiters of taste. The loyalty of the people for Hibari never fully loses its bitter taste of sour grapes. One can understand the hagiographic and fawning quality of almost all writing and documentaries on Hibari. It grows from a desire by loyal insiders to hold on to a possession that outsiders, who only came to appreciate its value too late, threaten to take away. By protecting Hibari's status as victim and object of scorn, her fans maintain their dogged loyalty. By fostering this image, Hibari guarantees her fans' devotion. She will never leave them for a more elegant world.

When she did leave them forever, she was ailing but had by then attained the status of myth. In 1987, Hibari entered the hospital for a four-month stay. The physical details of her illness have never been revealed. Nearing death, stricken with pain, she asked her longtime friend and collaborator Funamura Tōru to write her a song, for she had to sing again before she died. He wrote "Tangled Hair" (*Midaregami*), likening her to a lone lighthouse overlooking a powerful ocean. Funamura worried that the song might be too difficult for her and that she might be too weak to carry it off, but she insisted he hold nothing back. She performed this song—at her last public appearance—six months before she died, in front of 50,000 people at Tokyo Dome. This final rendition lifted Hibari to the glittering heights of schmaltz, or to the pinnacle of spiritual resonance, depending on one's view. Bedecked in black and silver feathers, with a feathered, glittering black headdress shooting four feet into the air, her shoulders clad in armor, Hibari became a bird, or a creature from another planet, ready to take off, or to be transformed (like Yamato Takeru, the mythological Japanese prince, into a white bird-god?) into another realm.

The scene is both extravagantly artificial and deeply sincere. "Hibari," she says, her voice quivering, truly as if in pain, "supported by your love, can today again lift her wings; today I give these feelings of gratitude to song and sing to the very end." Lush strings (from the world of the entertainment industry) accompany clarinets and a single lonely guitar (from the authentic world of *enka*); her feathered figure is projected on a massive screen high above her head, and there is anguish on her face, a heavy burden that weighs her down as she seems ready to lift off.

When Hibari sang as the "Tokyo Kid" at age twelve, she sang to a future that she faced with defiance and lightness of heart. Here, at the end of her life, after all her losses, after seven years of illness, at the close of Shōwa, she seems to sing to her past. The light breeze wafting across her childhood song is now a sad wind that gives it depth and gravity. She concludes the number shaking with words originally written for her as she lay in her sickbed: "Do not die." To whom is she saying, "Do not die"? To herself? To her countless, nameless fans? To a sad, Japanese spirit of lament?

Her final words express a longing for what once was, might have been, and perhaps can be—for the world of *enka*. The future has always evaded *enka*. When Hibari sang "Mournful Sake" in 1966, she was protesting against a future promised by economic well-being that would erase the past and its troubles—she was singing a song out of her time. The 1960s belonged to the Beatles and Beatles-inspired groups such as the Blue Comets and the Tigers; the 1970s to idol singers, stars such as Arai Yumi, Inoue Yōsui, and Nakajima Miyuki, and bands such as Happy End, the Brain Police (Zuinō Keisatsu), and Ostracize (Murahachibu); the 1980s to the Yellow Magic Orchestra, Michael Jackson, and Madonna. In the 1970s *enka* became frozen as a genre for the middle-aged and old, a distinct category of music separate from other forms of popular song, referring to prewar songs as well—many of which had fallen into disfavor in the early years after the war, when distance from the past seemed a priority. Now, at the end of Hibari's life, through the speeches of politicians, the disputations of intellectuals, and the advertising of the travel industry, the virtues of the "hometown" of authentic Japan in the provinces seemed not only acceptable but ideal.

To intellectuals, to liberals, to the young, *enka* was now denigrated as the song of boozy businessmen letting loose with karaoke machines in tiny urban bars. In the words of one prominent Japanese musicologist: "If today modern *enka* is despised as the music only of drunken company employees crying into their beer, it should not be forgotten that this now, apparently debased form was once an important vehicle for the dissemination of liberal ideas in a time of repression and resistance to progressive social change."[17]

Why, one wonders, did Hibari shed no tears during her last performance of "Mournful Sake"? According to Furuzawa Taku, it was "a blank self-abstraction from exhaustion and collapse, a prayer like water, the silence of her body, the figure of a simple and plain physical being that says, 'I am still alive.' "[18]

> With Misora Hibari's death, "Mournful Sake" disappeared eternally from the popular music repertoire. Among the over 1,000 songs recorded by Misora Hibari in her 52-year career, only this one song must never be sung outside the physical being of Hibari. Because this song could only have been nurtured by Misora Hibari, could only have been cultivated by her remorse. Because this song was the landscape of Misora Hibari's love, of all that lay outside her being. This song was the only landscape that could heal "Misora Hibari."[19]

To her fans, Misora Hibari has remained a voice from the past that echoes into the future, and *enka*, though an outmoded song style, does not die. Funamura Tōru wrote "Waterfront of Sorrow" (*Aishū hatoba*) in 1960 thinking of her. To him, she was the light of a buoy, crying into the mist, and the waves of the sea, murmuring a song "filled with memories, whose sounds linger and will not disappear."[20]

NOTES

1. Furuzawa Taku, "Inori: Ikiisogu Bara" [Prayer for the living rose], in *Misora Hibari: 'utau joō' no subete* [Misora Hibari: The singing queen], ed. Bungei Shunjū (Tokyo: Bungei Shunjū, 1990), 154.

2. Ibid., 158.

3. Mita Munesuke, *Kindai Nihon no Shinjō no Rekishi* [A history of emotions in modern Japan] (Tokyo: Kōdensha, 1992), 80–95.

4. Nippon Geinō Retsudan, *Misora Hibari o Kataru* [Speaking of Misora Hibari] (Tokyo: Nippon Geinō Retsudan, 1990), videotape.

5. Takeuchi Rō, *Misora Hibari* (Tokyo: Asahi Bunko, 1987), 186.

6. Ongaku no Tomosha, ed., *Shōwa kayōshi: Shōwa 21-Shōwa 51* [A history of Shōwa popular song, 1956–1976] (Tokyo: Ongaku no Tomosha, 1977), 186.

7. Nippon Geinō Retsudan, *Misora Hibari*.

8. Ongaku no Tomosha, *Shōwa kayōshi*, 182–83.

9. Mita, *Kindai Nihon*, 48.

10. Ibid., 96–113.

11. Hayashi Mariko, "Sayonara Misora Hibari-san" [Goodbye, Misora Hibari], in *Misora Hibari*, ed. Bungei Shunjū, 134.

12. Hisashi Inoue, "Kojin de kiita 'Kanashiki Kuchibue' " [The "Mournful Whistle" I heard at the orphanage], in ibid., 22.

13. Miyako Harumi, "Uta to itta ni narikireta Misora Hibari-san" [Misora Hibari, who became one with her song], in ibid., 135.

14. Takeuchi, *Misora Hibari*, 146–47.

15. Albert Murray, *Stomping the Blues* (New York: DeCapo Press, 1976), 51, 68.

16. Ongaku no Tomosha, *Shōwa kayōshi*, 10–11.

17. Mitsui Tōru, "The French Revolution and the Emergence of a New Form of Popular Song in Japan, 1789–1989," in *Musique, Histoire, Democratie*, vol. 1 (Paris: Editions de la Maison des Sciences de l'Homme, 1989), 65.

18. Furuzawa, "Inori," 165.

19. Ibid., 166.

20. Nippon Geinō Retsudan, *Misora Hibari*.

Index

Ainu people, 109–10
Akihito, Emperor, 210
American Railway Transportation
  (Johnson), 126
Aoki Yūsuke, 70
"The Apple Song" (*Ringo no uta*), 223
Arai Yumi, 227
Arakawa Akira, 105
Arisawa Hiromi, 177–78, 184
Artisans, rank in society, 1
Awaya Noriko, 222
Azabu Christian Church, 71

Baba Tatsui, 72
Balliett, Whitney, 220
Ban Masaji, 41
Beatles, 227
Blue Comets, 227
Bluestocking Society. *See* Seitosha
  (Bluestocking Society)
Brain Police (Zuinō Keisatsu), 227
Bryn Mawr College, 90–91, 92
Bunmei kaika (Civilization and
  enlightenment) slogan, 77, 81, 99,
  115
Byakuren, 161

Cabinet Information Bureau, 169
Capitalism, 135, 175, 177–79, 186–88
Censorship, 155, 175
Chicago, Rock Island & Pacific
  Railroad Company, 127
Child-rearing, 138–43, 146–47, 151
China: relations with Japan, 43, 44, 57,
  135, 155, 179, 184–85, 193, 199,
  204; relations with Ryukyu King-
  dom, 100–101
Chinese Eastern Railway, 129
Chōhei (friend of Mori Yoshiki), 35
Chōshū domain, 44, 99
Christianity, 68–69, 70–71, 75, 82
Civil Code of 1898, 144
Clark, William Smith, 81–82

Classes, 168, 179, 187, 190, 225–26;
  artisans, 1; merchants, 1–2, 43;
  middle class, 135–36, 138, 139, 140,
  149, 151–52, 156, 158, 166;
  outcasts, 1, 54; peasants, 1, 43, 77,
  104, 105, 110, 112, 139, 143, 184–
  85; samurai, 1, 2, 25–41, 43, 46, 52,
  77, 139
Cold War, 185
Confucianism, 43, 61, 62, 66, 71–72,
  75, 78, 101
Court life, 3, 9, 22, 45
Crawford, Joseph, 125–26
Culture, popular, 136, 155, 207. *See
  also Enka* music

Daidō Danketsu movement, 61, 65
Daimyo, 45; relations with samurai, 1,
  2, 38–39; relations with shoguns, 25,
  26, 28–29, 39–40, 44, 47, 48–49
Dajōdaijin, position of, 4, 6
Dear Dad (*Chichi koishi*) (film), 224
Defiance College, 71
Democracy, 61, 89, 186, 187, 189, 190,
  194, 195, 215
Dennery, Etienne, 181–82
Diet, 64–65, 67, 74, 77, 88–89, 95, 97,
  102, 115, 130–31
Domesticity, 81, 87–88, 97. *See also*
  Gender relations; Marriage
Dōseiai, 155, 159
Dutch. *See* Holland

Economic conditions: after Meiji
  Restoration, 25, 77; poverty, 111,
  177, 179, 181, 182; after World
  War II, 180, 185, 194–95, 197, 205–
  6, 210, 213; before World War II,
  135, 136, 182–83
Edo. *See* Tokyo
Education, 44, 111, 143–44, 145;
  importance of, 77–78, 99, 100, 136,
  137, 139, 175, 176, 189–90; Imperial

Education (*continued*)
　Rescript (1890), 78; after Meiji
　　Restoration, 43, 46, 71–73, 77–78,
　　99, 102–3, 115, 222; of women, 66–
　　67, 71, 78, 82–84, 86, 87, 95, 96, 97,
　　137, 147–48, 157, 165; after World
　　War II, 194, 195
Emerson, Ralph Waldo, 71
Emi Suiin, 119
Emperors, 1, 55–56, 137, 194; Akihito,
　210; Gokōmyō, 4, 5; Gomizunoo, 3,
　4, 5, 6–9, 11, 13, 14, 16, 20, 22;
　Gosai, 4, 5, 7, 13, 14–15, 18, 20, 22;
　Goyōzei, 22; Hirohito, 96, 136, 207,
　210, 214; Meishō, 4, 5, 7, 10, 21;
　Reigen, 4, 5, 10, 11, 14–17, 19, 22;
　relations with shoguns, 3, 15, 43, 44,
　49, 50; Taishō, 175, 176, 181
English language, 83, 84, 86, 87, 88,
　93, 116, 129
Enka music, 214, 219–20, 221–24, 227,
　228
Europe, 127, 167, 181–83, 187
Expo '70, 205–6
Extraterritoriality, 44, 77, 87

Fascism, 182, 189
Fatherhood, 138–44
Feminism, 167–68, 169
France, 101, 135, 181–82, 193, 221
Freedom, individual, 3, 4, 75, 115,
　136, 148; of women, 93–94, 97, 165,
　167–68, 169
Fujiwara clan, 6
Fukoku kyōhei (Rich country, strong
　army) slogan, 78, 115
Fukutomi Hanjo, 34
Fukuzawa Yukichi, 140–41, 148
Funamura Tōru, 226, 228
Furuichi Kōi, 85
Furuzawa Taku, 227–28
Fushimi, Princess, 11

Garland, Judy, 217
Gender relations, 2, 82, 97, 158–59,
　161, 162, 163, 168; after Meiji
　Restoration, 61, 69–70, 74, 75. *See
　also* Gender roles; Marriage
Gender roles: in child-rearing, 138–
　43, 146–47, 151; of men, 2, 78, 85,
　137, 138–40, 142–43, 144, 145, 148–

49, 151–52; of women, 2, 4, 6, 46–
　47, 78–79, 81, 82, 83, 85, 87–88, 89,
　93–94, 95, 96, 97, 111, 135, 137,
　138, 139–40, 142, 144, 145, 148,
　151–52, 155, 156–59, 161–62, 163,
　164–65, 171. *See also* Gender
　relations
Germany, 135, 181, 182, 183
Gokōmyō, Emperor, 4, 5
Gomizunoo, Emperor, 22; children
　born to, 4, 5; death of, 13, 14, 16;
　relationship with Konoe Motohiro,
　7, 8–9, 11; relationship with
　Shinanomiya, 3, 6–9, 11, 13, 16, 20
Gosai, Emperor, 4, 5, 7, 13, 14–15, 18,
　20, 22
Gōshi, 30–36
Gotō Kazuko, 93
Gotō Shinpei, 93, 116, 130–31
Gotō Shojiro, 64, 65
Goyōzei, Emperor, 22
Great Britain, 120, 127, 135, 182, 193;
　Labour Party, 186, 187
Great Depression, 135, 182–83
Growing Up (*Takekurabe*) (film), 221
Guam, 197–98, 199–204, 207–9, 211
Gumma prefecture, 65, 74

Hadley, Arthur Twining, 91
Hadley, Helen, 91
Happy End, 227
Hara Takashi, 175
Harper, William Rainey, 90
Harris, Townsend, 43–44
Hatashin Mihoko, 209
Hatoyama Haruko, 78–79, 81–97;
　attitudes toward motherhood, 85,
　86–87, 88, 94, 95, 96, 97; attitudes
　toward women's liberation, 93–94,
　97; death of, 96; education of, 82–
　84, 86, 88; as educator, 84, 85, 87,
　92, 95, 96; relationship with Hideo,
　94, 95; relationship with Ichirō, 94,
　95; relationship with Kazuo, 84–86,
　87–89, 93, 94–95; relationship with
　Kikuko, 85, 86, 87; visit to United
　States, 90–92; women's groups
　activities of, 92–93, 96
Hatoyama Hideo, 87, 88, 94, 95, 97
Hatoyama Ichirō, 86–87, 88, 94, 95,
　97

Hatoyama Kazuo: as politician, 88–89; relationship with Haruko, 84–86, 87–89, 93, 94–95; visit to United States, 90–92
Hatoyama Kikuko, 85, 86, 87, 94
Hattori Ryōichi, 222, 223
Hayashi Fumiko, 169
Hayashi Oyoyo, 28
Hayo (adoptive mother of Ishizaka Shōkō), 66
Heian Court, 162
Heike chanting, 21
Hereditary status. See Status, hereditary
Hida Hamagorō, 118–19
Higuchi Ichiyō, 221
Hio Academy, 66
Hiratsuka Raichō, 165
Hirohito, Emperor, 96, 136, 207, 210, 214
Hitler, Adolf, 182
Hokkaido, 110, 125
Holiday, Billie, 220
Holland, 3, 43, 101, 170, 193
Homosexuality, 155, 159, 160, 162, 163, 165, 166
Honda Co., 194
Hoshin Women's Club, 93
Hoshi Tōru, 65
Hugo, Victor, 68

Ichijō family, 6
Ichijō Fuyutsune, 14–15
Iha Fuyū, 110
Ii Naosuke, 49
Ikeda Hiroshi, 156
Imamura Junko, 93
Imperial College of Agricultural Science, 103
Imperialism, 149, 156, 169–70, 179, 184–85, 193, 199
Imperial Rescript on Education (1890), 78
Imperial University. See Tokyo University
Industrialization, 44, 78, 79, 115, 135, 139, 149, 155, 158
Inoue Hisashi, 220
Inoue Kaoru, 88, 92
Inoue Kinjirō, 92
Inoue Sabanoshin, 30–36
Inoue Yōsui, 227

Ireland, 182
Isawa Shūji, 222
Ishizaka Kōreki, 61, 66, 68, 71–74; conversion to Christianity, 75; death of, 74; political activities, 72; residence in United States, 62, 70, 73–74
Ishizaka Mina, 61, 66–71, 81; conversion to Christianity, 68–69, 71, 75; education of, 66–67; relationship with Kitamura Tōkoku, 62, 67–68, 69–71, 74, 75; relationship with Shōkō, 66, 69–70, 71
Ishizaka Shōkō, 44, 107, 175; death of, 75; political activities, 61, 62–65, 67, 72, 75; relationship with Mina, 66, 69–70, 71
Ishizaka Toshi, 62, 66, 74–75
Ishizaka Yama, 62, 66
Itagaki Taisuke, 63, 64, 67, 72
Itasaka Umazaemon, 33
Itō, Mrs. (Japanese resident of Germany), 92
Itō Akiko, 161
Itō Den'emon, 161
Itō Hirobumi, 91
Itō Masahi, 204
Itō Noe, 169
Iwamoto Gashō, 102
The Izu Dancer (Izu no odoriko) (film), 221

Jackson, Michael, 227
Jahana Noboru, 78, 79, 99–112, 175; education of, 78, 100, 102–3; and former aristocrats, 103–8, 110; as hero, 104–5, 110, 111–12; insanity of, 100; and Okinawa Agricultural Bank, 107–8, 109; and Okinawa Club, 107–8, 109; and peasants, 104, 105, 112; relationship with Narahara, 103–5, 107, 108, 111, 112; relationship with Ōta, 102, 106; as self-made man, 100; and sugar-cane, 103, 108–9
Japan: attitudes toward foreigners, 43, 44, 45, 48, 81, 87, 92, 97, 101, 118, 127, 128–30, 159, 178, 179; attitudes toward World War II, 170, 198, 203, 204, 205–6, 208, 216–17; Constitution of 1889, 44, 55–56, 73,

Japan (*continued*)
194; cultural homogeneity in, 110,
112; imperialist foreign policy of,
149, 156, 169–70, 179, 184–85, 193,
199; relations with China, 43, 44,
57, 135, 155, 179, 184–85, 193, 199,
204; relations with France, 135, 193;
relations with Great Britain, 135,
193; relations with Holland, 3, 43,
101, 170, 193; relations with Korea,
43; relations with Okinawa, 99, 100–
102, 106–7, 109–11; relations with
Russia, 44, 59, 127, 128, 135;
relations with Soviet Union, 193;
relations with United States, 43–44,
48, 101, 125, 135, 136, 149–50, 155,
185, 193–95, 199, 204–5, 213, 215;
rural attitudes in, 136, 137–38, 141;
under U.S. occupation, 125, 149,
185, 194–95, 205, 213, 215; Western
influence on, 3, 44, 52, 54, 62, 66,
70–71, 72–73, 74–75, 77, 81, 83, 85,
87, 97, 116–17, 118, 121, 125–26,
127, 139, 140–41, 143, 148, 158,
159, 178, 179, 181–83, 186, 187,
221, 222, 223; *zaibatsu* in, 115, 121,
135. *See also* Culture, popular;
Economic conditions; Education;
Newspapers and journals; Political
conditions
Japan Communist Party (JCP), 167,
179–80, 185, 190
Japanese National Railways, 131, 132
Japanese Women's Academic Society
(Dai Nihon jogakkai), 93
Japan League of Women's Associa-
tions, 96
Japan Socialist Party, 186, 188–89,
190
Japan Tourist Bureau, 129–30
Japan Women's Hygiene Association,
93, 96
JCP. *See* Japan Communist Party
Jiyūtō. *See* Liberal Party (Jiyūtō)
Johnson, Emory R., 126–27, 132
Jugō, position of, 4, 12

Kagawa prefecture, 103
Kagawa Shihoko, 93
Kagoshima prefecture, 100, 102, 103
Kanagawa prefecture, 63–65, 72

Kanpaku, position of, 4, 6, 14–15, 19,
21, 22
Kansai Railway, 121, 122–24, 126
Karōshi, 132
Kasagi Shizuko, 223–24
Kasuga Shrine, 7
Katsu Kaishū, 71
Kawabata Yasunari, 221
Kawade Kiyohisa, 224
Keio University, 148
Keynes, John Maynard, 180
Kikuchi Kan, 169
Kikuchi Yukie, 160, 161
Kikuike Chiyo, 94
Kinoshita Yoshio, 78, 79, 115–32; and
customer service on railroads, 116–
17, 122–25, 127, 132; death of, 131,
132; education of, 78, 116, 125; and
foreign tourism, 127, 128–30, 132;
personality, 131, 132; and railroad
gauge conversion, 130–31, 132; visit
to United States, 125–27
Kishi Nobusuke, 205
Kitajima Itoko, 93
Kitamura Eiko, 70, 71
Kitamura Tōkoku: conversion to
Christianity, 69; personality, 67–68;
"Pessimistic Poet and Women," 70;
political activities, 67, 68, 72, 73;
relationship with Ishizaka Mina, 62,
67–68, 69–71, 74, 75
Kobayashi Hideo, 168
Kobayashi Ichizō, 169–70
Kōchi, 26, 28
Kochinda, 100
Kōdōkai, 106–7
Kōga Masao, 219, 221
Koishikawa Young Women's Associa-
tion, 96
Kokuyū tetsudō no shōrai, 131
Komashaku Kimi, 167–68
Konagai Shōshū, 71–72
Kondo Isami, 62
Konoe family, 6, 7, 10–11, 19
Konoe Hiroko, 4, 9, 12–13, 17, 20
Konoe Iehiro, 4, 9, 17, 19, 21–22
Konoe Iehisa, 4, 22
Konoe Motohiro, 4, 20, 21; family of,
6, 7; personality, 13; relationship
with Gomizunoo, 7, 8–9, 11;
relationship with Gosai, 13, 14–15;

relationship with Nobuna, 17–19;
relationship with Reigen, 10, 11,
14–16, 17–18, 19; relationship with
Shinanomiya, 3, 6–7, 22; relation-
ship with Shin-Chūnagon, 11–12
Konoe Nobuna, 9, 17–19
Korea, 43, 68, 135, 193
Korean War, 194
Kōtoku Shūsui, 112
Kozuka Kinhichi, 208, 209
Kōzu Sensaburō, 84
Kujō family, 6
Kumei Tadao, 169
Kumeo (nephew of Nishimiya Hide),
55, 58
Kurino Shinichirō, 85
Kyōgen theater, 20, 21
Kyōritsu Women's School, 87, 90, 93,
95
Kyoto, 1, 9, 10–11, 20–21
Kyūshū University, 180, 185

Labor unions, 186
Ladd, Mrs. George Trumbull, 91, 94
Land reform, 149, 194
League of Japanese Patriots, 73–74
League to Establish a National
Assembly, 64
Lenin, V. I., 183, 187
Lesbianism, 155, 159, 160, 162, 163,
165, 166
Liberal Democratic Party, 205
Liberal Party (Jiyūtō), 64, 67

MacArthur, Douglas, 194
Madonna, 227
The Maiden of the Apple Farm (Ringo
goen no shōjo) (film), 224
Manchuria, 135, 136, 149, 167, 182,
184, 193, 199, 205
Marriage, 27–28, 45, 56, 74, 137, 152,
156, 166; as arranged, 6, 12, 70, 84–
85, 144, 148–49, 160, 165; child-
rearing in, 138–43, 146–47, 151; as
chosen, 69–70, 75, 94; domesticity,
81, 87–88, 97; Ryōsai kenbo (good
wife, wise mother), 81, 95, 96, 148,
157, 158, 159, 161, 164, 165
Marxism, 177–80, 183, 185–91
Matsui Dōsetsu, 33
Matsumoto Sōichirō, 116

Matsuura Daisuke, 147
Matsuura Isami, 136, 137–52; death of,
151; and education of children, 143–
44, 147–48; education of, 145, 147;
as father, 138–44; and marriage of
children, 148–49; relationship with
Kou, 142, 143, 147, 152
Matsuura Kou, 138, 139–40, 141–42,
150; death of, 151; relationship with
Isami, 142, 143, 147, 152
Matsuura Miyo, 146–47
Matsuura Moto, 147
Matsuura Yūya, 145–46, 147
McKinley, William, 90, 91
Meiji Restoration, 49, 50, 99; changes
resulting from, 44, 45, 51–52, 54,
59, 61, 62–63, 66, 71, 74, 75, 81, 82,
83, 112, 115, 194–95; economic
conditions after, 25, 77; education
after, 43, 46, 71–73, 77–78, 99, 102–
3, 115, 222; gender relations after,
61, 69–70, 74, 75; hereditary status
abolished after, 44, 52, 61, 137;
military after, 44, 78, 115, 139
Meishō, Emperor, 4, 5, 7, 10, 21
Men: as fathers, 138–44. See also
Gender roles, of men
Merchants, 1–2, 43; rank in society, 1
Meyer, Balthasar, 125
Middle class, 135–36, 138, 139, 140,
149, 151–52, 156, 158, 166
Military, 169–70, 203–4, 219; Fukoku
kyōhei (Rich country, strong army)
slogan, 78, 115; after Meiji Restora-
tion, 44, 78, 115, 139; rank in
society, 1; before World War II,
136, 155, 168. See also Daimyo;
Samurai
Mill, John Stuart, 72
Miller, H., 127
Minagawa Bunzō, 204
Minobe Ryōkichi, 180, 190
Minobe Tatsukichi, 180
Misora Hibari, 194, 213–28; and "I
Am a Child of the City" (Watashi wa
machi no ko), 224; and "Apple
Ballad" (Ringo oiwake), 215, 224; and
Dear Dad (Chichi koishi), 224; death
of, 214; and Growing Up
(Takekurabe), 221; and "The
Homeland Tsugaru," 216; and The

Misora Hibari (*continued*)
Izu Dancer (*Izu no odoriko*), 221; and
The Maiden of the Apple Farm (*Ringo
goen no shōjo*), 224; and "The Mother
of Kudan" (*Kudan no haha*), 215–16;
and "Mournful Sake" (*Kanashii sake*),
216–21, 226, 227–28; and *Mournful
Whistle* (*Kanashiki kuchibue*), 215,
224–25; relationship with
Funamura, 226; as shaman, 214–16;
and *Sword Slashing* (*Chanbara kenpō*),
221; and "Tangled Hair," 226–27;
and *Tokyo Kid*, 224, 225, 227
Mito domain, 45, 46, 49–51, 52, 58
Mitsubishi Co., 121
Mitsuko (daughter of Gomizunoo),
9
Miyaji Harue, 40
Miyake Shigeri, 164
Miyake Yasuko, 164
Miyako Harumi, 220–21
Miyamoto Yuriko, 167, 169
Miyazaki Ryūsuke, 161
Moku (Tosa senior administrator),
34–35
Monday Club, 93
Monma Chiyo, 161–65, 166, 167,
170, 171
Mori Aninori, 92
Mori Hirosada, 25–28
Mori Hirotake, 28
Mori Kumenoshin, 30
Mori Masana, 41
Mori Omase, 28
Mori Otsune, 28
Mori Umeno, 27–28
Mori Yoshiki, 1, 2, 25–41; duties, 29–
30, 33–39, 38, 40–41; personality,
40–41; relationship with Hirotake,
28; relationship with Yamauchi
Toyochika, 29–30; relationship with
Yamauchi Toyokazu, 29–30; and
rural samurai, 30–36
Morris, Ivan, 111
Mosai Academy, 71–72
Motherhood, 139–42, 151–52, 156–
57, 164–65; attitudes of Hatoyama
Haruko toward, 85, 86–87, 88, 94,
95, 96, 97; *Ryōsai kenbo* (good wife,
wise mother), 81, 95, 148, 157, 158,
159, 161, 164, 165

Mournful Whistle (*Kanashiki kuchibue*)
(film), 215, 224–25
Murano Tsune'emon, 72
Murray, Albert, 222
Music, 20, 21, 62, 74–75; boogie
woogie, 223–24; *enka*, 214, 219–20,
221–24, 227, 228; *ryūkōuta*, 222; in
United States, 219, 220, 221, 222
Myōhōin, Prince, 4, 15, 18

Nabeshima, Mrs. (Japanese resident of
Germany), 92
Nabeshima Nagako, 93
Nagano Prefectural Assembly, 120
Nagoya, 122
Nakahata Satoru, 202, 208
Nakajima Miyuki, 227
Nakajima Nobuyuki, 63
Nanokawa villagers, 29–30
Nan'yōsha, 107
Narahara Shigeru, 103–5, 107, 108,
111, 112
National Assembly. *See* Diet
Nationalism, 70, 136, 148, 179, 203,
223
National Mobilization Law, 183
Natsume Sōseki, 143
Nature, appreciation of, 1, 20–21, 22
Newspapers and journals: *Bungakkai*
(Literary World), 168; *Bunshō Sekai*
(Literary World), 157; and death of
Misora, 214; *Fujin Kōron* (Women's
Review), 170; *Fujin Kurabu*
(Women's Club), 156, 168; *Fujin
sekai* (Women's World), 94; *Fujo
shinbun*, 96; *Japan Weekly Mail*, 119,
123, 125; *Jiji shinpō*, 119; *Kaizō*
(Reconstruction), 166; *Kurosōbi*
(Black Rose), 165–66; *Okinawa jiron*,
107; *Onna* (Women), 93; *Ōsaka
Asahi Shinbun*, 169; *Ōsaka Mainichi
Shinbun*, 169, 170; *Peace Economics*
(*Heiwa Keizai*), 190; *Ryūkyū Shinpō*,
100, 102, 106; *Seitō*, 97; *Sensha*
(Tank), 169; *Shinchō* (New Tide),
157; *Shin Niho* (New Japan), 73–74;
Shōjo Gahō (Girls Illustrated), 157;
Shōjokai (Girls' Circle), 157; *Shōjo no
Tomo* (Girls' Friend), 157; *Shōjo
Sekai* (Girls' World), 157; *Shufu no
Tomo* (Housewife's Friend), 167,

169; *Sukōru* (Squall), 169; *Tairiku Shinpōsha*, 184–85; *Tōkyō Asahi Shinbun*, 161; *Tōkyō keizai zasshi*, 119, 120; *Tōkyō Nichinichi*, 95, 125, 168, 169; and Yokoi Shōichi, 198, 206–7, 209–11; *Yomiuri Shinbun*, 171
Nichigon, Archbishop, 18
Nijō family, 6
Ninomiya Sontoku, 110, 143
Nippon Railway Company, 121
Nishimiya Hide, 44, 45–59, 81; business activities, 52–54, 55, 56, 57; relationship with Kumeo, 55; relationship with Nobutaka, 52, 53–55, 56, 57, 58; relationship with Tokugawa Yoshiko, 47, 48, 49–50, 51, 56, 57
Nishimiya Nobutaka, 52, 53–55, 56, 57–58, 59
Nishimura Yoshiko, 186
Nitobe Inazō, 82
Nō dance, 20, 21
Nonaka Jōhei, 37–38
Nonomura Chūemon, 33
North Eastern Railway Company, 127
Notsuda, 62–63, 65, 72, 74–75

Obata Hideyoshi, 200
Occupation Government (SCAP), 149, 185, 194, 205, 213, 215
Ogawa Teru, 57, 58
Ōi Kentarō, 72
Ōimikado (adoptive father of Konoe Nobuna), 17–18
Okinawa, 77, 79; attitudes of mainland Japanese toward, 99, 109–11; former aristocrats in, 102, 103–8, 109–10; immigration from, 110, 111, 112; peasants in, 104, 105, 112; relations with Japan, 99, 100–102, 106–7, 109–11; Ryukyu Kingdom, 100–102; *somayama* in, 104–5, 107, 112; sugarcane in, 103, 108–9; taxes in, 102, 111
Okinawa Agricultural Bank, 107–8, 109
Okinawa Club, 107–8, 109
Okuda Shinzō, 176
Onodo Hiroo, 208
Onoe Kikugorō V, 117
Osaka, 122, 205–6, 222

Ostracize (Murahachibu), 227
Ōsugi Sakae, 169, 175, 176–77
Ōta Chōfu, 102, 106, 107, 109–10
Outcasts, 54; rank in society, 1
Ōyama Sutematsu, 92–93

Patriotic Women's Society, 93, 96
Peace Preservation Laws, 77, 165, 175, 180, 183–84
Peasants, 43, 77, 110, 139, 143, 184–85; and Jahana, 104, 105, 112; rank in society, 1
Pen Corps (Pen butai), 169
Penrod, Christina, 71
People's Rights movement, 63, 64, 65, 107, 175
Perry, Commodore Matthew C., 43, 44, 48
Piaf, Edith, 221
Police, 184
Political conditions: after World War II, 204–5; Daidō Danketsu movement, 61, 65; government repression, 73–74, 77, 136, 155, 168–69, 175, 176–77, 180, 181, 183–84, 185; after Meiji Restoration, 61, 62–65, 67–68, 72, 73, 75, 115, 143; People's Rights movement, 63, 64, 65, 107, 175; political parties, 64, 67, 77, 115, 130–31, 132, 167, 179–80, 185, 186, 187, 188–89, 190, 205; and Yokoi Shōichi, 210
Poverty, 111, 177, 179, 181, 182
Presley, Elvis, 220
Prime minister, office of, 77, 97, 175, 205
Prince, Miss (teacher at Tokyo Girls' School), 92, 93
Progressive Party, 67
Publishing industry, 78, 136, 155. See also Newspapers and journals

Quakerism, 71

Railroads, 78, 115–32; Bullet Trains, 132; Chicago, Rock Island & Pacific Railroad Company, 127; Chinese Eastern Railway, 129; customer service on, 116–17, 118–21, 122–25, 127, 132; freight traffic on, 117; gauges of, 130–31, 132; in Great

Railroads (*continued*)
  Britain, 120; Japanese National
    Railways, 131, 132; Kansai Railway,
    121, 122–24, 126; nationalization of,
    115, 127–28; Nippon Railway
    Company, 121; North Eastern
    Railway Company, 127; privately
    owned, 115, 120–24, 126, 127–28,
    131, 132; privatization of, 131;
    San'yō Railway Company, 121–22;
    state owned, 115, 116, 120, 121,
    122–25, 128–29, 131, 132; Trans-
    Siberian Railway, 129; in United
    States, 120, 125–26
Reigen, Emperor, 4, 5, 10, 11, 14–17,
    19, 22
Riso (mother of Mori Omase), 28
Rōnō-ha, 180, 183–84
Roosevelt, Theodore, 90, 91
Russia, 127, 129, 130, 179
Russo-Japanese War, 44, 59, 124, 128,
    135
Ryōsai kenbo (good wife, wise mother),
    81, 95, 96, 148, 157, 158, 159, 161,
    164, 165
Ryūkōuta, 222
Ryukyu Kingdom, 100–102

Sakhalin, 110
Sakisaka Itsurou, 183
Sakurai (Konoe family butler), 22
Samurai, 25–41, 43, 46, 52, 77, 139;
    rank in society, 1; relations with
    daimyo, 1, 2, 38–39; right to punish
    rudeness with death, 27, 30–36;
    rural samurai (*gōshi*), 30–36, 37–38
Sand, Jordan, 87
Sanger, Margaret, 165
Sanuki, 103
San'yō Railway Company, 121–22
Sapporo Agricultural College, 82
Satsuma domain, 44, 99, 100–101,
    102, 103
Sawaki Hidae, 214–15
SCAP. *See* Occupation Government
Seelye, Laurenus Clark, 91
Seitōsha (Bluestocking Society), 165,
    169
Seiyūkai party, 130–31
Senjinkun, 203–4
Sesshō, position of, 4

Sexuality, 155, 158–59, 160, 161–64,
    165, 166, 171, 207
Shiba Shirō, 73
Shichi Mikio, 201, 202, 208
Shimabara rebellion, 26
Shimoda Utako, 96
Shinagawa Women's School, 71
Shinanomiya Tsuneko, Princess, 2, 3–
    4, 5, 6–22, 45, 81; artistic interests,
    20, 21; children of, 9, 12–13, 17–19,
    21–22; individual freedom of, 3, 4;
    nature loved by, 20–21, 22; person-
    ality, 6, 13–14, 15, 19; relationship
    with Gomizunoo, 3, 6–9, 11, 13, 16,
    20; relationship with Gosai, 7, 14–
    15, 18, 20; relationship with Hiroko,
    12–13, 17, 20; relationship with
    Iehiro, 17, 19, 21–22; relationship
    with Konoe Motohiro, 3, 6–7,
    22; relationship with Meishō, 7, 21;
    relationship with Myōhōin, 18;
    relationship with Nobuna, 17–
    19; relationship with Reigen, 10,
    14–17; relationship with Shin-
    Chūnagon, 4, 11–12; relationship
    with Tōfukumon'in, 7, 10, 12;
    relationship with Yōtokuin, 7;
    Shichiku villa, 9, 21, 22
Shin-Chūnagon, 4, 5, 11–12
Shinkei, Prince, 21
Shoguns. *See* Tokugawa shoguns
Shōjo, 158–60, 166, 167
Shosaburō (Tosa senior administrator),
    34
Shō Tai, 106
Shōwa, Emperor. *See* Hirohito,
    Emperor
Siberian Intervention (1918), 130,
    135
Silk, exports of, 78
Sinatra, Frank, 219
Sino-Japanese War, 44, 57, 128, 135
Smiles, Samuel, 83
Smith College, 91, 92
Socialism, 168, 175, 183, 185–90
Sogan (Konoe family friend), 18
Somayama, 104–5, 107, 112
Sono (Fujiwara) family, 4
Sono Kuniko. *See* Shin-Chūnagon
Sonshō, Prince, 10
Sony Corp., 194

Soviet Union, 167, 179, 181, 183, 187, 193, 204
Spencer, Herbert, 72
Status, hereditary, 1, 25, 26, 27–28, 43, 77; abolished after Meiji Restoration, 44, 52, 61, 137
Sugarcane, 103, 108–9
Sword Slashing (*Chanbara kenpō*) (film), 221

Taga Tsutomu, 82
Taishō, Emperor, 175
Taiwan, 135
Takahama Kyoshi, 170
Takahashi (Governor of Okinawa), 111
Takahashi Masako, 186
Takahashi Masao, 135, 136, 175–91; death of, 191; as economist, 185; education of, 175, 176, 177, 180; as educator, 189–90; imprisonment of, 183–84; Marxism of, 177–80, 183, 185–91; *Peace Economics*, 190; *Politics and Economics at a Turning Point*, 187; relationship with Arisawa, 177–78, 184; relationship with Dennery, 181–82; relationship with Minobe Ryōkichi, 180, 190; relationship with Minobe Tatsukichi, 180; relationship with Okuda, 176; and Rōnō-ha, 180, 183–84; *Talks on Socialism*, 186; visit to Europe, 181–83
Takamine Chōkyō, 102, 106
Takamura Taigo, 30–36
Takarazuka Revue, 170
Takashima (ambassador to United States), 90
Takatsukasa family, 6
Takebashi Girls' School, 83, 93
Takehisa Yumeji, 157–58
The Tale of Genji, 20
Tamura Toshiko, 159
Tea ceremony, 27, 46, 47, 54, 55
Terada Kaoru, 94, 95
Terada Sakae, 94
Textile industry, 78
Thomas, M. Carey, 90
Tigers (musical group), 227
Tocqueville, Alexis de, 72
Tōfukumon'in, 7, 10, 12

Tōjō Hideki, 203–4, 205
Tōkai Sanshi, 73
Tokudaiji Kintomo, 22
Tokugawa Akitake, 50
Tokugawa Nariaki, 44, 45, 46, 47–48
Tokugawa shoguns, 1, 45, 77, 101; Hidetada, 7; Ienobu, 4; Ieyasu, 12; policies toward foreigners, 43–44; relations with daimyo, 25, 26, 28–29, 39–40, 44, 47, 48–49; relations with emperors, 3, 15, 43, 44, 49, 50; Tsunayoshi, 13; Yoshinobu, 49, 50, 51, 53, 57, 99
Tokugawa Tsunatoyo, 12, 20
Tokugawa Yoshiko, 47, 48–50, 51, 56, 57
Tokyo, 59, 81, 117–18, 147, 150; earthquake (1923), 95, 168–69, 175; Olympics in, 205; during Tokugawa shogunate, 26, 28–29
Tokyo Girls' School, 92
Tokyo Kid (film), 224, 225, 227
Tokyo League of Women's Associations, 96
Tokyo School of Forestry, 103
Tokyo Senmon Gakkō, 67, 88
Tokyo University/Imperial University, 72, 73, 88, 116, 148, 176, 180, 181
Tokyo War Crimes Trials, 205
Tokyo Women's Normal School, 83–84, 87, 93
Tomigusuku Seiwa, 106
Tosa domain, 25, 26, 28–41
Tourism, foreign, 127, 128–30, 132
Transportation systems, 78
Trans-Siberian Railway, 129
Travel, 116, 117–18, 120, 138; to Europe, 181–82, 187; to United States, 62, 70, 73–74, 84, 90–93, 125–27, 167, 181
Trotsky, Leon, 183
Tsuda Umeko, 90–91, 92–93
Tuberculosis, 131, 132

Uchimura Kanzō, 82
Union Christian College, 71
United States: Japanese visitors to, 62, 70, 73–74, 84, 90–93, 125–27, 167, 181; popular music in, 219, 220, 221, 222; railroads in, 120, 126–27; relations with Japan, 43–44, 48, 101,

United States (*continued*)
125, 135, 136, 149–50, 155, 185,
193–95, 199, 204–5, 213, 215
University of Chicago, 90
University of Pennsylvania, 126
University of Wisconsin, 125
Uryū Shigeko, 92–93
U.S.-Japan Security Treaty (1960),
204–5

Van Metre, Thurman, 126

Wada Hirō, 185
Wage labor, 135
War Crimes Trials, 205
Waseda University, 67
Watanabe Sakuta, 38
Weston, Miss (British resident of
Japan), 93
Wharton School of Finance and
Commerce, 126
Women: education of, 66–67, 71, 78,
82–84, 86, 87, 95, 96, 97, 137, 147–
48, 157, 165; individual freedom for,
93–94, 97, 165, 167–68, 169; and
Misora, 215–16; Western influence
on, 81, 83, 92, 97; during World
War II, 169–70, 193–94, 213. *See
also* Gender roles, of women
Women's Literature Prize
(Joryūbungakusho), 170
Women's Patriotic Association
(Aikokufujinkai), 156
Women's Suffrage League, 94
Woodworth family, 71
World War I, 135
World War II, 74, 135, 138, 149–50,
184–85, 193–95, 219, 222–23;
attitudes of Japanese toward, 170,
198, 203, 204, 205–6, 208, 216–17;
U.S. occupation after, 125, 149, 185,
194, 205, 213, 215; women during,
169–70, 193–94, 213; and Yokoi
Shōichi, 197–98, 199–204
Wycoff, Mrs. (wife of American
educator in Tokyo), 84

Yale University, 90, 91
Yamada Shōichi, 199
Yamato Takeru, 226
Yamauchi clan, 26, 38–39

Yamauchi Toyochika, 28, 29
Yamauchi Toyokazu, 30, 40
Yamauchi Toyooki, 40–41
Yasukuni Shrine, 213, 215–16
Yasuoka Shōtarō, 197, 198
Yellow Magic Orchestra, 227
Yokohama Women's Academy, 66–67,
68
Yokoi Eijirō, 199
Yokoi Shōichi, 197–211; death of, 211;
relations with press, 198, 206–7,
209–11
Yokoi Tsuru, 199
Yoshida Kuraji, 30–31
Yoshitake Teruko, 162, 165
Yoshiya Masa, 156–57, 164–65
Yoshiya Michiaki, 157
Yoshiya Nobuko, 136, 155–71; *Ataka-
ke no hitobito* (The people of the
Ataka household), 170; "Atarashiki
hi" (A new day), 169; *Bōfū no bara*
(Stormy rose), 167; "Dannasama
muyō" (A husband is unnecessary),
166; death of, 171; education of,
157; feminism of, 167–68;
Hanamonogatari (Flower tales), 157–
58, 159–61, 169, 170; lesbianism of,
155, 160, 161–62, 163, 165, 166;
"Moyuru hana" (Burning flower),
161; *Mura to heitai* (Village and
soldiers), 169; "Narazu no taiko"
(Soundless drum), 157; *Nyonin heike*
(Heike women), 171; "Onibi"
(Will-o'-the-wisp), 170; *Onna no
yūjō* (Women's friendship), 156,
168; political views, 167, 168;
relationship with Kikuchi, 160,
161; relationship with Kobayashi,
169–70; relationship with Masa,
156–57, 164–65; relationship with
Monma, 161–65, 166, 167, 170,
171; relationship with Takehisa,
157–58; relationship with Tamura,
159; *Toki no koe* (The voice of the
times), 171; *Tokugawa no fujintachi*
(Tokugawa women), 170, 171; visit
to United States, 167; during
World War II, 169–70; *Yaneura no
nishojo* (Two virgins in an attic),
160
Yoshiya Sadakazu, 157

Yoshiya Tadaaki, 157, 160
Yoshiya Yūichi, 157
Yōtokuin (sister of Gomizunoo), 7
Yotsutsuji family, 17

Yuasa Yoshiko, 167
Yūkansha, 64, 65

Zaibatsu, 115, 121, 135